Science, Technology, and Society

The Impact of Science from 2000 B.C. to the 18th Century

Science, Technology, and Society

The Impact of Science from 2000 B.C. to the 18th Century

Judson Knight, Neil Schlager, Editors

VOLUME 2

Mathematics

Physical Science

U·X·L®

THOMSON
GALE™

Detroit • New York • San Diego • San Francisco • Cleveland • New Haven, Conn. • Waterville, Maine • London • Munich

THOMSON
GALE

Science, Technology, and Society: The Impact of Science from 2000 B.C. to the 18th Century

Judson Knight, Neil Schlager, Editors

Project Editor
Christine Slovey

Editorial
Carol Nagel, Diane Sawinski

Permissions
Shalice Shah-Caldwell

Imaging and Multimedia
Robert Duncan, Robyn Young

Product Design
Tracey Rowens

Composition
Evi Seoud

Manufacturing
Rita Wimberly

For more information, contact
The Gale Group, Inc.
27500 Drake Rd.
Farmington Hills, MI 48331-3535
Or you can visit our Internet site at http://www.gale.com

LIBRARY OF CONGRESS CATALOGING-IN-PUBLICATION DATA

Science, technology, and society: the impact of science from 2000 B.C. to the 18th century / Judson Knight, Neil Schlager, editors.

p. cm.

Includes bibliographical references and index.

ISBN 0-7876-5653-4 (set : hardcover) — ISBN 0-7876-5654-2 (v. 1) — ISBN 0-7876-5455-0 (v. 2) — 0-7876-5656-9 (v. 3)

1. Science—History. 2. Science—Social aspects—History. 3. Science and civilization—History. 4. Technology—History. 5. Technology—Social aspects—History. 6. Technology and civilization—History. I. Knight, Judson. II. Schlager, Neil, 1966–

Q125 .S434756 2002 2002005432
509—dc21

Printed in the United States of America
10 9 8 7 6 5 4 3 2 1

Contents

VOLUME 1

chapter one Life Science

Contents

VOLUME 3

chapter four

Technology and Invention

Reader's Guide

S*cience, Technology, and Society: The Impact of Science from 2000* B.C. *to the 18th Century* presents more than eighty topical and biographical essays designed to help students understand the impact that science had on the course of human history between 2000 B.C. and the eighteenth century. Essays examine scientific discoveries and developments and the individuals who made them, showing how social trends and events influenced science and how scientific developments changed people's lives.

Format

Science, Technology, and Society: The Impact of Science from 2000 B.C. *to the 18th Century* is divided into four chapters across three volumes. The Life Science chapter appears in Volume One. The Mathematics and Physical Science chapters appear in Volume Two. And the Technology and Invention chapter appears in Volume 3. The following sections appear in each chapter:

Chronology: A timeline of key events within the chapter's discipline.

Overview: A summary of the scientific discoveries and developments, trends, and issues within the discipline.

Essays: Topic essays describing major discoveries and developments within the discipline and relating them to social history.

Biographies: Biographical profiles providing personal background on important individuals within the discipline, and often introducing students to additional important issues in science and society during the 3700-year period covered.

Brief Biographies: Brief biographical mentions introducing students to the major accomplishments of other notable scientists, researchers, teachers, and inventors important within the discipline.

Research and Activity Ideas: Offering students ideas for reports, presentations, or classroom activities related to the topics discussed in the chapter.

For More Information: Providing sources for further reasearch on the topics and individuals discussed in the chapter.

Other features

Sidebars in every chapter highlight interesting events, issues, or individuals related to the subject. More than 180 black-and-white photographs help illustrate the discoveries and the individuals who made them. In addition, cross-references to subjects discussed in other topic essays are indicated with "see references" in parentheses while cross-references to individuals discussed elsewhere in the title are indicated by boldface type and "see references" in parentheses. Each volume concludes with a cumulative subject index so that students can easily locate the people, places, and events discussed throughout *Science, Technology, and Society: The Impact of Science from 2000 B.C. to the 18th Century.*

Comments and Suggestions

We welcome your comments on *Science, Technology, and Society: The Impact of Science from 2000 B.C. to the 18th Century* and suggestions for other science topics to consider. Please write: Editors, *Science, Technology, and Society: The Impact of Science from 2000 B.C. to the 18th Century*, U•X•L, 27500 Drake Rd., Farmington Hills, Michigan 48331-3535; call toll-free: 1-800-877-4253; fax to (248) 414-5043; or send e-mail via http://www.gale.com.

Advisory Board

Special thanks are due to U•X•L's *Science, Technology, and Society* advisors. The following teachers and media specialists offered invaluable comments and suggestions when this work was in its formative stages:

Dr. Josesph L. Hoffman
Director of Technology
West Bloomfield School District
West Bloomfield, Michigan

Dean Sousanis
Science Chairman
Almont High School
Almont, Michigan

Eric Wisniewski
Math and Science Teacher
Edsel Ford High School
Dearborn, Michigan

Chronology

C. 7000 B.C.E.
First consistent, reliable fire-making technology is developed.

C. 3500 B.C.E.
The Sumerians develop the wheel.

C. 3500–2000 B.C.E.
Early mathematicians of Sumer in Mesopotamia discover the foundations of arithmetic, later developed independently by the Chinese, Indians, and Maya.

C. 2630 B.C.E.
Egyptian architect Imhotep begins building the Step Pyramid, a tomb for the pharaoh Djoser (or Zoser), launching several centuries of pyramid building in Egypt.

C. 1600 B.C.E.
The Phoenicians develop the alphabet.

C. 1500 B.C.E.
Medical practices based on the Vedic religion, a predecessor to Hinduism, appear in India.

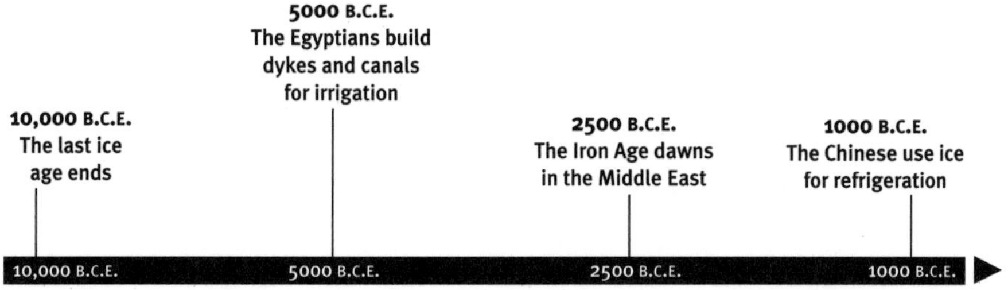
10,000 B.C.E. The last ice age ends
5000 B.C.E. The Egyptians build dykes and canals for irrigation
2500 B.C.E. The Iron Age dawns in the Middle East
1000 B.C.E. The Chinese use ice for refrigeration
10,000 B.C.E.
5000 B.C.E.
2500 B.C.E.
1000 B.C.E.

Chronology

c. 600 B.C.E.
Thales of Miletus originates both Western philosophy and the physical sciences by stating that water is the basic substance of the universe.

c. 540 B.C.E.
Persian emperor Cyrus II orders the building of the Royal Road, the first major highway system, which serves as a model for later Roman roads and the interstate highways of today.

c. 530 B.C.E.
Greek philosopher and mathematician Pythagoras establishes a community of followers in a Greek colony on the southern coast of Italy.

c. 400 B.C.E.
Greek physician Hippocrates and his followers establish a medical code of ethics. Hippocrates attributes diseases to natural causes and uses diet and medication to restore the body.

c. 350 B.C.E.
Greek philosopher Aristotle establishes the disciplines of biology and comparative anatomy and makes the first serious attempt to classify animals.

c. 300 B.C.E.
Greek mathematician Euclid writes a geometry textbook entitled *Elements*, which brings together all the known geometric ideas of its time, and is destined to remain the authority on mathematics for some twenty-two hundred years.

c. 300 B.C.E.
The Romans begin developing sophisticated techniques of road building. They also launch the construction of aqueducts capable of carry large quantities of water many miles. Both activities will continue for more than five hundred years.

c. 250 B.C.E.
Greek mathematician and engineer Archimedes invents a number of useful mechanisms, including Archimedes' screw, a device for raising water that is still used in parts of the world today.

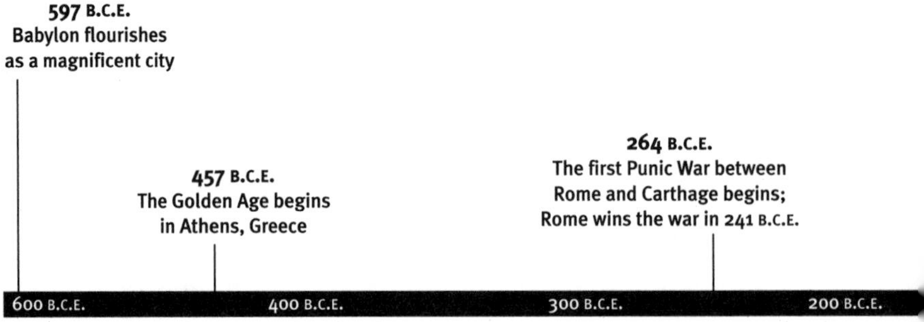

597 B.C.E.
Babylon flourishes as a magnificent city
457 B.C.E.
The Golden Age begins in Athens, Greece
264 B.C.E.
The first Punic War between Rome and Carthage begins; Rome wins the war in 241 B.C.E.
600 B.C.E.
400 B.C.E.
300 B.C.E.
200 B.C.E.

C. 140 B.C.E.
Hipparchus, a Greek astronomer, develops the fundamentals of trigonometry.

C. 260 B.C.E.
Aristarchus of Samos, a Greek astronomer, states that the Sun and not Earth is the center of the universe.

C. 350 B.C.E.
Greek philosopher Aristotle proves that Earth is spherical and establishes principles of physics that, though incorrect, will remain influential for the next two thousand years.

C. 425 B.C.E.
Democritus, a Greek philosopher, states that all matter consists of tiny, indivisible particles called atoms.

105 C.E.
Chinese inventor Ts'ai Lun perfects a method for making paper from tree bark, rags, and hemp.

C. 150 C.E.
The Greco-Roman astronomer Ptolemy (Claudius Ptolemaeus) writes his highly influential *Almagest,* which offers a geocentric (Earth-centered) model of the universe that will be widely accepted for the next fifteen hundred years.

C. 160–C. 199 C.E.
Greek physician Galen becomes the most influential figure in medicine and remains so for the next millennium.

C. 400 C.E.
Christian noblewoman Fabiola establishes in Rome (in present-day Italy) the first hospital in western Europe.

400 C.E.
Invaders from central Asia introduce the stirrup to Europe. By allowing a soldier to remain sitting on a horse while delivering a powerful blow, the stirrup makes possible the age of knights and feudalism that follows.

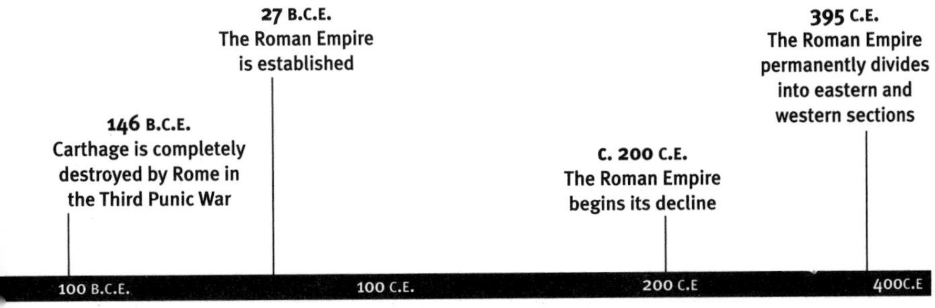

27 B.C.E.
The Roman Empire is established
395 C.E.
The Roman Empire permanently divides into eastern and western sections
146 B.C.E.
Carthage is completely destroyed by Rome in the Third Punic War
C. 200 C.E.
The Roman Empire begins its decline
100 B.C.E.
100 C.E.
200 C.E
400C.E

499
Aryabhata, a Hindu mathematician and astronomer, writes his *Aryabhatiya,* which describes the Indian numerical system.

c. 600
Block printing makes its first appearance in China.

820
Al-Khwarizmi, an Arab mathematician, writes a mathematical text that introduces the word "algebra" (*al-jabr* in Arabic), as well as Hindu-Arabic numerals, including zero.

c. 800–c. 1300
Medical knowledge flourishes in the Muslim world. Among the distinguished figures of this period are Persian physician known as Rhazes (ar-Razi); Arab physician and philosopher Avicenna (Ibn Sina); and Arab physician Averroës (Ibn Rushd).

c. 1000
The magnetic compass, invented much earlier, is perfected and put into increased use in China.

c. 1000
Arab physicist Alhazen (Abu 'Ali al-Hasan Ibn al-Haytham) argues against the prevailing belief that the eye sends out a light that reflects off of objects.

c. 1000–1170
The medical school of Salerno in Italy, established around 800 C.E., becomes the first institution in Europe to grant medical diplomas. By 1000 it is thriving and brings in students from around the region. In 1170 a professor at the school, Roger of Salerno, publishes the first book on surgery in the West.

1202
In *Liber Abaci,* Italian mathematician Leonardo Fibonacci introduces Hindu-Arabic numerals to the West.

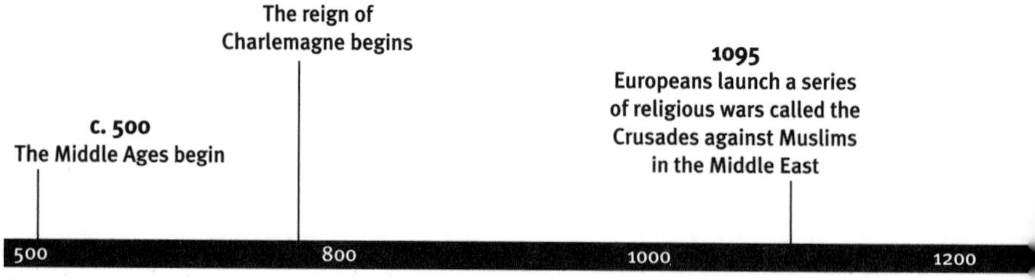
768
The reign of
Charlemagne begins
1095
Europeans launch a series
of religious wars called the
Crusades against Muslims
in the Middle East
c. 500
The Middle Ages begin
500
800
1000
1200

1224
Holy Roman Emperor Frederick II issues laws regulating the study of medicine, elevating the status of real physicians and diminishing the number of frauds. Later, in 1241, he becomes the first major European ruler to permit dissection of cadavers (cutting open dead bodies for medical study) formerly prohibited by religious law.

1288
The first known guns are made in China. Firearms are first mentioned in Western accounts twenty-five years later, in 1313.

c. 1315
The first mechanical clocks appear in Europe.

c. 1450
German inventor Johannes Gutenberg invents a printing press with movable type, an event that will lead to an explosion of knowledge as new ideas become much easier to disseminate.

1543
In his *De revolutionibus orbium coelestium* (The revolutions of the heavenly spheres), completed in 1530 but not published until the time of his death, Polish astronomer Nicolaus Copernicus proposes a heliocentric, or Sun-centered universe, thus initiating the Scientific Revolution.

1543
Belgian physician Andreas Vesalius publishes his illustrated book of anatomy, *De humani corporis fabrica* (On the structure of the human body), one of the most important works in medical history.

1572
Danish astronomer Tycho Brahe observes a supernova, or exploding star, an event that puts to rest the long-held Aristotelian notion that the heavens are perfect and unchanging.

1587
Italian astronomer Galileo Galilei begins experiments that lead to his law of falling bodies, showing that, contrary to Aristotle, the rate that a body

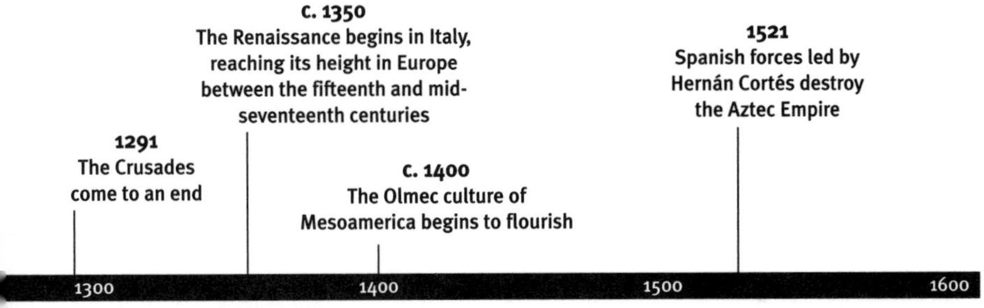

c. 1350
The Renaissance begins in Italy, reaching its height in Europe between the fifteenth and mid-seventeenth centuries
1521
Spanish forces led by Hernán Cortés destroy the Aztec Empire
1291
The Crusades come to an end
c. 1400
The Olmec culture of Mesoamerica begins to flourish
1300
1400
1500
1600

falls is independent of its weight, and that all objects will fall at the same rate in a vacuum.

1589
William Lee of England invents the first knitting machine.

1594
Scottish mathematician John Napier develops the idea of logarithms, which will eventually make possible the calculation of difficult multiplication and division problems.

1609
German astronomer Johannes Kepler introduces his laws of planetary motion.

1619
At just twenty-two years of age, French mathematician René Descartes establishes the basics of modern mathematics by applying algebra to geometry and formulating analytic geometry. Eighteen years later, Descartes will publish this breakthrough work in *Discourse on Method.*

1628
English physician William Harvey, considered the founder of modern physiology—the scientific study of the functions, activities, and processes of living things—demonstrates how blood circulates in *Exercitatio anatomica de motu cordis sanguinis in animalius* (On the movement of the heart and blood in animals).

1654
Blaise Pascal sends fellow French mathematician Pierre de Fermat a letter requesting help in solving a problem involving dice and games of chance. This leads to a lively exchange that results in the creation of probability theory.

1661
English physicist and chemist Robert Boyle publishes *The sceptical chymist,* a work regarded by many as the beginning of scientific chemistry.

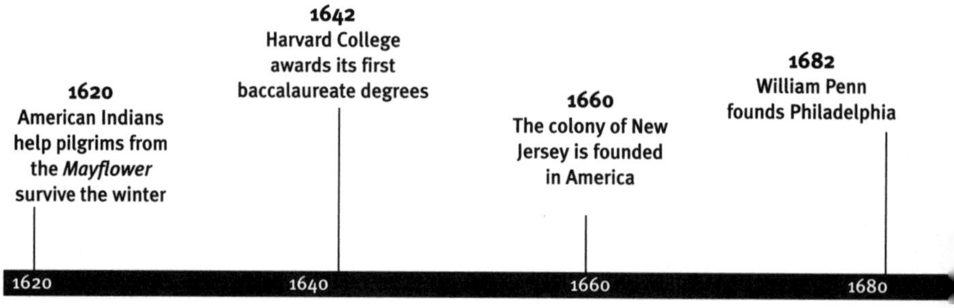
1620
American Indians help pilgrims from the Mayflower survive the winter
1642
Harvard College awards its first baccalaureate degrees
1660
The colony of New Jersey is founded in America
1682
William Penn founds Philadelphia
1620
1640
1660
1680

1669
British physicist and mathematician Isaac Newton develops a version of calculus, but does not publish his work for many years.

1681
The Languedoc Canal, also known as the Canal du Midi, in southern France is completed. This 150-mile (241-kilometer) waterway will be considered the greatest feat of civil engineering between Roman times and the nineteenth century.

1684
German philosopher and mathematician Gottfried Wilhelm von Leibniz develops his own version of calculus, which he immediately publishes. The years that follow will see a heated debate between supporters of Newton and Leibniz as to who was the true inventor of calculus.

1687
Isaac Newton publishes *Philosophiae naturalis principia mathematica,* generally considered the greatest scientific work ever written, in which he outlines his three laws of motion and offers an equation that becomes the law of universal gravitation.

1735
Swedish botanist Carolus Linnaeus (Carl von Linné) outlines his system for classifying all living things.

1735
German mathematician Leonhard Euler solves the famous Königsberg bridge problem, thus pioneering the areas of graph theory and topology and introducing concepts used today in everything from computer networking to highway design.

1769
Scottish inventor James Watt obtains a patent for his steam engine, which improves on ideas Thomas Newcomen developed half a century earlier.

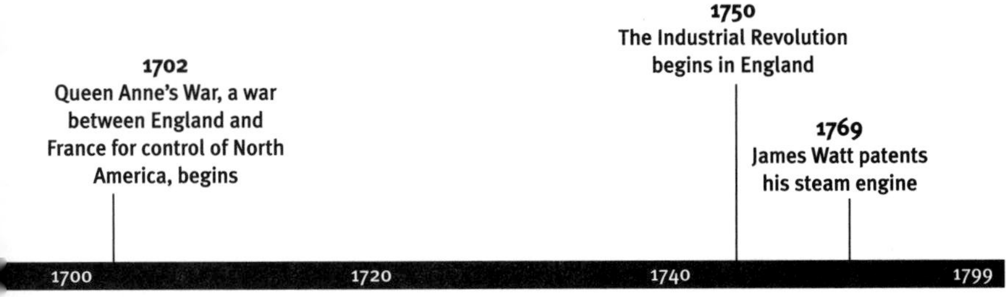
1702
Queen Anne's War, a war between England and France for control of North America, begins
1750
The Industrial Revolution begins in England
1769
James Watt patents his steam engine
1700
1720
1740
1799

Words to Know

A

abacus An early form of hand-operated calculator that uses movable beads strung along parallel wires inside a frame.

acceleration A change in velocity over time. The acceleration due to gravity, for instance, is 32 feet (9.8 meters) per second per second, meaning that for every second an object falls, its velocity is increasing as well.

acupuncture The insertion of thin needles into specific points of the body in order to relieve pain or treat illness.

alchemy A set of mystical beliefs based on the idea that ordinary matter can be perfected. In the Middle Ages this became a semi-scientific discipline concerned, for instance, with attempts to turn various metals into gold.

algebra A branch of mathematics in which arithmetic operations (for example, addition or multiplication) are generalized. In algebraic equations, symbols represent numbers of unknown value, and the equations themselves are used to find these values.

alternative medicine Medical practices that are not officially recognized by the mainstream medical community.

anatomy The study of the structure of organisms, including the human body.

apothecary One who prepared and sold medicines in medieval times.

applied mathematics The use of mathematics for a specific purpose, as in business or engineering. This is in contrast to pure mathematics.

aqueduct A long pipe, usually mounted on a high stone wall that slopes gently, which is used to carry water from the mountains to the lowlands.

astrolabe A small instrument, used during ancient and medieval times, for calculating the positions of bodies in the heavens.

astronomical clock A clock that, in addition to telling the time, is designed to show the positions of the Sun, Moon, and other celestial bodies.

astrology The study of the positions and the movements of the stars, planets, and other heavenly bodies in the belief that these affect people's lives.

Ayurvedic A term describing a form of medicine, closely tied with the Hindu religion, practiced from ancient times in India.

B

bank In nautical terms, refers to the number of oarsmen along a vertical line. On a trireme, a ship with three tiers, there were three banks. Later ships, however, used more men on a single oar without adding tiers.

bestiary An ancient or medieval catalogue of animal life. Bestiaries were highly unscientific and typically included numerous fictional creatures such as the unicorn.

biology The scientific study of living organisms. Actually a collection of disciplines that includes botany and zoology, biology is (along with medicine) one of the two principal areas of study in the life sciences.

block printing A process whereby a printer carves out the material to be printed on a piece of wood, then inks the wood block and presses it onto paper to create a printed image.

botany A branch of biology concerned with plant life.

C

caduceus A staff with two entwined snakes and two wings at the top, the internationally recognized symbol for medicine.

calculus The branch of mathematics that deals with rates of change and motion.

Cartesian coordinate system A method for identifying points on a plane by assigning to each point a unique set of numbers indicating its location. In the Cartesian system, values of *x* and *y* respectively indicate horizontal and vertical distance from the center, designated as (0,0). Cartesian graphs may also be three-dimensional, with a *z*-axis perpendicular (at a right angle to) both *x* and *y*.

case history A record of a particular patient's illness and treatment, often used in medical texts for the purpose of teaching or illustrating a concept.

celestial Of the skies or heavens.

Cesarean section A medical procedure in which a baby is surgically removed from its mother's uterus.

chemistry An area of the physical sciences concerned with the composition, structure, properties, and changes of substances, including elements, compounds, and mixtures.

civil engineering An area of engineering concerned with the design and building of large public works projects such as roads and bridges.

circulatory system The heart, blood, and blood vessels.

circumference The distance around a circle.

civilization A term referring to a society that has all or most of the following: a settled way of life, agriculture, cities, an organized political system, polished tools, and writing.

combinatorics The study of combining objects by various rules to create new arrangements of objects.

conic section The cross-section of a cone when cut by a plane.

constellation A group of stars. In many cases the stars involved are at incredible distances from one another, but they seem, from Earth's perspective, to form groups.

contagion The transmission of a disease by direct or indirect contact.

cosmology A branch of astronomy concerned with the origin, structure, and evolution of the universe.

cosmos The universe.

cube root The cube root of a given number is a number that, when multiplied by itself twice, will produce that number. Thus 2 is the cube root of 8 since $2 \times 2 \times 2 = 8$.

D

decimal fraction A method of representing numbers that are less than 1 by using a decimal point and place value. The number 0.01 is a decimal fraction, whereas 1/100 is a common fraction.

decimal system The number system in use throughout most of the world today, based on 10.

diameter The distance across a circle, as drawn along a path that passes through the center of that circle.

diffraction That which occurs when light rays pass close to an object and bend or separate as a result.

dissection Cutting open dead bodies in order to study their internal characteristics.

domesticate To adapt something (usually a plant or animal) so that it is useful and advantageous for humans.

E

eclipse An event in which one celestial body covers, or otherwise makes it impossible to see, another. In a solar eclipse, the Moon passes between Earth and the Sun, covering the Sun. In a lunar eclipse, Earth comes between the Sun and the full Moon, placing the Moon in Earth's shadow.

ecliptic The great circle of the heavens, which is the apparent path of the Sun as it seems to move across the sky, or the path of Earth as seen from the Sun.

element A substance, made up of only one kind of atom, that cannot be broken down chemically into another substance. Scientists developed this definition around the year 1800; prior to that time, a number of misguided theories prevailed. Most notable among these was the Greek notion of four elements: earth, air, fire, and water.

embryo An unborn animal in the early stages of development. For humans, the embryonic stage is defined as the period of eight weeks following conception, or the fertilization of the egg.

epidemic A disease that affects large numbers of people.

Euclidean geometry Geometry based on the principles laid down by Euclid (c. 330–260 B.C.E.) in his *Elements*, which is concerned primarily with flat, two-dimensional space in which nonparallel lines eventually converge.

F

fluid mechanics The study of fluids (liquids or gases) and their properties. This includes hydrostatics, or the study of fluids at rest, and hydrodynamics or fluid dynamics, the study of fluids in motion.

forceps A medical instrument, shaped like tongs, used to extract a baby during difficult births, as well as for other surgical applications.

G

genus A group of species distinguished by common characteristics.

geocentric Earth-centered.

geology The scientific study of Earth, particularly as revealed through its rocks.

geometry The branch of mathematics concerned with the properties and relationships of points, lines, angles, surfaces, and shapes.

gynecology The branch of medicine concerned with diseases and physical care of women.

H

heliocentric Sun-centered.

herbal A book concerned with plants and their medicinal uses.

herbalist Someone who deals in medicinal herbs. Herbalists played a major role in medieval medicine and continue to do so in alternative medicine today.

Hindu-Arabic numerals The number system in use throughout most of the world today, which uses ten digits, including zero.

horoscope A chart that uses the positions of planets and constellations for the purpose of creating an astrological forecast.

hull The body of a ship.

humors Four fluids (phlegm, blood, yellow bile, and black bile) that, according to Hippocrates and his followers, made up the human body. Imbalances in these humors were supposedly responsible for all illnesses.

hypotenuse The longest side of a right triangle.

hysterectomy An operation in which a woman's uterus is removed.

I

Industrial Revolution A period of rapid development that began in about 1750 and transformed the economies of the West from agriculture-based to manufacturing-based systems.

inertia The tendency of objects in motion to remain in motion, and objects at rest to remain at rest, unless acted upon by some outside force.

infrastructure A system of public works, such as roads and sewers, necessary to the functioning of a society.

inoculation The prevention of a disease by the introduction to the body, in small quantities, of the virus or other microorganism that causes the disease.

inscribe In geometry, to draw a figure inside another one in such a way that it touches, but does not overlap, the boundaries of the larger figure.

intercalation The insertion of an extra month in a year to make the calendar line up with the seasons.

irrational number A number that cannot be expressed as the ratio of any two whole numbers because in decimal form, irrational numbers such as pi (π) neither terminate (come to an end) nor fall into a repeating pattern.

K

kinematics The study of how objects move.

L

life expectancy A calculation, based on statistical data, of the average life span of an organism.

lock A device on a canal that allows a vessel to negotiate changes in altitude by raising or lowering the water level.

logarithm The power to which a given number, called a base, must be raised to yield a given product, for instance, $10^2 = 100$. In logarithmic terms this would be expressed thus: $\log_{10}100 = 2$.

logic A system of reasoning for reaching valid conclusions about concepts, and for assessing the validity of a conclusion that has been reached.

lunar calendar A measure of the year based on twelve lunar months (the time it takes the Moon to revolve around Earth), which lasts about 354.37 days.

luni-solar calendar A combination of lunar and solar calendars, which uses intercalation to align the two.

M

machine Any device that transmits, modifies, or magnifies force for a specific purpose. Machines typically either alter the amount of force applied, or the direction along which it is applied. A simple machine is a machine with only one or two parts.

magic square A square set of boxes—the number must always be a square number such as 9, 16, or 25—containing different numbers. In a magic square, the sum of the numbers in each row, column, or diagonal is the same.

matter A physical substance that occupies space, possesses mass, and is ultimately convertible to energy. Matter can be a gas, liquid, or solid.

mechanics A branch of physics concerned with the study of bodies in motion.

medieval Having to do with the Middle Ages (c. 500–c. 1500 C.E.).

menstruation The monthly discharge of blood and other materials from the uterus of a nonpregnant female primate (a class of animals including apes as well as humans) of breeding age.

metallurgy The science and technology of metals.

midwife A person who assists women in childbirth. In premodern times, midwives were almost always female and seldom had formal medical training.

movable-type printing A process in which a printer uses precast pieces of type, representing letters and other symbols, which are inserted into a frame and used to print a document.

N

negative number A number smaller than 0.

Neolithic Revolution A term describing a series of changes that occurred between about twenty thousand and six thousand years ago, when humans began to produce much more sophisticated, polished tools, as well as pottery and woven materials.

non-Euclidean geometry A form of geometry, developed in the 1800s, that is concerned primarily with curved (and sometimes three-dimensional) space in which it is possible that nonparallel lines do not converge.

notation Symbols to represent numbers or operations such as addition and subtraction.

number theory The study of the properties of numbers, and the relationships between them.

numerology The belief that numbers have special meanings of a spiritual nature, and can be used to predict the future.

O

obstetrics The branch of medicine concerned with childbirth.

occupational health An area of medicine concerned with the health hazards related to specific professions.

optics The study of light and vision.

ovary The part of the female anatomy in which eggs (which can be fertilized by sperm to create offspring) are produced.

P

periodical A publication, such as a newspaper or magazine, that comes out on a periodic basis, for example, every day or every month.

pharmacology A branch of medical science concerned with medicines and drugs.

philosophy The area of study that seeks to provide a general understanding of reality.

phonogram A written symbol that represents a specific syllable.

physics An area of the physical sciences that is concerned with matter, energy, and the interactions between them.

physiology The scientific study of the functions, activities, and processes of living things.

pi The ratio between the circumference of (distance around) a circle and its diameter (distance across). Pronounced "pie" and represented by the Greek letter π, pi has a value of 3.14159265+. This is its value to eight decimal places; in fact pi is an irrational number.

pictogram A written symbol that looks like the thing it represents.

place value The use of a number's position to indicate its size. In a number such as 1239, for instance, the 2 does not stand for 2, but for 200. Whereas the Hindu-Arabic numeral system in use today has a built-in concept of place value, the Roman numeral system used during the Middle Ages (c. 500–c. 1500) did not.

plane method The technique of performing geometric work using only a compass and an unmarked straightedge.

polygon A closed shape with three or more sides, all straight.

postulate A basic principle or established rule. Sometimes called an axiom.

prehistoric Anything that existed before the development of written language.

prime number A number that can be divided only by itself and 1.

probability theory A branch of mathematics devoted to predicting the likelihood that a particular event will occur. Such predictions are typically based on statistical data.

prognosis A prediction regarding the course and outcome of a disease based upon previous observation of similar cases.

proof A step-by-step process of proving certain ideas in geometry by referring to already established propositions.

public health A set of policies and methods for protecting and improving the health of a community through efforts that include disease prevention, health education, and sanitation.

pulmonary circulation The movement of blood from the right ventricle of the heart into the lungs via the pulmonary artery, and from the lungs to the left ventricle through the pulmonary veins.

pure mathematics Mathematics for its own sake, rather than for a specific application. Compare with applied mathematics.

pythagorean theorem A rule, attributed to the Greek mathematician Pythagoras (c. 580–c. 500 B.C.E.) but probably derived much earlier, which states that for every right triangle, the square of the hypotenuse is equal to the sum of the squares of the other two sides.

Q

quack Someone who falsely claims to possess medical skill and the ability to provide proper treatment.

quarantine The isolation or separation of people or items in order to prevent the spread of communicable diseases.

R

ratio The relationship between two numbers or values. All fractions are ratios, but some ratios such as π (pi, the relationship between the circumference and diameter of a circle) cannot be expressed as fractions.

reflection That which occurs when light rays strike a smooth surface and bounce off at an angle equal to that of the incoming rays.

Reformation A religious movement in the 1500s that ultimately led to the rejection of Roman Catholicism by various groups and the formation of Protestant religious denominations.

refraction The bending of light as it passes at an angle from one transparent material into a second transparent material. Refraction accounts for the fact that objects under water appear to have a different size and location than they have in air.

retrograde motion The apparent backward movement, or reversal of direction, by outer planets in the solar system. In fact retrograde motion is simply an optical illusion, created by the fact that Earth is orbiting the Sun much faster than the outer planets are.

right triangle A triangle with one right angle, or 90° angle. (Since the total measurement of the three angles in a triangle is 180°, no triangle can have more than one right angle.)

S

scientific method A set of principles and procedures for systematic study, introduced primarily by Galileo Galilei, and still used in the sciences. The scientific method consists of four essential parts: the statement of a problem to be studied; the gathering of scientific data through observation and experimentation; the formulation of hypotheses or theories; and the testing of those hypotheses. The results of testing may lead to a restatement of the problem, or an entirely new problem to be analyzed, which starts the process over again.

Scientific Revolution A period of accelerated scientific discovery that completely reshaped the world. Usually dated from about 1550 to 1700, the Scientific Revolution saw the origination of the scientific method and the introduction of ideas such as the heliocentric universe and gravity. Its leading figures included Nicolaus Copernicus, Galileo Galilei, and Isaac Newton.

scribe A member of a small and very powerful group in ancient society who knew how to read and write.

scurvy An illness caused by a lack of vitamin C that results in swollen joints, bleeding gums, loose teeth, and an inability to recover from wounds.

sexagesimal system A number system based on 60.

smallpox A viral infection accompanied by fevers and chills, and characterized by the formation of a rash over large parts of the body. As the effects of the illness continue, the rash turns to pus-filled bumps or papules that, when infected, can cause death. Even those who survive, however, bear the scars left by the eruption of the papules.

solar calendar A measure of the year based on Earth's revolution around the Sun, which takes 365.2422 days. This is the calendar used in most of the world today.

species A category of closely related organisms. A species is usually defined by the ability of its members to breed with one another and by their inability to breed with members of other species.

square The square of a number is that number multiplied by itself. Thus 25, for instance, is the square of 5, since $5 \times 5 = 25$.

square root The square root of a given number is a number that, when multiplied by itself, will produce that number. Thus 2 is the square root of 4 since $2 \times 2 = 4$.

standardize To establish a common standard with which measurements, or measuring devices, must be consistent.

star catalogue A listing of the known stars with their names, positions, and movements.

statistics A branch of mathematics concerned with the collection and analysis of numerical data.

T

technology The application of knowledge to make the performance of physical tasks easier.

terrestrial Of the Earth.

theorem A proposition based on one or more postulates.

thermodynamics The study of the relationships between heat, energy, and work. (Work, closely related to the concept of power, is a term in physics that has a definition different from its everyday meaning.)

tier A level. In discussing ancient ships, the levels of rowers, one atop the other, powering the craft.

tool A handheld device that aids in the accomplishment of tasks.

trigonometry The study of the properties of triangles—in particular, the relationships between the various sides of a right triangle—as well as the properties of points on a circle.

U

uterus An organ in the body of a female mammal that holds offspring during their stages of development prior to birth.

V

vacuum An area devoid of matter, even air.

vagina A canal leading from the exterior of a woman's body to the uterus.

ventricle A chamber in the heart.

velocity Speed in a certain direction.

vernacular The language of the people. During the Middle Ages, when educated people communicated with each other in Latin, "vernacular" referred to everyday national languages such as Italian, English, German, or French.

W

watershed A ridge of high land that divides areas drained by different river systems.

whole number A number, such as 1, or 23, or 2,765,014, that includes no fractions.

Z

zodiac An imaginary band in the heavens, divided into twelve constellations or astrological signs.

zoology A branch of biology concerned with animal life.

Science, Technology, and Society

The Impact of Science from 2000 B.C. to the 18th Century

chapter two

Mathematics

CHRONOLOGY

c. 3500–2000 B.C.E.
Early mathematicians of Sumer in Mesopotamia discover the foundations of arithmetic, later developed independently by the Chinese, Indians, and Maya.

c. 530 B.C.E.
Greek philosopher and mathematician Pythagoras establishes a community of followers in a Greek colony on the southern coast of Italy.

c. 300 B.C.E.
Greek mathematician Euclid writes a geometry textbook entitled *Elements,* which brings together all the known geometric ideas of its time, and is destined to remain the authority on mathematics for some 2,200 years.

c. 140 B.C.E.
Hipparchus, a Greek astronomer, develops the fundamentals of trigonometry.

c. 100 B.C.E.
Negative numbers are used in China.

499 C.E.
Aryabhata, a Hindu mathematician and astronomer, writes his *Aryabhatiya,* which describes the Indian numerical system.

820
Al-Khwarizmi, an Arab mathematician, writes a mathematical text that introduces the word "algebra" (*al- jabr* in Arabic), as well as Hindu-Arabic numerals, including zero.

1202
In *Liber Abaci,*Leonardo Fibonacci introduces Hindu-Arabic numerals to the West.

1594
Scottish mathematician John Napier begins to develop the idea of logarithms, which will eventually make possible the calculation of difficult multiplication and division problems.

1619
At age twenty-two, René Descartes establishes the basics of modern mathematics by applying algebra to geometry and formulating analytic geometry. Eighteen years later, Descartes will publish this breakthrough work in *Discourse on Method.*

1654
Blaise Pascal sends Pierre de Fermat a letter requesting help in solving a problem involving dice and games of chance. This leads to a lively interchange that results in the creation of probability theory.

1669
British physicist and mathematician Isaac Newton develops a version of calculus, but does not publish his work for many years.

1684
German philosopher and mathematician Gottfried Wilhelm von Leibniz develops his own version of calculus, which he immediately publishes. The years that follow will see a heated debate between supporters of Newton and Leibniz as to who was the true inventor of calculus.

1735
German mathematician Leonhard Euler solves the famous Königsberg bridge problem, thus pioneering the areas of graph theory and topology, and introducing concepts used today in everything from computer networking to highway design.

From the earliest days of prehistory (before writing developed in about 3500 B.C.E.), human beings needed the simplest form of mathematics: counting. Markings on cave walls and other artifacts left by our distant ancestors indicate that people had a basic idea of assigning numerical values to things. They did this by making a number of marks corresponding to the number of things being counted, much as people make hash marks today. Of course, people today only use hash marks in certain situations, usually when adding numbers by ones. In most cases, it is more appropriate to use something humans lacked until a few thousand years ago: symbols to represent numbers.

The beginnings of mathematics in the East

Even more fundamental to the development of mathematics than these symbols, however, is the concept of numbers in the abstract—the idea of "five," for instance, as opposed to the idea of five people, five stones, or five trees. The history of mathematics began in Mesopotamia (part of modern-day Iraq) in about 3500 B.C.E., with the use of number symbols. Only by about 2500 B.C.E., however, did the people of Sumer in Mesopotamia begin to use symbols that stood simply for numbers, rather than for numbers of particular things.

The influence of Mesopotamian mathematics spread to Egypt, which, as surviving documents show, possessed a relatively sophisticated understanding of mathematics by about 2000 B.C.E. The Egyptians had a decimal number system, used fractions, and apparently practiced basic forms of geometry and even algebra. Like the Sumerians, who used numbers primarily for business, the Egyptians were most interested in math for its applications, in their case, for engineering and surveying.

Chinese mathematics

The earliest surviving Chinese mathematical works, dating from about 300 B.C.E., contain detailed astronomical calculations, as well as problems involving surveying, agriculture, and other everyday matters. Yet not all mathematics in China was so practical: the Chinese were interested in number patterns, and developed the first magic squares—sets of boxes

A tablet from ancient Babylon shows a math problem written in cuneiform, the oldest known form of writing.

containing numbers that produce the same sum whether added horizontally, vertically, or diagonally.

In a number of regards, premodern Chinese mathematics excelled far beyond those of Mesopotamia, Egypt, or ancient Greece and Rome, which provided the cultural foundations for the modern West (that is, western Europe and North America). For example, Chinese mathematicians used negative numbers (numbers less than zero) in about 100 B.C.E., but these were unknown in western Europe until about 1500 C.E.. Also in about 100 B.C.E., Chinese mathematicians were making use of formulas that made it relatively easy to find the square and cube roots of numbers, something western Europeans also would not be able to do until about sixteen hundred years later. Square and cube roots of numbers are other numbers that, when multiplied by themselves once or twice respectively, equal the original number.

Chinese mathematicians also derived a very accurate value for the ratio between the circumference of a circle (the distance around the circle) and its diameter (the distance across it). This ratio is represented by the Greek letter pi (π). Though Mesopotamian and Egyptian mathematicians knew about pi, the Chinese estimate of it was much more accurate.

The origins of zero

In contrast to the numerous achievements of Chinese mathematicians, their counterparts in India are remembered primarily for one thing: the creation of the number system used today. This is not totally fair, since Hindu mathematicians such as **Aryabhata** (476–550; see biography in this chapter) achieved a number of distinctions; however, creating that number system was of such great importance that it overshadows all other accomplishments.

Of particular importance within the Hindu-Arabic numeral system was the creation of a symbol for nothing: zero. This may seem like an obvious idea now, but it was not always so; indeed, the Greeks, for all their achievements in mathematics, never used zero as a number. The Babylonians had a concept of zero, but only as a placeholder, or a symbol to hold an empty column—as the zero does, for instance, in 102 or 403. Far away in Central America, the Mayan people also developed the idea of zero, like the Babylonians, merely as a placeholder. Only the Hindu mathematicians of India treated it as an actual number, a revolutionary concept that would eventually change the world.

Mathematics in Greece

These developments in Mesopotamian, Egyptian, Chinese, Indian, and Mayan mathematics took place over about four thousand years, from the beginnings of the Mesopotamian number system in about 3500 B.C.E. to about 500 C.E., when the Hindu numeral system began to spread to the Arab world. By contrast, the heyday of Greek mathematics lasted only from 600 to 100 B.C.E. Nonetheless, the strides made by Greek mathematicians had an enormous impact on the development of mathematics.

One reason for their prominence is that the Greeks were the first to systematically move beyond applied mathematics, or mathematics that serves a purpose such as business or engineering, to pure mathematics. That is, mathematics for its own sake, or for the simple joy of uncovering the relationships between numbers. Thanks to this shift in thinking, mathematicians began exploring new fields of study without worrying whether their discoveries would have any immediate practical application.

As long as mathematicians were only inclined to explore ideas that had practical applications, they were not likely to discover new and untested concepts. Greek mathematicians working in geometry, however, took an interest in figuring out the relationships between the sides and angles of a triangle, without being concerned as to whether they could use these ideas for any practical purpose. Yet as scientists would later discover, such concepts could be put to a number of practical uses, for instance in figuring out the amount of force required to move objects in certain situations, or for calculating the distance between two points without having to measure that distance. Likewise, the designs of curves in trigonometry would later be applied in the designs of arches and other architectural elements, while algebra made it possible to calculate a number of different values in the same problem. Pulling loads, designing buildings, calculating distances, and paying workers are all very practical uses of mathematics, but without the exploration of mathematical ideas for their own sake, the means of making these calculations might never have been discovered.

Philosophy and mathematics

The Greeks' approach to the study of mathematics bore a close relation to the study of truth itself—philosophy. Thus many of the earliest figures of Greek mathematics, such as **Pythagoras** (c. 580–c. 500 B.C.E.; see biography in this chapter), were also philosophers. Pythagoras and his followers, the Pythagoreans, believed that numbers were at the heart of life and reality, and that everything from music to astronomy could be explained in numerical terms.

A similar interest in the ultimate meaning of things, which was characteristic of many ancient Greek thinkers, is also reflected in Zeno's paradoxes. A set of puzzles devised by the philosopher Zeno of Elea (c. 495–c. 430 B.C.E.), the paradoxes were intended to show that change is impossible, yet the results were quite different from what Zeno intended. Because they involved subdividing space into ever smaller increments, the paradoxes are often regarded as an early example of ideas that would play a part in the development of calculus two thousand years later. Furthermore, as philosophers eventually realized, Zeno's paradoxes ultimately served to show the limitations of logic.

Logic can be defined as a system of reasoning, closely related to mathematics, for reaching valid conclusions about concepts, and for assessing conclusions that have been reached. The philosopher **Aristotle** (384–322 B.C.E.; see biography in Life Science chapter) devised a set of rules for logic, so that statements could be treated like equations and analyzed with regard to their logical validity. These rules ultimately formed the basis for the style in which **Euclid** (c. 330–c. 260 B.C.E.; see biography in this chapter) presented the teachings of geometry.

Euclidean geometry and the three unsolved problems

Logic is only as good as the assumptions used in a logical argument, yet mathematicians such as Euclid used the methods of logic to construct consistent mathematical rules and methods. Euclid wrote one of the most influential books of all time, *Elements of Geometry,* in which he laid down the principles of geometry. Geometry is the branch of mathematics concerned with the properties and relationships of points, lines, angles, surfaces, and shapes. The principles of Euclidean geometry themselves are extremely logical, and they build upon one another in the same way that the parts of a logical argument do.

Applying a concise, easy-to-understand style, Euclid built each postulate, or statement, on commonly accepted truths. From these postulates, he then derived theorems, or more complex sets of principles. To prove the theorems, he used logical arguments based on the postulates.

Not everything in geometry was as straightforward as the ideas laid down in Euclid's *Elements*. Despite all their advances in geometry, the Greeks remained stumped by three geometric problems: squaring a circle (that is, constructing a square with the same measurements as a particular circle); trisecting (dividing into three parts) an angle; and doubling a cube (making a cube twice as large as another cube, something that cannot be done simply by doubling the lengths of the sides). These, the great unsolved problems of Greek mathematics, proved to be among the most challenging concepts in the history of ancient mathematical thought.

Mathematicians later discovered that all of these problems could be solved, but not with the method the Greeks were trying to use, something called the plane method, which relied solely on two simple tools: a compass and an unmarked straightedge. All three problems seem to have emerged in the 400s B.C.E., when these were the only tools available to mathematicians. As the years passed and various mathematicians tried their hands at one or more problems, they developed a number of methods for solving them, including angles and formulas that would be used in other areas of geometry. Yet no mathematician could solve the problems using only the plane method.

Trigonometry and algebra: From Greece to the Muslim world

Among the legacies the Greeks left behind was trigonometry, the study of the properties of triangles, in particular, the relationships between the various sides of a right triangle (a triangle with one angle equal to 90°), as well as the properties of points on a circle. Though today trigonometry is firmly placed among the various mathematical disciplines, it originated from astronomy. Trigonometry is used in measuring angles and distances on a spherical surface such as a globe, and because the orbits of planets and other bodies in the heavens are curved like spheres (though they are not perfectly spherical), trigonometry proved important to astronomical calculations. The first thinker to treat trigonometry as a form of mathematics was the Greek astronomer Hipparchus (flourished 146–127 B.C.E.), sometimes regarded as the father of trigonometry, but trigonometry did not emerge as a subject completely independent of astronomy until about 1300 C.E.

Even before Hipparchus, however, **Eratosthenes** (c. 276–c. 194 B.C.E.; see biography in this chapter) used trigonometry to provide an extremely accurate estimate of Earth's size. Unfortunately, Eratosthenes' discovery went unnoticed while an inaccurate measurement made by the much more influential Greco-Roman astronomer **Ptolemy** (c. 100–c. 170; see biography in Physical Science chapter) became the accepted measurement. Ptolemy's work had an enormous influence on medieval thinking through his *Almagest,* translated and widely used by Muslim thinkers of that era. Ptolemy's mistakes would have an enormous impact on mathematics and science until about 1500.

OPPOSITE PAGE
A model of the orbits of the planets by Johannes Kepler. Trigonometry originated from astronomy as a method for measuring the orbits of planets and did not emerge as an independent mathematical subject until the 1300s.
(Reproduced courtesy of the New York Public Library Picture Collection.)

Another astronomer, Abu'l-Wefa (940–998) of Persia, contributed to the study of trigonometry. By the time of Abu'l-Wefa, the golden age of Greek mathematics had long since passed, and the Muslim lands of the Middle East had taken the lead in the world of mathematics and science. Muslim thinkers such as Abu'l-Wefa greatly expanded the concepts of trigonometry passed to them by the Greeks, bringing the discipline to much greater maturity. In later centuries, trigonometry would aid in navigation and sail design, thus making possible the great voyages of the Age of Exploration (c. 1450–1700), when sailors from Spain, Portugal, England, France, Holland, and other countries explored and colonized much of Asia, Africa, and the Americas.

Algebra

Another mathematical discipline, algebra, is almost entirely the creation of Muslim mathematicians such as **al-Khwarizmi** (c. 780–c. 850; see biography in this chapter). The Greek thinker Diophantus (210–290), known primarily for his work in number theory (the properties of numbers, and the relations between them), introduced some early concepts in algebra, but it was Hindu and Muslim mathematicians who developed the core ideas. Al-Khwarizmi himself gave algebra its name, *al-jabr,* or "balancing."

Algebra is usually defined as a generalization of arithmetic, a way of letting symbols (for example, x and y) represent numbers to find an unknown value. Unlike geometry or trigonometry, it is not directly concerned with shapes. Nonetheless, later progress in the discipline would establish a relationship between algebraic equations and various curves and points on a graph.

An example of the challenges in algebra approached first by Muslim mathematicians and later by their counterparts in Europe was the solving of cubic equations, or equations in which the highest exponent is 3. (An exponent is the "power" to which a number is raised, as represented by a small symbol to the upper right of the number. For example, 10^4 or 10 to

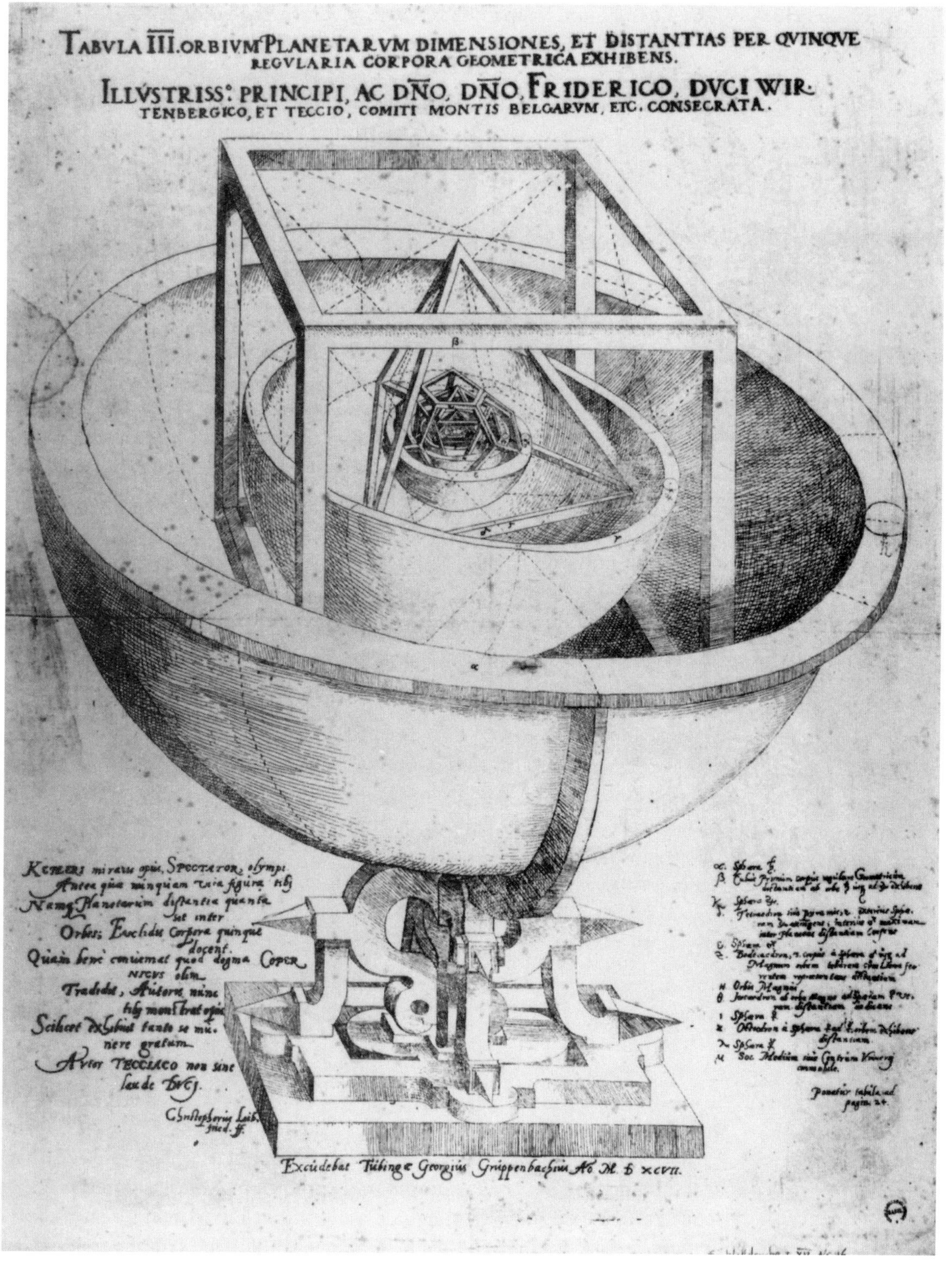
TABVLA III. ORBIVM PLANETARVM DIMENSIONES, ET DISTANTIAS PER QVINQVE REGVLARIA CORPORA GEOMETRICA EXHIBENS.
ILLVSTRISS: PRINCIPI, AC DÑO, DÑO, FRIDERICO, DVCI WIRTENBERGICO, ET TECCIO, COMITI MONTIS BELGARVM, ETC. CONSECRATA.

the fourth power is equal to 10 multiplied by itself three times: 10 × 10 × 10 × 10 = 10,000.)

Persian poet and mathematician Omar Khayyam (1048–1131) was first to solve cubic equations, but Omar's work, which combined Babylonian, Greek, and Hindu ideas, did not reach Europe for many centuries. Therefore the Italian mathematicians who solved cubic equations in the 1500s (see sidebar, "The Tartaglia-Cardano 'Grudge Match'" on page 260) thought they were the first.

Hindu-Arabic numerals come to the West

Europeans did not even begin to approach the challenges of algebraic equations until the 1500s, by which time they had adopted the Hindu-Arabic number system. Though created in India, this system was popularized in the Middle Ages (c. 500–c. 1500) by Arab mathematicians such as al-Khwarizmi. Therefore, when Europeans gained their first exposure to these numerals in the 1200s, they mistakenly called them "Arabic numerals."

The first European thinker to adopt the Hindu-Arabic numeral system, and to advocate its use, was Italian mathematician **Leonardo Fibonacci** (c. 1180–c. 1240; see biography in this chapter). A brilliant European mathematician of the medieval period, Fibonacci is considered primarily responsible for popularizing the use of Arabic-Hindu numerals, replacing the cumbersome numeral system that still remained in use from the days of the Roman Empire (c. 27 B.C.E–c. 500 C.E.).

Roman numerals

Developed in about 500 B.C.E., Roman numerals were used for about two thousand years. This was unfortunate, because the Roman system had no place value. When numbers are represented by Hindu-Arabic numerals, it is easy to see at a glance that a number such as 1,000 is larger than 3. With Roman numerals, however, such relationships are not obvious at all; for example, because III (3) is longer than M (1,000), III might seem to be the larger number.

The Roman numeral system made addition and subtraction difficult, while multiplication and division were virtually impossible. One of the only benefits of the system was the fact that it encouraged the development of early computing devices such as the counting board, as well as improvements on the abacus. An early form of hand-operated calculator that used movable beads strung along parallel wires inside a frame, the abacus had been invented thousands of years earlier in Babylonia. On the other hand, the use of counting boards probably helped extend the life of the inefficient Roman system: only in about 1500, three centuries after Fibonacci, did Europeans finally adopt the Hindu-Arabic numeral system.

Logarithms

Within a century after the adoption of the Hindu-Arabic system, Scottish mathematician John Napier (1550–1617) had devised an idea that would prove invaluable to the development of the computer. Napier discovered that numbers could be expressed in terms of what he called a "power." For example, 100 is equal to 10 times 10, or 10^2. This is the same as saying "10 squared," "10 raised to the power of 2," or simply "10 to the power of 2." In the number 10^2, 10 is called the base, and 2 the exponent.

Napier further discovered an amazing fact: that, as long as the same base number is used, numbers can be multiplied by adding exponents, and divided by subtracting exponents. This made relatively easy work of what were once extremely time-consuming multiplication and division problems. Used in the slide rule, invented in 1622 by English mathematician William Oughtred (1574–1660), logarithms provided the only practical means of solving difficult arithmetic problems until the development of the hand-held calculator in the 1970s.

John Napier discovered logarithms, the only practical means of solving complex arithmetic problems until the development of the hand-held calculator. **(Reproduced courtesy of the Library of Congress.)**

Zero and other concepts

Logarithms are an example of the discoveries made possible by the Hindu-Arabic numerals. By simplifying the use of numbers, these numerals opened up unexplored frontiers, expanding the limits of mathematicians' imagination. Hindu-Arabic numerals also introduced a number literally unknown in the West up to that time: zero.

Most ancient mathematical systems had lacked a concept of zero, and even those that had the concept generally treated zero as merely a placeholder. Only the Hindu number system gave zero the status of a full-fledged numeral. This innovation made it much easier to accurately record numbers and the steps involved in equations, thus making it much easier to perform calculations, and thus opening the way for mathematical progress in other areas. For example, it is not very easy to express a problem such as 1,000,003 times 50,020 without all the zeroes involved. Also, it is very hard to record steps in a problem if one cannot show how and where the zeroes appear. Even with small numbers such as 20, it would be hard to express the value of that number without making some reference to zero. Obviously, 20 is more than 19 and less than 21, and without some way to clearly designate place value even such a simple number could become confusing.

Along with the introduction of zero came a revolution in mathematical symbolism. Until the late 1400s, mathematicians performed their work without the use of convenient signs such as +, −, or ÷. Instead of symbolizing these, they used words, which made equations much more difficult.

Advances in the 1600s and 1700s

The number of mathematical advances that took place in the seventeenth and eighteenth centuries is astounding, and together these helped make possible the industrialized society of the modern world. Most often these new concepts, which ultimately had great practical applications, came about as the result of a mathematician's interest in something that did not immediately seem useful—a game of dice, for instance, or a popular brain teaser.

A fascination with dice and games of chance led Pierre de Fermat to conduct the first important work in probability theory and statistics. (Reproduced by permission of The Granger Collection, New York.)

The mathematics of gambling, for example, fascinated French mathematicians **Pierre de Fermat** (1601–1665; see biography in this chapter) and **Blaise Pascal** (1623–1662; see biography in this chapter), the fathers of statistics and probability theory, fields of mathematics today applied in science and engineering, political polling, and insurance. In the 1700s, Swiss mathematician **Leonhard Euler** (1707–1783; see biography in this chapter) became intrigued by a puzzle known as the Königsberg bridge problem.

The town of Königsberg included two islands in the middle of a river connected to the mainland, and to each other, by a total of seven bridges. The question was whether it was possible to cross all seven bridges without backtracking or crossing a bridge twice—something that Euler proved impossible. In his work on this brain teaser, he pioneered the areas of graph theory (the mathematical study of networks) and topology (a branch of mathematics concerned with the properties of geometric figures when these are stretched or compressed), introducing concepts used today in everything from computer networking to highway design.

Calculus

Perhaps the most significant, and certainly the most intellectually challenging, of all mathematical developments in the 1600s and 1700s was the creation of calculus, the branch of mathematics that deals with rates of change and motion. Calculus was the brainchild of two men who worked independently, British physicist and mathematician **Isaac Newton** (1642–1727; see biography in Physical Science chapter) and German philosopher and mathematician **Gottfried Wilhelm von Leibniz** (1646–1716; see biography in this chapter).

Questions as to who deserved credit for calculus inspired bitter disputes among European mathematicians for many decades. This was not the only controversy surrounding calculus. Because it involved the division of physical space into almost inconceivably small units, calculus made a number of European thinkers uncomfortable. Many criticized the very basis of the new discipline, but these critiques ultimately strengthened calculus, because they forced mathematicians to develop a better understanding of its ideas.

During the 1700s, Euler and others expanded understanding of calculus, and applied it to numerous practical fields. Calculus helped make possible the enormous scientific advances that would follow in the nineteenth and twentieth centuries. Scientists applied calculus in studying the motion of heavenly bodies, the mechanical properties of solids and fluids, and later, the movement of rockets and satellites. Calculus has applications in areas as down-to-earth as manufacturing, in which it helps maximize profits while minimizing costs, yet it is also essential to the study of subatomic particles, and to the technology of space flight.

ESSAYS

THE BIRTH OF MATHEMATICS IN THE NEAR EAST

The first society to establish a formal method of arithmetic was the civilization of Sumer (shoo-mer) in Mesopotamia, now part of Iraq. The Sumer people flourished from about 3500 to 2000 B.C.E. Overlapping the era of Sumerian culture was that of another Mesopotamian civilization, Babylonia, which originated around 3000 B.C.E. and remained powerful until almost 500 B.C.E.

Mathematics first developed in Sumer, where it was used for a very practical purpose: merchants needed to keep track of their money and inventory, or the goods they kept in stock. There was no concept of mathematics as something abstract, or separate from everyday applications. The Sumerians did not initially have the concept of 5 as a number without

Words to Know

decimal system: A number system, such as the one in use throughout most of the world today, based on 10.

notation: Symbols to represent numbers or operations such as addition and subtraction.

place value: The use of a number's position to indicate its size. In a number such as 1239, for instance, the 2 does not stand for 2, but for 200. Whereas the Hindu-Arabic numeral system in use today has a built-in concept of place value, the Roman numeral system used during the Middle Ages (c. 500–c. 1500) did not.

sexagesimal system: A number system based on 60.

being tied to an object; they only understood the idea of 5 chickens, for instance, or 5 cows. Sumerian bookkeepers used special sets of symbols to represent the types of objects being counted, whether it was a herd of goats, a measure of grain, or an area of land. They would use the symbol for a particular type of object, and would repeat this symbol an appropriate number of times to represent the quantity of that object.

Gradually, the Sumerians refined their use of various symbols until by about 2500 B.C.E. they recorded most items according to a single system of notation. Interestingly, the notation they chose, which resembled hash marks, was the same they had originally used to count a group of objects in which none is the same type of thing, for instance, one chicken plus one cow plus one clay jar. Thus they had begun thinking of numbers separate from the things being counted, a necessary step in order to address more difficult mathematical questions.

From this period dates the world's oldest known math problem, which states that a certain number of men each receive seven *ka* (approximately the size of a modern liter, or 0.264 gallons) of grain from a granary containing 1,152,000 *ka*. The answer—164,571 men with three *ka* left over—appears on a surviving clay tablet, while another tablet shows an incorrect answer by a student struggling to learn mathematics. The student's mistakes show historians how math was done forty-five hundred years ago.

A Sumerian clay tablet with incised cuneiform characters tallying sheep and goats.
(Reproduced by permission of the Corbis Corporation.)

The sexagesimal system

Over the next four hundred years or so, the Sumerians developed their writing from pictographs into a form known as cuneiform (kyoo-NAY-i-form). They also created a set of number symbols. For notation, the Mesopotamian number system used only two symbols, a vertical wedge for 1 and a corner wedge for 10. Numbers up to 59 were made by bundling these signs; after that, 60 was written as a 1 in the sixties column.

Thus the Sumerians created the first number system with place value; that is, the value of the number changes depending on its position (see essay "Early Number Systems" in this chapter). Later, when the Babylonians adopted the Sumerian system, they attempted a version of the decimal point as used today. The Babylonians never actually developed a "sexagesimal point," but they did have the concept of using a 3, for instance, to represent 3 or 3/10 (0.3) or 3/100 (0.03). Because they lacked a symbol to go between whole numbers and fractional numbers, which is the function of a decimal point, the Babylonians simply had to figure out where the point should go, based on the context. For example, π, which is the ratio between the circumference of (distance around) a circle and its diameter (distance across), is about 3.14, but if there were no decimal point, this would be written as 314, and anyone seeing the number would have to guess from the context that it was 3.14, and not 314 or 31.4.

The number system developed by the Sumerians, and passed on to the Babylonian civilization of Mesopotamia, used 60 as its basis. This is called a sexagesimal system. In the system applied by most societies today, called the decimal system, a number adds another place—that is, another digit to the left—after increasing by a power of 10. (Ten to the first power is 10; 10^2, or 10 to the second power, is 100; 10^3 is 1000.)

By contrast, in the sexagesimal system, place value was related to multiples of 60. This may seem odd, yet aspects of the sexagesimal system, inherited from the Babylonians, remain in place today, most notably the sixty-second minute, and the sixty-minute hour. Thus our way of keeping time is a base-60 system. In a base-10 system, the next number after 9

City of Babylon c. 479 B.C.E. The Babylonians were among the most advanced astronomers of the ancient world. **(Reproduced by permission of Archive Photos, Inc.)**

always ends in a 0, whether this is 99 and 100, or 5,799 and 5,800. Likewise, in the base-60 system of the clock, the next number after 59 is always 00; for example, 12:59 and 1:00.

Though it might seem a bit cumbersome, the Sumerians and Babylonians used a sexagesimal system because 60 has a large number of divisors, or numbers that divide into it in whole numbers: 2, 3, 4, 5, 6, 10, 12, 15, 20, and 30, for a total of ten divisors. By contrast, 10 has only two divisors, 2 and 5, and even 100 has only seven: 2, 4, 5, 10, 20, 25, and 50. With ten divisors, 60 could easily be divided into whole numbers, and this made calculations much easier in a world without calculators.

As for the Babylonians, who were among the most advanced astronomers of the ancient world, they found the sexagesimal system useful because 60, when multiplied by 6, comes close the number of days in a year. At that time, astronomy had not yet separated from the unscientific pursuit of astrology, and the Babylonians also found it useful that 360 divided easily by 12, the number of signs in the Zodiac.

The legacy of this system

The most important legacy of Mesopotamian mathematics can be found in the units by which time is still measured. When the Greeks under Alexander the Great (356–323 B.C.E.) conquered the Persian empire, which included all of Mesopotamia, Babylonian learning traveled westward to Greece. Among those ultimately influenced by Babylonian astronomy was the Greco-Roman astronomer **Ptolemy** (c. 100–170; see biography in Physical Science chapter), who adopted the sexagesimal system. Because his ideas dominated European astronomy until about 1500, the division of hours and minutes into units of sixty became ingrained in the Western mind.

Scientists throughout the world—and indeed all peoples of the industrialized world outside the United States—use the decimal-based metric system for measurement, yet the only area of measure that has never effectively converted to the metric system is time. Just as the Babylonians divided a degree into 3,600 seconds, so there are 3,600 seconds in an hour today. These numbers, as well as the number of hours in a day, work better in the sexagesimal system than in the decimal system, yet they remain in use because people are accustomed to the sexagesimal divisions of a day. Even if a day were re-divided into tens or hundreds there is still the fact that the length of a year can never be turned into a metric figure, since it is based on Earth's movement around the Sun. This movement takes 365.25 days, and since the metric system is based on units of 10, and 365.25 divided by 10 does not yield a whole number, there is no useful way to convert the length of the year into metric units. Therefore it makes more sense to stick with the 86,400-second day, a legacy of ancient Babylonia.

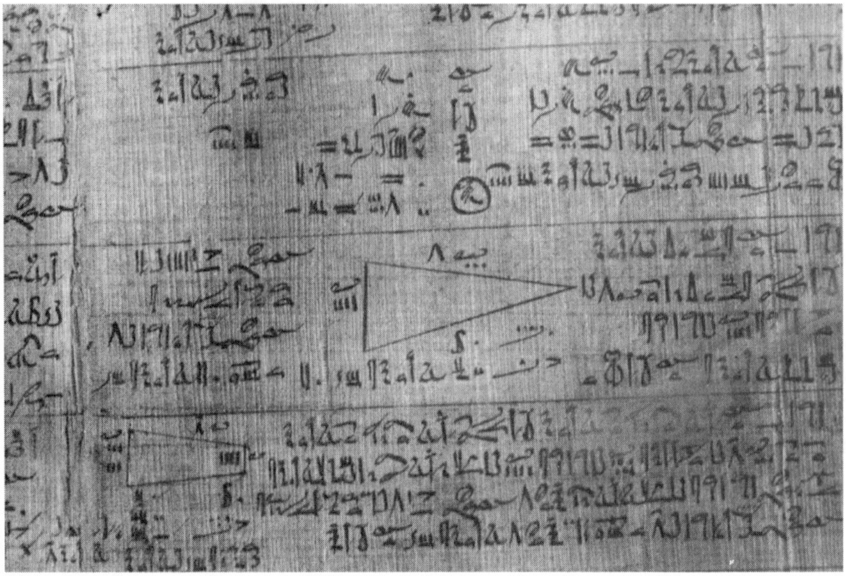

An Egyptian papyrus inscribed with calculations of the area of a triangular field. (Reproduced by permission of The Granger Collection, New York.)

Egyptian mathematics

The Egyptian civilization surpassed that of Mesopotamia in some regards, though not in terms of mathematics. However, the Egyptians did leave behind two important records of their mathematical work, documents created from a material more durable than the clay tablets of Mesopotamia.

The Egyptians developed an early form of paper, made from the leaves of the papyrus plant, and among the papyri that survive from ancient Egypt are two mathematical texts. The first, which originated in about 1850 B.C.E., is now housed at the Moscow Museum of Fine Art in Russia, and is known as the Moscow Papyrus. The second is attributed to the mathematician Ahmes (c. 1680–c. 1620 B.C.E.), but is named after the man who found it, Scottish archaeologist A. Henry Rhind. Though composed in about 1650 B.C.E., the Rhind Papyrus appears to be a copy of a document that dates from the same era as the Moscow Papyrus.

Before the development of papyrus, Egyptian records had been carved in stone using hieroglyphs. Mathematical notation from that period shows a complex system of representing numbers, but written numerals were simplified with the creation of a simpler set of written characters, called hieratic, after about 2500 B.C.E. The hieratic number system appears to have been decimal, and incorporated the idea of place value. Like the Sumerians, the Egyptians were concerned with practical applications for math, and the problems recorded on the papyri deal with everyday matters such as how to divide six loaves of bread among ten men.

MATHEMATICS IN CHINA, INDIA, AND BEYOND

Advances in mathematics by the Sumerians most likely influenced Egyptian mathematics, and vice versa (see essay "The Birth of Mathematics in the Near East" in this chapter.) Yet mathematics also developed among ancient cultures that had little or no contact with other societies.

Such was the case with India, whose mathematicians developed the Hindu-Arabic numeral system (1, 2, 3...) used today. At least the Indians had some contact with Mesopotamia and lands to the west, but the Chinese were far more isolated. Because they were separated from India by high mountains, and from western Asia and Europe by wide distances, the Chinese had no idea that other civilizations even existed until about 100 B.C.E. Yet the mathematicians of China managed to make a number of breakthroughs in areas such as measuring the size of a circle.

Even more isolated were the Maya, who flourished in what is now Guatemala, Belize, and Mexico from about 300 to 925 C.E. Despite their separation from the rest of the world, the Maya developed an advanced mathematical system that included zero, an idea also introduced by the mathematicians of India.

China

Chinese mathematicians of the first century C.E. used decimal fractions, or fractions represented as decimal numbers with place value; for example, 0.5 instead of the common fraction 1/2. Thus they achieved something neither the Greeks nor the Romans ever did. In fact, decimal fractions would not appear in Europe until the 1500s.

The Chinese were the first to use negative numbers, which they had been applying since the first century B.C.E. European mathematicians as late as the 1400s still dismissed these as unreal numbers, arguing that it is impossible to have less than nothing. But as the Chinese recognized, a negative number is very real. If a person overdraws her bank account by $20, she has a balance of -$20, and this is quite different from a zero balance. Thus, negative numbers proved useful in finance, where it is certainly possible to have less than nothing. And though the ancient Chinese did not have thermometers and temperature scales as we know them now (these were invented in Europe after about 1600), negative numbers are used today for measuring temperatures below zero.

In addition to finding methods for extracting square and cube roots (the numbers that must be multiplied by themselves once or twice respectively in order to equal a particular product), the Chinese even created a basic form of algebra. They also calculated amazingly accurate figures for pi, the

Words to Know

abacus: An early form of hand-operated calculator that used movable beads strung along parallel wires inside a frame.

algebra: A branch of mathematics in which arithmetic operations (for example, addition or multiplication) are generalized. In algebraic equations, symbols represent numbers of unknown value, and the equations themselves are used to find these values.

circumference: The distance around a circle.

cube root: The cube root of a given number is a number that, when multiplied by itself twice, will produce that number. Thus $2 \times 2 \times 2 = 8$, and 2 is the cube root of 8.

decimal fraction: A method of representing numbers that are less than 1 by using a decimal point and place value. The number 0.01 is a decimal fraction, whereas 1/100 is a common fraction.

diameter: The distance across a circle, as drawn along a path that passes through the center of that circle.

Hindu-Arabic numerals: The number system in use throughout most of the world today, which uses ten digits, including zero.

negative number: A number smaller than zero.

pi: The ratio between the circumference of (distance around) a circle and its diameter (distance across); that is, the circumference divided by the diameter. Pronounced "pie" and represented by the Greek letter π, pi has a value of 3.14159265+. This is its value to eight decimal places; in fact pi is an irrational number, meaning that it goes on and on without repeating or ending.

place value: The use of a number's position to indicate its size. In a number such as 1,239, for instance, the 1 refers to 1 thousand rather than just 1, and 2 refers to 2 hundreds. Whereas the Hindu-Arabic numeral system in use today has a built-in concept of place value, the Roman numeral system used during the Middle Ages did not.

ratio: The relationship between two numbers or values. All fractions are ratios, but some ratios such as π (pi, the relationship between the circumference and diameter of a circle) cannot be expressed as fractions.

square root: The square root of a given number is a number that, when multiplied by itself, will produce that number. Thus $2 \times 2 = 4$, and 2 is the square root of 4.

The abacus, an ancient counting machine, arrived in China from the Middle East in the 1600s. **(Reproduced by permission of the Corbis Corporation.)**

ratio between the circumference of a circle and its diameter (the distance around the circle divided by the distance across it). The mathematician and astronomer Tsu Ch'ung-chih (Zu Chongzhi; 429–500) first calculated pi at 355/113 or 3.1415929, which is correct to six decimal places (that is, all numbers before the last 9.) Having an accurate equivalent for π made it possible to more accurately calculate the size of a circle. This in turn made it easy to build wagon wheels that were all the same size, to design perfectly circular buildings, or to calculate the amount of land in a circular lot.

Chinese math classics

An unknown author of the first century of the common era wrote the great classic of Chinese mathematical literature, *Nine Chapters on Mathematical Procedures,* which contains the bulk of Chinese mathematical knowledge up to that time. While the book addressed the writing of numbers, its primary emphasis was on the use of early calculators. Though China is famous for its use of the abacus, this counting machine did not appear in China until the 1600s; instead, the ancient Chinese used counting rods, sticks of bamboo that represented numbers and helped maintain place value in computations.

Over the next ten centuries, Chinese mathematicians devoted much of their energy to commenting on and expanding the *Nine Chapters,* but by about 1000 C.E. it had become clear that they needed to update the book in light of work by mathematicians in more recent centuries. The fact that the Chinese government established an Office of Mathematics to undertake those revisions is a reflection of the high emphasis placed on the ability to perform practical calculations such as those necessary for business or building. The mathematicians on the committee produced *Ten Classics of Mathematics* (c. 1050), which improved on the *Nine Chapters.*

By the 1100s, Chinese mathematicians had spread their efforts into new areas, including geometry and the solutions to equations. In *Mathematical Treatise in Nine Sections,* a publication whose title honored the *Nine Chapters,* Ch'in Chiu-shao (1202–1261) addressed equations in algebra and other topics.

At the same time Ch'in Chiu-shao was working in southern China, Li Yeh (1192–1279) in northern China published an important geometry text known as *Sea-Mirror of Circle Measurements.* Also significant was *Precious Mirror of the Four Elements,* a work of algebra by Chu Shih-chieh (c. 1280–1303). These works greatly influenced mathematical knowledge in China, where such learning was applied for purposes such as surveying land, or in laying out the foundations for buildings.

Negative numbers and magic squares

By the early 1300s, Chinese mathematicians began paying increasing attention to the role of negative numbers. The Chinese were the first to develop symbolism for representing negatives, either depicting them in different colors from positive ones, or denoting then by drawing a diagonal line through the number. Despite their advances in this field, however, the Chinese did not long pursue these studies, primarily because they failed to recognize any practical value in them. Like the Egyptians and Sumerians before them, they were primarily concerned with forms of mathematics that offered immediate real-life applications.

An exception to this trend was the Chinese interest in magic squares, which according to tradition had been discovered by an early king in about 2000 B.C.E. The magic square is a set of four, nine, sixteen, or twenty-five boxes arranged in a square pattern. (Actually, the number of boxes can be any number, as long as it is a square.) The "magic" comes from placing numbers in the squares which, when added by row, column, or diagonal, yield the same sum.

During the 1400s, Yang Hui (c. 1238–c. 1298) constructed a number of highly complex magic squares. In his *Cheng chu tong bian ben mo* (1275), he presented an early version of a number diagram that was later perfected by and named for French mathematician and philosopher **Blaise Pascal** (1623–1662; see biography in this chapter). Yang Hui created his own version of Pascal's triangle, as the number diagram came to be called, a good four centuries earlier.

Yang Hui's book also emphasized systematic mathematical education, rather than the traditional path of simple memorization common in China at the time. In fact his work represented the final flowering of the great age of Chinese mathematics. Most later Chinese mathematical texts were sim-

Magic Squares. **(Reproduced by permission of Hans J. Neuhart, Electronic Illustrators.)**

8	1	6
3	5	7
4	9	2

16	2	3	13
5	11	10	8
9	7	6	12
4	14	15	1

17	24	1	8	15
23	5	7	14	16
4	6	13	20	22
10	12	19	21	3
11	18	25	2	9

32	29	4	1	24	21
30	31	2	3	22	23
12	9	17	20	28	25
10	11	18	19	26	27
13	16	36	33	5	8
14	15	34	35	6	7

30	39	48	1	10	19	28
38	47	7	9	18	27	29
46	6	8	17	26	35	37
5	14	16	25	34	36	45
13	15	24	33	42	44	4
21	23	32	41	43	3	12
22	31	40	49	2	11	20

64	2	3	61	60	6	7	57
9	55	54	12	13	51	50	16
17	47	46	20	21	43	42	24
40	26	27	37	36	30	31	33
32	34	35	29	28	38	39	25
41	23	22	44	45	19	18	48
49	15	14	52	53	11	10	56
8	58	58	5	4	62	63	1

ply summations of earlier writings, and mathematics in China became increasingly stagnant.

The decline of Chinese mathematics

The Chinese had once been far ahead of the West in their understanding of mathematics, but by the late 1600s, Western ideas had begun to reach China. From that point on, the West would hold the lead; yet contact with the West also stimulated a resurgence of Chinese interest in mathematics.

The abacus arrived in China from the Middle East during the 1600s, and it is possible that the Chinese exported some ideas to the Middle East and Europe as well. Certainly China had extensive contact with the outside world during the Han and T'ang dynasties (207 B.C.E.–220 C.E. and 618–907 C.E. respectively), and probably passed mathematical knowledge to those regions during that time. As to what the Chinese may have passed on to the West, historians are not certain. Some writers claim that the Europeans' use of decimal fractions was based on the Chinese model, and others maintain that Chinese mathematicians (rather than those of India) actually invented the number zero. If these claims are true, they have certainly never been proven.

On the other hand, it is certain that the Chinese made a great number of mathematical advances; that they later seemed to forget their own past achievements; and that Chinese mathematical work was surpassed first by that of Arab mathematicians in about 900 C.E., and later by European mathematicians in about 1500 C.E.. Ironically, the Chinese would later learn mathematics from European teachers, in many cases not knowing that the ideas they were being taught had been discovered in China first.

India

Despite the many advances made by Chinese mathematics, India would have a much greater impact on modern understanding of numbers. Though the mathematicians of Mesopotamia are credited with developing the first place-value system, the Indians' use of place value is of greater historical significance, since theirs was a decimal system (base-10) rather than a sexagesimal (base-60) one, and is the precursor to the modern number system used throughout the world today. The decimal system is the dominant mathematics system in use throughout the world today in which a place is added for multiples of 10, i.e. 10, 100, 1000, etc. In a sexagesimal, or base-60, system a place is added for multiples of 60.

In fact, the modern number system is a direct descendant of the one first developed in ancient India. The 200s B.C.E. saw the first appearance of the numbers Europeans later mistakenly called "Arabic numerals." They are more properly called Hindu-Arabic numerals in recognition of the fact that

Mayan Mathematics

Though it was ultimately from India that Europeans adopted the zero, Hindu mathematicians were not the only ones to develop the concept. Across the ocean, in a land of whose existence the rest of the world was ignorant until about 1500, mathematics developed independently among the Mayan people of what is now Mexico, Belize, and Guatemala.

Some time during what is known as the Preclassic stage of Mayan history (c. 800 B.C.E.–c. 300 C.E.), the Maya invented a system of mathematics, as well as the calendars on which they applied it. In fact, the two are so closely linked that they are seldom discussed separately.

The vigesimal (base-20) Mayan counting system is reflected in the twenty-day months of their two calendars. One calendar was for religious purposes, and consisted of thirteen months, for a total of 260 days. The other calendar, which governed public life, consisted of eighteen months, along with five nameless days," for a total of 365 days. Every fifty-two years, the two calendars aligned.

The Mayan calendar was accurate to about five minutes per year, an impressive fact when compared with the Julian calendar, which remained in use throughout Europe until the 1600s, and which had an annual error of eleven minutes. Indeed, the very fact that the Maya developed a system of mathematics entirely on their own, without input from any other civilization, is remarkable.

Not only did the Maya have a concept of place value, but they also used the zero as a placeholder for an empty column, as in a number such as 502. Despite the many advances credited to Greek mathematicians, European mathematics would not fully incorporate these ideas until about 1500—just as European explorers were on the brink of conquering what remained of the once-great Mayan civilization.

they originated in India among mathematicians of the Hindu religion, and later spread to the Arab world. After several modifications, these numerals evolved into the standard 1, 2, 3, 4, 5, 6, 7, 8, 9 still used in modern times.

Instead of using more symbols for higher numbers, they introduced a place-value system for multipliers of 10. This made it much easier to perform calculations involving large numbers than it would have been using Roman numerals or any of the other number systems in use at the time. To multiply 438 by 3,000, for instance, is a matter of breaking the problem down into a few simple steps, based on place value: multiply 3 by 400, 3 by 30, and 3 by 8; add these products together; then multiply the total by 1,000, a step that requires the placement of three zeroes at the end of the number obtained in the earlier steps.

This is much simpler than the same problem in Roman numerals, which would be represented as MMM multiplied by CDXXXVIII. Because Roman numerals had no place-value, and calculations were so difficult, Romans had to use an abacus or some other calculating device. With the numeral system developed in India, however, such calculations could be done in written form, and some problems were rendered so easy that a good mathematician could practically do them in his or her head.

Development of the zero concept

By far the greatest mathematician of premodern India was **Aryabhata** (476–550; see biography in this chapter), who summed up existing mathematical knowledge in a collection of writings called the *Aryabhatiya* in 499. Aryabhata's most significant work lay in his explanation of the Hindu numeral system. By his time, Indian mathematicians had created a means of designating place value in the name of a number. Today a number such as 742 is understood to mean seven hundreds, four tens, and two ones; similarly, Hindu mathematicians used their own terminology to designate the hundreds place, the tens place, and so on.

Indian mathematicians also found a way to designate an empty column. In a number such as 502, for instance, the tens column needs a numeral to represent it; otherwise, it would be indistinguishable from 52 or 5,002 or 50,002. Aryabhata and other Indian mathematicians began using a symbol called *sunya,* or "empty," for a place with no numerical value; today this idea is known as zero. Having a symbol for zero ended a great deal of confusion over numbers.

Still, it took some time for zero to gain acceptance as anything more than a placeholder. The Hindu mathematician Sridhara (c. 850) maintained that zero is as meaningful a number as any other and Bhaskara (1114–1185) contemplated the challenging problem of dividing by zero. Bhaskara concluded that a particular number, three, divided by zero is equal to infinity. In fact, there is no solution to the problem, because even if infinity were multiplied by zero, the result would not be a number other than zero. Three (or any other number) divided by zero cannot be equal to infinity, since infinity multiplied by zero cannot be equal to any number other than zero. Therefore, Bhaskara was incorrect, but he was still ahead of other mathematicians in realizing that division by zero is a tricky matter, quite unlike division by any other number.

Bhaskara was the first mathematician to note that the multiplication or division of a positive number by a positive, or a negative by a negative, yields a positive result, and that a positive and a negative divided or multiplied gives a negative result. (For example, $2 \times 2 = 4$, as does -2×-2, but $2 \times -2 = -4$. Similarly, $4 \times 2 = 2$; and $-4 \times -2 = 2$, but $4 \times -2 = -2$.) In addition, he built on the work of earlier mathematicians, including Aryabhata, in developing algebra. He even used letters to represent unknown numbers, as mathematicians still do.

The lasting contributions of Indian math

As with Aryabhata, Bhaskara's most important work lay with the development and explanation of zero. In fact, this was the most significant contribution of Indian mathematicians. The Indians were not the only ones to come up with this concept; the mathematicians of ancient Mesopotamia seem to have used the zero, as did those of the Mayan civilization. However, the Hindu mathematicians were the first to use zero as more than just a placeholder, treating is as a number in its own right.

As important as zero was, it was just one numeral out of ten in the Hindu-Arabic numeral system, which proved to be by far the most influential numeral system in all of history. Because it is so easy to use, it became the preferred system for civilizations everywhere, and remains in use today in America and throughout the world. (See essay "Hindu-Arabic Numerals and Mathematical Symbolism" in this chapter.)

☐ THE GREEKS' NEW APPROACH TO MATHEMATICS

While civilizations in Mesopotamia, India, China, and Central America developed many fundamental mathematical ideas that the Greeks themselves would never grasp, such as the concept of zero, negative numbers, and a workable number system using place value, the Greeks are widely admired for their brilliance as mathematicians. At the high point of Greek mathematics, from about 550 to about 250 B.C.E., they showed the world how to look at numbers and mathematical processes in an entirely different way, and in the process freed up mathematics for future progress.

In contrast to the applied mathematics of the Sumerians and others, who used numbers for specific purposes such as business and engineering, the Greeks practiced pure mathematics, that is, mathematics for its own

Words to Know

applied mathematics: The use of mathematics for a specific purpose, as in business or engineering. This is in contrast to "pure" mathematics.

geometry: The branch of mathematics concerned with the properties and relationships of points, lines, angles, surfaces, and shapes.

hypotenuse: The longest side of a right triangle.

irrational number: A number that is not the ratio of any two whole numbers. In decimal form, irrational numbers such as pi (π) neither terminate (come to an end) nor repeat.

logic: A system of reasoning for reaching valid conclusions about concepts, and for assessing the validity of a conclusion that has been reached.

number theory: The study of the properties of numbers, and the relationships between them.

pi: The ratio between the circumference of (distance around) a circle and its diameter (distance across). Pronounced "pie" and represented by the Greek letter π, pi has a value of 3.14159265+. This is its value to eight decimal places; in fact pi is an irrational number.

proof: A step-by-step process of proving certain ideas in geometry by referring to already established propositions.

sake. The Sumerians had been the first to treat numbers in the abstract: instead of thinking in terms of five chickens or five goats, they were able to conceive of 5 and other numbers as ideas unto themselves. The Greeks took this even further, treating mathematics as something that did not necessarily relate to everyday uses. In so doing, they established the tradition of exploring mathematical ideas simply for the joy of working with numbers.

Greek society was among the first in which the search for truth through philosophy also played a significant role. Philosophy is the area of study that explains general principles about truth, reality, meaning, wisdom, and right and wrong. Philosophy in its Western form was born in

pure mathematics: Mathematics for its own sake, rather than for a specific application. Compare with applied mathematics.

Pythagorean theorem: A rule, attributed to the Greek mathematician Pythagoras (c. 580–c. 500 B.C.E.) but probably derived much earlier, which states that for every right triangle, the square of the hypotenuse is equal to the sum of the squares of the other two sides.

ratio: The relationship between two numbers or values. All fractions are ratios, but some ratios such as π (pi, the relationship between the circumference and diameter of a circle) cannot be expressed as fractions.

right triangle: A triangle with one right angle, or 90° angle. (Since the total measurement of the three angles in a triangle is 180°, no triangle can have more than one right angle.)

square: The square of a number is that number multiplied by itself. Thus 25, for instance, is the square of 5, since $5 \times 5 = 25$.

square root: The square root of a given number is a number that, when multiplied by itself, will produce that number. Thus $2 \times 2 = 4$, and 2 is the square root of 4.

whole number: A number, such as 1 or 23 or 2,765,014, that includes no fractions.

Greece. Like mathematics, philosophy is concerned with systems and relations of ideas. Logic, an area of philosophy developed by the Greeks, is particularly important to the study of mathematics. Thus it is fitting that some of the earliest Greek philosophers were men who also contributed, either directly or indirectly, to the foundations of mathematical study.

The Pythagoreans

The first Western mathematician of note was **Pythagoras** (c. 580–c. 500 B.C.E.; see biography in this chapter), who in 530 B.C.E. established a community of followers in a Greek colony on the southern coast of Italy. The

Pythagoreans were no ordinary group of mathematical students; indeed, they were more like a religious cult than a school. Among the beliefs and practices they espoused was the transmigration of souls, or reincarnation, along with a disciplined lifestyle that included vegetarianism.

The most influential of the Pythagorean beliefs was their notion that all of reality was mathematical, and that the relationships between numbers revealed a mystical order at the heart of life. This inspired thinkers to look at numbers differently. Today, we take it for granted that mathematics is necessary in the study of science, but this was not always the case. The Pythagoreans helped Greek philosophers and others to realize that numbers help us to understand the world. In addition, by according such a great deal of philosophical importance to numbers and the relationships between them, the Pythagoreans opened the way to new discoveries of their own, in areas as wide-ranging as acoustics (the study of sound) and astronomy.

Pythagoras developed a system of musical scales and chords based on ratios between numbers. **(The Bettmann Archive. Reproduced by permission of the Corbis Corporation.)**

The Pythagoreans studied the properties of numbers, the reflection of numerical properties in geometrical figures, and the existence of numerical relationships in the natural world. Such investigations led the Pythagoreans to observe a geometrical relationship in right triangles that has come to be know as the Pythagorean theorem. In fact, this relationship had been noticed centuries earlier by the mathematicians of Babylonia. Whatever the source, the Pythagorean theorem states that for every right triangle (a triangle with a 90-degree angle), the square (a number multiplied by itself) of the hypotenuse (longest side) is equal to the sum of the squares of the other sides. Thus if a right triangle has one side that is three inches long, and another side four inches long, the hypotenuse will measure five inches: $3^2 + 4^2 = 5^2 = 9 + 16 = 25$. This pattern is true for all right triangles, regardless of the size of the sides of the triangle. This Pythagorean theorem remains one of the touchstones of elementary geometry.

Music and astronomy

The Pythagoreans' investigations also led them to develop a system of musical scales and chords, based on ratios between numbers. This system became the basis for Western music. Today scientists recognize that every musical note has a certain frequency, or number of vibrations per second, and have confirmed that harmonic combinations of notes are those that have ratios involving smaller, rather than larger, numbers.

For instance, middle C on a piano and the first harmonic (one octave above it) sound perfectly musical when played together, and it so happens that the ratio between their two frequencies (264 and 528 vibrations per second respectively) is exactly one to two, or 1:2 in modern notation. On the other hand, the ratio between the frequencies of E and F involves relatively large numbers (15:16), and when those two notes are played together, they produce a grating sound unpleasant to most ears. Thus, a 1:2 ratio between string lengths, which involves relatively small numbers, has a more pleasant sound than a 15:16 ratio, which involves numbers that are much larger than 1 or 2. The Pythagoreans were also profoundly interested in astronomy, which in their minds was not entirely unconnected with music. In the orderly movements of the stars, they saw a harmony like that of music.

The lasting impact of the Pythagoreans

The Pythagoreans flourished throughout southern Italy until the mid-400s B.C.E., and during this time they gained considerable political power. Ultimately, however, this power proved their undoing, because it led to raids and violent suppression by local rulers. In the aftermath, the surviving Pythagoreans scattered throughout the Greek-speaking world, passing their ideas on to others.

The works of the Greek philosophers Plato (427–347 B.C.E.) and **Aristotle** (384–322 B.C.E.; see biography in Life Science chapter) strongly reflected Pythagorean views. At the heart of Plato's philosophy, for instance, was the Pythagorean idea that the physical world is only a reflection of some deeper, spiritual reality. It is also possible that Pythagoreans, and not the followers of the esteemed Greek physician Hippocrates (c. 460–c. 377 B.C.E.; see biography in Life Science chapter), actually composed the Hippocratic Oath that provides a code of conduct for doctors even in modern times. (See "Greek Physicians Transform the Life Sciences" in the Life Sciences chapter.)

Certainly Pythagorean thought has indirectly influenced many efforts to equate or explain nature with mathematics, and among these is the modern science of digitization. By electronically representing sound, images, and information as numbers, digitization achieves the Pythagorean ideal of understanding the world (or at least a part of it) in terms of numbers. If Pythagoras could be alive today and hear digital sound, which brings together his two favorite things—music and numbers—he would no doubt be pleased.

Zeno's paradoxes

An example of the interplay between mathematics and philosophy can be found in a set of puzzles formulated by the philosopher Zeno of Elea (c. 495–c. 430 B.C.E.). Actually, these puzzles are called paradoxes, a paradox being an idea that seems contradictory or opposed to common sense, yet is in fact correct. The story behind Zeno's paradoxes is ironic, because they achieved results quite different from those he intended. Setting out to make one philosophical point, he inadvertently made quite a different one: instead of showing that change is impossible, as he had planned, Zeno accidentally illustrated the fact that the use of incorrect data can lead to false results, even if the best logical principles are applied.

Zeno was a student of the philosopher Parmenides (par-MIN-uh-deez; born about 515 B.C.E.), who taught that Non-Being is an impossibility; only Being exists. In Parmenides's view, Being was timeless and changeless, a claim that was difficult to maintain in light of the many examples of change in the world. So Zeno set out to defend his teacher's position with a series of paradoxes that, he hoped, would prove that change is impossible.

The paradoxes and their impact

In one paradox, Zeno referred to an arrow being shot from a bow. At every moment of its flight, it could be said that the arrow was at rest within a space equal to its length. Though it would be thousands of years before slow-motion photography, in effect Zeno was asking his listeners to imagine a snapshot of the arrow in flight. If it was at rest in that snapshot, then when did it actually move?

Another paradox involved Achilles, hero of Homer's *Iliad* and the "swiftest of mortals," in a foot race against a tortoise. Because he was so much faster than the tortoise, Achilles allows the creature to start near the finish line—a big mistake, because as Zeno set out to prove, Achilles could then never pass the tortoise. Zeno argued that by the time Achilles got to the point where the tortoise started, as long as the tortoise kept moving, the creature would have moved on to another point, and when Achilles got to that second point, the tortoise would have moved on to yet another point, and so on. There would be no point at which Achilles could pass the tortoise.

These and Zeno's other paradoxes impressed philosophers with the importance of logic. Logic is closely tied with mathematics, because both involve the application of very strict rules, which relate ideas to one another, and if one applies the right rules in either mathematics or logic, one will get the correct answer every time. Also, just as mathematics uses equations, logic uses something called a syllogism, which is like an equation. (Syllogisms are discussed in the next section, "Aristotle and Logic.")

Note that the paradoxes served to emphasize the importance of logic, but they did not, of course, prove that change is impossible, or that Achilles could never catch up with the tortoise—claims that are obviously untrue. On the surface, Zeno's paradoxes seem convincing, but actually, what he managed to do was to play a logical trick. In each problem, Zeno treated either space or time as though they were made up of an infinite number of points, infinite arrow "snapshots," and infinite points between Achilles and the tortoise.

If this were true, then Zeno's claim that Achilles could not catch up with the tortoise would be true as well. But this is not the case: no matter how small the increments of measurement one uses, only a finite, or limited, amount of those measures are involved. Even if the distance between Achilles and the tortoise were measured in angstrom units (a modern unit of measurement so small it is used to gauge the size of atoms), the number would be very, very large, but it would not be unlimited. Achilles would not have to cross infinite points to get to the tortoise, and since he is obviously moving at a faster rate of speed, he would eventually pass the tortoise no matter how much of a head start the slower creature had.

Thus Zeno's paradoxes indirectly influenced mathematics by encouraging the study of logic as a means of unraveling the puzzles. They also directly influenced mathematical thinking by raising the idea of very small intervals. When something is almost infinitely small, it is referred to as infinitesimal. The idea of ever more infinitesimal quantities, approaching but never quite reaching nothingness, did not mix well with Pythagorean notions. Indeed, it would be centuries before Western mathematics would consider the ideas raised by Zeno, and thus today, his paradoxes are often regarded as an early hint toward the idea of calculus (see essay "Angles, Curves, and Surfaces" in this chapter).

Aristotle and logic

Logic can be defined as a system of reasoning for reaching valid conclusions about concepts, and for assessing a conclusion that has been reached. Aristotle first developed a set of rules for using logic. He created a system called a syllogism (SIL-uh-jizm), of which the classic example is "All men are mortal [i.e., will die]; Socrates is a man; therefore, Socrates is mortal." Each of the statements in a syllogism should be capable of being judged true or false. The first two statements, known as premises, provide evidence for the third statement, known as the conclusion. What Aristotle demonstrated is that if the premises are true then the conclusion must follow. Such arguments are said to be deductively valid.

Likewise, if one of the premises is not true, then the conclusion does not follow with necessity, such as "All Greeks are liars; Socrates is a Greek;

therefore, Socrates is a liar." The first premise is not provable as true or false and so it does not support the final conclusion.

At the same time, it is possible to create an argument that is not valid, using premises that are true: "All Greeks come from Europe; Socrates comes from Europe; therefore, Socrates is Greek." The faultiness of this logic becomes apparent if one draws a diagram, using a big circle to represent people from Europe. Inside of that circle would be two smaller ones, labeled Greeks and Socrates. The diagram demonstrates that there is no reason to assume that the Socrates circle fits inside of the Greek circle.

The impact of logic

The application of logic provided mathematicians and scientists with a way of developing their ideas, testing their reasoning, and evaluating correct relationships between concepts. One of the most useful contributions Aristotle made was his introduction of symbolic notation of a kind that would later be used in mathematics.

The syllogism above that begins "All men are mortal" can be rendered symbolically as "all As are Bs; C is an A; therefore, C is a B." By contrast, the error of the "All Greeks come from Europe" syllogism becomes clear when it is represented by symbols: "All As are Bs; C is a B; therefore C is an A." Aristotle thus conceived of the format used today in equations such as "2 + 2 = 4." He also set the stage for the idea of the proof, which would become a fundamental aspect of geometry and other mathematical disciplines.

EARLY NUMBER SYSTEMS

In order to perform mathematical work, it is necessary to have two things: a system of numbers that uses some particular number as its reference point, and a way of representing those numbers in writing. Long before civilizations developed written languages, they grappled with the first problem, and the answers were not always obvious. A number system is a structured arrangement of numbers that make it possible to count and perform mathematical problems. Every number system uses a particular number as its base, a number that provides it with a frame of reference, or a starting point. In the decimal number system used by Americans, the number 10 is that base, meaning that numbers are viewed in groups of 10, and once you reach a multiple of 10, then the counting "starts over" (in a sense) at 1, with the next number a multiple of 10 plus 1, the number after that a multiple of 10 plus 2, and so on. But in a base 60 system, such as the system we use for keeping time (with sixty seconds in a minute, and sixty minutes in an hour), the counting starts over after reaching 60. Therefore the next minute after 10:59 is 11:00, and the next minute after that is 11:01.

Words to Know

abacus: An early form of hand-operated calculator that used movable beads strung along parallel wires inside a frame.

applied mathematics: The use of mathematics for a specific purpose, as in business or engineering. This is in contrast to pure mathematics.

decimal fraction: A method of representing numbers that are less than 1 by using a decimal point and place value. The number 0.01 is a decimal fraction, whereas 1/100 is a common fraction.

decimal system: A number system, such as the one in use throughout most of the world today, based on 10.

Hindu-Arabic numerals: The number system in use throughout most of the world today, which uses ten digits, including zero.

notation: Symbols to represent numbers or operations such as addition and subtraction.

place value: The use of a number's position to indicate its size. In a number such as 1,239, for instance, the 1 stands for 1000, the 2 for 200, the 3 for 30, and the 9 for 9. Whereas the Hindu-Arabic numeral system in use today has a built-in concept of place value, the Roman numeral system used during the Middle Ages did not.

pure mathematics: Mathematics for its own sake, rather than for a specific application. Compare with applied mathematics.

sexagesimal system: A number system based on 60.

whole number: A number, such as 1 or 23 or 2,765,014, that includes no fractions.

Today people use the decimal system, based on the number 10, but in other times and places, civilizations have used numeral systems based on other numbers, including 2, 5, 20, 60, and 100. Most such numeration systems were probably based on body parts used for counting, the first and most primitive form of calculator. Thus the decimal system probably relates to the number of fingers on a person's two hands.

A base-5 system, with its relationship to the number of fingers on a single hand, would seem to make sense, but the only known group with a base-5 numeration system is a tribe of Arawak Indians in South America. More common was the base-20 or vigesimal system, used by the Maya of Central America, and probably based on the combined number of fingers and toes. There have even been number systems based on the number of arms a person has. Binary counting systems, used by early peoples, are simple in that they include only two numerals. But they are also complex, in that they make possible the operation of highly sophisticated machines: computers, which interpret binary symbols as a series of "on" and "off" signals.

In addition to settling on a basis for a number system, there is also the problem of developing symbols to represent those numbers. This proved to be an even greater challenge. For thousands of years, Western civilization followed the idea established by the Greeks, and later developed by the Romans, of using letters to represent numbers. The much more efficient system of Hindu-Arabic numerals (1, 2, 3... 9), by contrast, is a relatively recent adaptation, having evolved in the period between about 200 B.C.E. and 500 C.E.

Mesopotamian and Egyptian numerals

Some numeral systems clearly were not based on body parts. Examples include the Chinese system, which used 100 as its frame of reference, and the sexagesimal (sek-suh-JEZ-uh-mul) or base-60 system developed by the Sumerians of ancient Mesopotamia (now part of Iraq). It has been speculated that the Sumerians, who developed the sexagesimal system between about 3500 and 2000 B.C.E., based it on units of measure common in their society.

On the other hand, they may have chosen it because 60 can be divided by 2, 3, 4, 5, and 6, 10, 12, 20, and 30 with a whole number as the result. (By contrast, 10 can only be divided by two numbers, 2 and 5, to yield a whole number.) Whatever the case, the Sumerians' sexagesimal system, which they passed on to the Babylonians, would prove highly influential because of its use in astronomy. Aspects of it remain in place today, in the way that a circle—and, more importantly, time in a day—is divided. A circle is divided into 360 degrees, an hour into sixty minutes, and a minute into sixty seconds, and these traditions all go back to Babylonia and the sexagesimal number system. (See essay "The Birth of Mathematics in the Near East" in this chapter).

The Sumerians' number system was the first one with the idea of place value. A place-value system assigns a particular value to the position of a numeral in a longer number. For example, in the decimal system, a num-

The Binary Number System

The simplest, yet in some ways the most advanced, numeration system is binary, or base-2. Early peoples, and some native peoples in remote corners of the world today, apparently based this system on the two arms of the human body. During the 1600s, German philosopher and mathematician **Gottfried Wilhelm von Leibniz** (1646–1716; see biography in this chapter) began to develop a highly sophisticated binary number system based on an ancient Chinese text. This became the basis for the system of 1's and 0's that computers today use in interpreting bundles of data.

The decimal system uses a ones column, a tens column, a hundreds column, and so on by multiples of 10. By contrast, the binary system has a ones column, a twos column, a fours column, an eights column, and so on by multiples of 2. Expressed in binary form, 2 is 10; 3 is 11; 4 is 100; and so forth. While this might appear extremely difficult to someone raised with decimal numbers, it is ideally suited to computers, which rapidly process the numbers as a series of electrical pulses.

ber's position defines whether it is a multiple of 1, 10, 100, 1000, and so on. In the number 1,234, the 4 occupies the ones slot, or numbers 0 through 9; the 3 occupies the slot representing tens, or numbers 10 through 99; the 2 occupies the slot representing hundreds, or numbers 100 through 999; and the 1 occupies the slot representing thousands, or numbers 1000 through 9999.

The use of place-value makes it easy to recognize the value of a number at a glance. Thus the Sumerian system was more advanced than the Roman numeral system, which came thousands of years later. When the Babylonians adopted the Sumerian system, they attempted to represent what we would call decimal fractions; for example, 0.5 instead of 1/2. However, since theirs was a sexagesimal system, perhaps the term "sexagesimal fractions" would be more accurate. They did not actually use a point like our decimal point, but relied on the written context to convey the proper size of a number. For instance (to put it in modern terms), if a text said "He drank 2 gallons of water with his dinner," in all likelihood this would mean 0.2 gallons, since it is hard to imagine a person drinking 2 gallons of water with a meal.

Number systems based on written language

The Sumerians and Egyptians are noted as the first cultures to develop writing, and both adopted written forms of their number systems based on their respective forms of written language. Thus the Sumerians, whose wedge-shaped form of writing was known as cuneiform (kyoo-NAY-i-form), created a set of cuneiform written number symbols. The Babylonians later adopted these symbols, which used a 1 in the sixties column to represent 60. This is reflected in the way that modern people represent time in a day: to indicate, say, 71 minutes, the preferred form would not be 71:00 but 1:11:00, meaning 1 hour, 11 minutes, 0 seconds.

OPPOSITE PAGE
The Greek alphabet. Modern science and math use the Greek alphabet to symbolize various concepts. **(Reproduced by permission of the Gale Group.)**

The Egyptians developed a number system based on hieroglyphics at around the same time as the Sumerians created their cuneiform notation; however, most of the written records that survive are in the form of hieratic, a simpler script that appeared in about 2500 B.C.E. Unlike their counterparts in Mesopotamia, the Egyptians used a decimal system, with special symbols to represent each new power of 10 up to 10 million.

Greek numerals

Greek mathematics used two types of notation, or symbols for representing numbers. The first of these used groups of vertical strokes (rather like hash-marks) for numbers. The second Greek system of notation applied an idea unknown to the early Egyptians and Sumerians: the alphabet. Hieroglyphics and cuneiform (much like the Chinese written language today) used different characters to represent different words, a method that could become rather complicated. In about 1500 B.C.E. the Phoenicians, a seafaring people from what is now Lebanon, developed an alphabet. The Greeks adapted the Phoenician alphabet, which they passed on to the Romans, and which later became the basis for the modern-day English alphabet of twenty-six letters. The Greeks also used the alphabetic characters to represent numbers.

Alphabetic notation

The first letter of the Greek alphabet, alpha, represented 1; the second letter, beta, represented 2; and so on. (In fact, the word "alphabet" is derived from the first two letters of the Greek alphabet.) Influenced by the Egyptians, the Greeks had adopted a decimal system, setting a pattern for all later Western mathematics. Accordingly, after iota (the tenth letter in the Greek alphabet), the Greek symbol for 11 was iota-alpha (10 and 1) 12 was iota-beta (10 and 2) and so on up to 19. Specific letters of the alphabet were reserved for numbers divisible by 10: thus 20 was *k* or kappa, 30 was *l* or lambda, and so on up to the last letter, omega, which represented 100. Special marks added to the existing numbers expressed multiples of 100, and other symbols indicated 1,000 and 10,000.

Even today, mathematicians use letters of the Greek alphabet as mathematical symbols; for instance, π or pi (pronounced pie) a number equal to the ratio between the circumference (distance around) of a circle and its diameter (distance across). Long before the adoption of such symbols, however, the Greeks' method of notation would have an enormous influence on the notation system developed by the Romans that remained in use for almost two thousand years.

Roman numerals

Developed around 500 B.C.E., the Roman numeral system is somewhat familiar to most people today, but it has only limited uses, which are linked more with tradition than with usefulness. Among the areas in which the system is used are the outlines for term papers, or the designation of the title of a ruler (for example, Henry VIII). It is also used with the copyright symbol at the end of a motion picture to indicate the year of its release. For instance, the 1998 Academy Award winner *Titanic*, released in 1997, was designated MCMXCVII.

The Roman system uses seven basic numerals. The symbol I stands for 1, and is probably based on the shape of a single finger indicating that digit. (In fact, the word "digit" is taken from a Latin root meaning "finger.") Next is V or 5, most likely drawn from the shape of an upraised hand with five fingers. The x for 10 probably developed by joining two symbols for 5, and symbols for higher numbers (L for 50, C for 100, D for 500, and M for 1,000) came from Latin words for those numbers. For example, the Latin word for "hundred" was *centum*, while *mille* meant "thousand." (These words are the basis for the English terms "century" and "millennium.")

Greek Alphabet

Αα	Alpha
Ββ	Beta
Γγ	Gamma
Δδ	Delta
Εε	Epsilon
Ζζ	Zeta
Ηη	Eta
Θθ	Theta
Ιι	Iota
Κκ	Kappa
Λλ	Lambda
Μμ	Mu
Νν	Nu
Ξξ	Xi
Οο	Omicron
Ππ	Pi
Ρρ	Rho
Σσς	Sigma
Ττ	Tau
Υυ	Upsilon
Φφ	Phi
Χχ	Chi
Ψψ	Psi
Ωω	Omega

Arabic	Roman	Arabic	Roman	Arabic	Roman
1	I	16	XVI	90	XC
2	II	17	XVII	100	C
3	III	18	XVIII	200	CC
4	IV	19	XIX	300	CCC
5	V	20	XX	400	CD
6	VI	21	XXI	500	D
7	VII	22	XXII	600	DC
8	VIII	23	XXIII	700	DCC
9	IX	24	XXIV	800	DCCC
10	X	30	XXX	900	CM
11	XI	40	XL	1,000	M
12	XII	50	L	2,000	MM
13	XIII	60	LX	3,000	MMM
14	XIV	70	LXX	4,000	$M\overline{V}$
15	XV	80	LXXX	5,000	$\overline{V}$

A table of Roman numerals and their Hindu-Arabic equivalents. (Reproduced by permission of the Gale Group.)

Problems with Roman numerals

The *Titanic* example above shows just how awkward Roman numerals can be when representing large numbers: 1997 uses only four characters or symbols, whereas MCMXCVII requires twice as many. This problem of long, cumbersome numbers was a shortcoming in the Roman system from the beginning, and the Romans developed several rules in an attempt to overcome it. Among these was the use of a smaller numeral preceding a larger one to indicate subtraction. Thus instead of using IIII to indicate 4, they adopted the use of IV, meaning "5 minus 1." Yet this rule never became fully standard, which is why many grandfather clocks with Roman numerals use a IIII instead of a IV. Likewise, documents from the Middle Ages (c. 500–c. 1500) often include a VIIII, instead of IX, to symbolize 9.

Also difficult was the matter of representing extremely large numbers such as 1 million. For this purpose, the Romans used a bar, called a *vinculum,* over numerals to indicate that the numerals shown should be multiplied by 1,000. Thus an M with vinculum indicated 1 million, and a VI under a vinculum represented 6,000.

Despite these efforts toward simplifying the Roman system, it was exceedingly complicated, and the fact that it lacked a concept of place value made multiplication extremely difficult. Consider the problem of multiplying 3,000 by 438, which would be relatively easy with the place-value number system people use today. The problem can be reduced to a few simple steps: multiply 3 by 400, 3 by 30, and 3 by 8; add these products together; then multiply the total by 1,000, a step that requires the placement of three zeroes at the end of the number obtained in the earlier

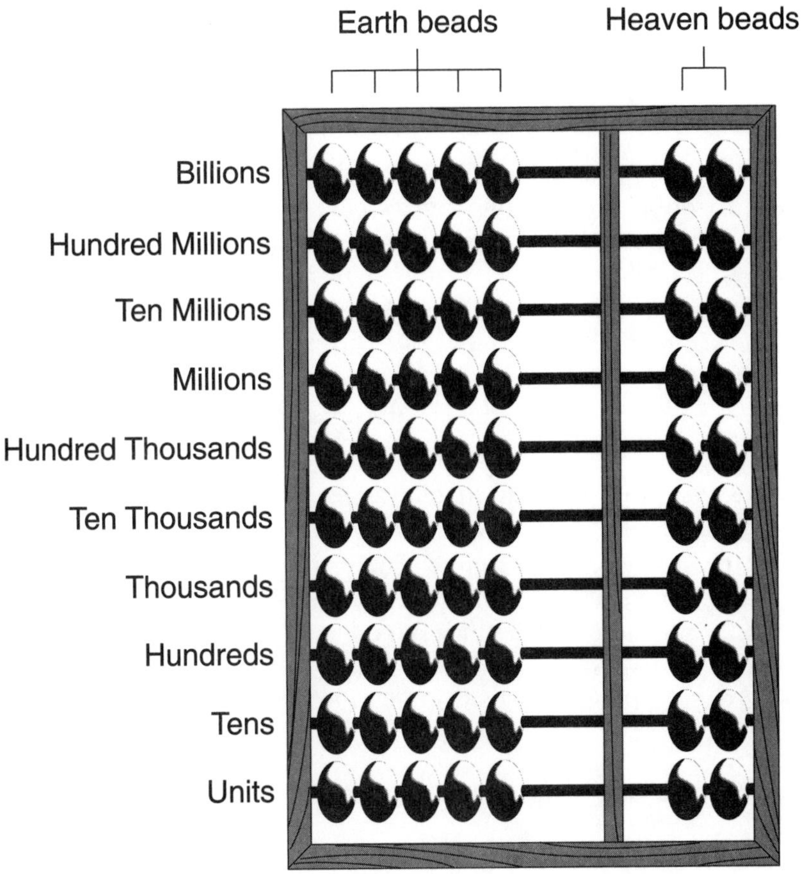

A diagram of a Chinese abacus. Drawing by Hans and Cassidy. Reproduced by permission of Gale Group.

steps. Under the Roman system, however, the problem would be represented as MMM (or III with a vinculum) multiplied by CDXXXVIII. Performing the actual calculation would be a nightmare, because the Roman system does not allow for a ones column, a tens column, and so on.

The Romans also lacked a means of representing fractions by symbols such as 1/2. They would have had to write it out as "one-half," or rather, "six-twelfths," since their system of fractions was based on 1/12. They called this unit an *uncia,* from which the English word "ounce" is derived. Thus they would have expressed 1/4 as 3 unciae, or 3/12. As for fractions in which the denominator, or bottom number, was not divisible by 12 (for example, 1/5), they simply lacked the means of representing these.

Effects of the Roman system

For all its problems, the Roman numeral system worked well enough for the Romans, who, unlike the Greeks, were not concerned with pure mathematics; that is, math for its own sake, rather than for a specific application. By contrast, the Romans were interested primarily in applied mathematics, for purposes such as keeping government and business accounts, maintaining military records, and aiding in the construction of buildings and other engineering projects.

The fact that multiplication and division under the Roman system were fairly difficult operations spurred development of early calculators called counting boards. Actually, the first calculator, the abacus, developed in Babylonia in about 3000 B.C.E. It used movable beads strung along parallel wires within a frame, and incorporated the concept of place value so that one string represented ones, the next tens, and so on. The Roman counting board, which was used throughout Europe during the Middle Ages (c. 500–c. 1500), applied much the same principle.

Between 200 B.C.E. and 200 C.E., as the Romans conquered an empire that stretched from Scotland to modern-day Iraq, their numeral system spread throughout much of the known world. For a thousand years after the decline and fall of the empire, European mathematics experienced very little progress. Only after about 1500 would the much more practical and effective Hindu-Arabic numeral system (1, 2, 3... 9) finally replace Roman numerals. (See essay "Hindu-Arabic Numerals and Mathematical Symbolism" in this chapter.)

HINDU-ARABIC NUMERALS AND MATHEMATICAL SYMBOLISM

Many early peoples, including the Babylonians, Egyptians, Greeks, Romans, Chinese, and Maya of Central America, developed number systems. However, if a modern person encountered a mathematical text from one of these civilizations, he or she would have a hard time understanding it, and not just because it was written in another language.

One of the amazing things about mathematics, as it exists today, is that it includes a set of symbols that translate across cultures. Different languages have different words for the number 2, but people around the world still understand the symbol 2, making mathematics a sort of universal language. This universal language of written math had a specific origin—in India, home of the nine symbols for the counting numbers as well as the remarkable concept of zero.

The Hindu-Arabic numerals would change the world, and their appearance in the West (that is, western Europe) spurred on the development of other written symbols that made the use of mathematics considerably easier. Today people take these symbols, such as the equals sign, for granted; yet without them, mathematics would much more difficult.

Words to Know

decimal fraction: A method of representing numbers that are less than 1 by using a decimal point and place value. The number 0.01 is a decimal fraction, whereas 1/100 is a common fraction.

Hindu-Arabic numerals: The number system in use throughout most of the world today, which uses ten digits, including zero.

notation: Symbols to represent numbers or operations such as addition and subtraction.

place value: The use of a number's position to indicate its size. In a number such as 1239, for instance, the 2 does not stand just for 2, but stands for 200. Whereas the Hindu-Arabic numeral system in use today has a built-in concept of place value, the Roman numeral system used during the Middle Ages did not.

Hindu-Arabic numerals

While Europeans continued to use the cumbersome Roman numeral system which used letters to represent numbers, such as I, II, II, IV, V, etc. (see essay "Early Number Systems" in this chapter), the Chinese developed their own number system of "rod numerals"—sets of vertical and horizontal strokes, rather like the hash marks by which modern people represent numbers in units of 5 (four hash marks with a diagonal slash through them). As with the Roman system, Chinese development of "rod numerals" was accompanied by advances in early calculators, with accountants and mathematicians using small movable rods to aid them in their calculations.

By far the most important numeral system in the East (that is, east Asia)—in fact, the most important in all of history—was the one that arose in India by about the third century B.C.E. That period saw the first appearance of what were called the Brahmi symbols, the first form of what would become known as Hindu-Arabic numerals. Unlike the Roman or Chinese systems, the Indian system used distinct single numerals for each number from 1 to 9. Because each numeral occupied only one position (for instance, 3 is just one symbol, unlike the Roman numeral III), this made it easy to designate place value. Place value refers to the value of a

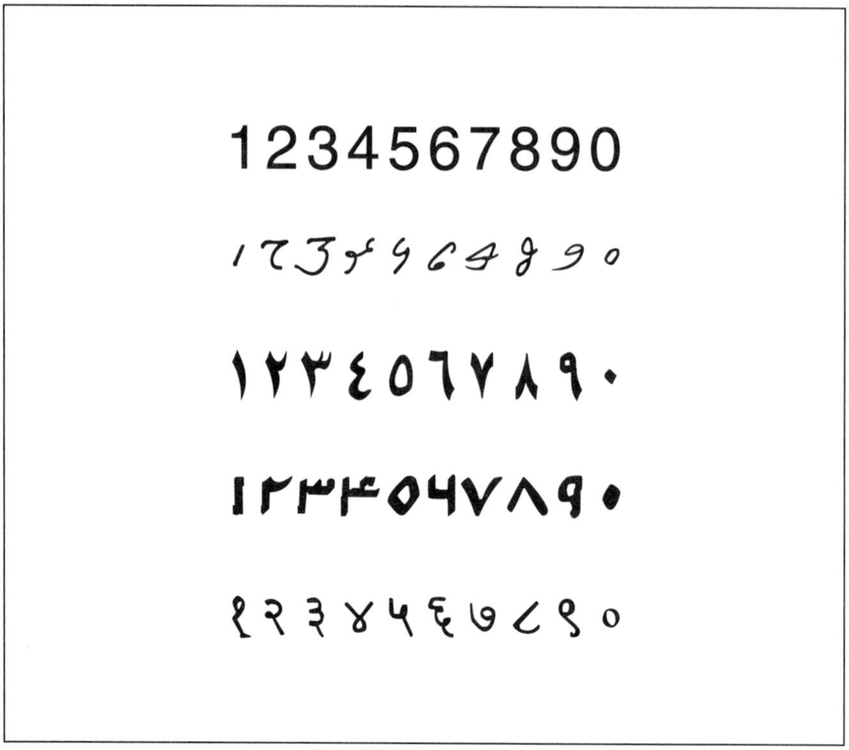

An illustration of the development of Hindu-Arabic numerals. From top to bottom are: modern western Arabic, early western Arabic, modern eastern Arabic, early eastern Arabic, and later Devanagari. **(Illustration by GGS Information Services. Reproduced by permission of the Gale Group.)**

number changing depending on its placement, as in the number 327, the 3 stands not for 3, but for 300, and the 2 stands not for 2 but for twenty.

The Hindu numeral system traveled westward to the Arab world, where the writings of Arab mathematician **al-Khwarizmi** (c. 780–c. 850; see biography in this chapter) helped introduce these numbers to the West. Europeans, thinking that the system had originated in the Middle East, mistakenly called the numbers "Arabic numerals." These Hindu-Arabic numerals (as they are more properly called) fascinated Italian mathematician **Leonardo Fibonacci** (c. 1170–c. 1240; see biography in this chapter), who, as the son of a government official in north Africa, learned about them from merchants he met. Later he explained the system in his highly influential work *Liber abaci* (Book of calculations; 1202).

The Hindu-Arabic numerals change the world

In the period after Fibonacci's time, Hindu-Arabic numerals began gaining acceptance, and by about 1500 they had fully replaced Roman numerals throughout Europe. It is impossible to overstate the impact brought about by this change. In the world of business, for instance, the Hindu-Arabic numeral system made banking and trade much, much easier by simplifying computations, and thus influencing the rise of commerce.

Within the realm of science and technology, the more efficient system of arithmetic made possible the calculation of mathematical and astronomical tables that were used in surveying, construction, and navigation. For mathematicians themselves, Hindu-Arabic numerals made it much easier to work with numbers, and to consider the properties of the numbers themselves rather than becoming bogged down in the difficulties of simply writing out equations.

For all the impact of the nine Hindu-Arabic numerals that indicate actual counting numbers (that is, 1 through 9), these are almost overshadowed by a tenth symbol, introduced in India. The importance of this symbol is surprising, because it stands, quite literally, for nothing. Yet as Europeans discovered after they adopted the zero, "nothing" can be quite important.

Zero

Zero is such a part of modern mathematics and life that people tend to take its use for granted, yet unlike the other numbers, it was not an obvious idea. The Greeks, for instance, despite their many advances in mathematics, never grasped the concept; or rather, they were never willing to treat "nothing" as a number with mathematical value.

This Greek rejection of zero, indeed, fear of the very concept, had deep roots. Greek philosophy had no place for the idea of nothingness, or a vacuum. In addition, Pythagorean mathematics stressed the perfection of numbers, and nothing could be more imperfect, from the Greek perspective, than nothingness. (See essay "The Greeks' New Approach to Mathematics" in this chapter.)

Because of the Greeks' influence on Western thinking, zero did not exist as part of European mathematics for thousands of years. This is particularly ironic in light of the fact that the concept of zero first originated long before the time of the Greeks, and appeared independently in several other civilizations.

The Babylonian zero

The concept of zero first arose in Babylonia, where mathematicians recognized that it was sometimes necessary to insert "nothing" as a placeholder; that is, a numeral to designate an empty column. For instance, in the number 302, the tens column is empty, but without a zero to fill it, the number might be mistaken for 32. To designate empty columns, the Babylonians originally used blank spaces, and therefore would have written this number as 3 2.

Babylonian notation did not indicate the number of "nothing" columns, so it was impossible to tell at a glance whether 3 2 meant 302 or

Just What Year Is It?

A "millennium" celebration in Vietnam on December 31, 1999.

Strange as it may seem, until Europeans adopted Hindu-Arabic numerals after about 1500 C.E., they had no concept of zero. The introduction of the zero changed history, yet the world still lives with at least one consequence of the fact that Europeans lacked the concept of zero for so long.

All over the planet, even in countries where Christianity is not the majority religion, many nations use the Western calendar, which is based on the birth of Jesus Christ. In the Western calendar, dates are sometimes designated as B.C. (before Christ) and A.D. (*anno domini,* Latin for "in the year of

3,002 or even 30,002. Nor did the Babylonians use zeroes at the end of the number, so a number such as 32 could (depending on the context) mean 32 or 320 or 3,200 or more. By the 200s B.C.E., the Babylonians had partially overcome these problems by developing a symbol for zero, but they never used it at the end of a number. Nor did they ever treat zero as an actual number, rather than a placeholder.

Zero among the Maya

Far away, in Central America, the Maya also developed the idea of zero. Like the Babylonians, the Maya were also noted for their sophisticated calendars, but in some ways their achievement is even more remarkable in view of the limitations facing their civilization. A few other civilized peoples existed in the region around the Maya; for instance, in the city-state of Teotihuacán, but the Maya did not enjoy the wealth of contacts with our Lord") now more commonly referred to as B.C.E. (before the Common Era or Christian Era) and C.E. (the Common Era or Christian Era).

However, the Byzantine historian Dionysius Exiguus (c. 500–c. 560), who developed the system, based his calculations on incorrect information. He believed that Christ had been born 753 years after the founding of Rome, when in fact, 747 years appears to be a more correct figure; therefore Christ was actually born in 6 B.C.E., not 0 B.C.E. /C.E., as one would expect.

Nor was there a year "zero," because Dionysius had no concept of such a thing. In his reckoning of events, the next date after December 31, 1 B.C.E. was January 1, 1 C.E. The effects of this became apparent two thousand years later, as people prepared for the end of the millennium on December 31, 1999, which was not actually the end of the millennium.

Since there was no 0 C.E., the end of the first century came on December 31, 100, and the end of the twentieth century on December 31, 2000. Nevertheless, people around the world celebrated the end of the millennium at midnight on December 31, 1999, when all the calendars changed to 2000.

other societies available to the Babylonians and other peoples of the Old World. In addition to their lack of contact with other civilizations, the Maya were, quite literally, a stone-age people in the sense that they never developed metal tools and weapons. They had no domesticated draft animals, or animals that could pull loads and thus assist in plowing, building, and other labors. They never even discovered the wheel; nor, in fact, did any society in the Americas prior to the arrival of European explorers in about 1500.

Those explorers dismissed the Maya and other civilizations in the Americas as savages, even though they had highly organized societies, written languages, and a legacy of elaborate architectural monuments. Not only that, but the Maya had long before discovered a concept still new to the Europeans of the sixteenth century: the zero.

The Hindu zero compared with others

Like the Babylonians, the Maya treated zero as a mere placeholder. The same was true of the Chinese, who also had the notion of zero, though they may have adopted the idea from India rather than developing it on their own. In any case, the Indian or Hindu zero was by far the most advanced version of the concept, and it is from the Hindu zero that the modern idea originates.

The first known use of a word for zero in Hindu mathematical writings occurred in 458 C.E., and the first appearance of the symbol itself dates to 628 C.E. The Hindu mathematician Brahmagupta (598–c. 665) explained the use of zero and other Hindu numerals in *Brahamasphuta Siddhanta*. His work, as well as that of other Indian mathematicians, shows an understanding of zero far beyond that reached by their counterparts in Babylonia and Central America.

Instead of treating zero simply as a placeholder, the Hindus used it as a number; and rather than thinking of zero as "nothing," they viewed it as the absence of something. These may seem like hair-splitting distinctions, but they made a major difference. All other numbers could be defined in terms of 1; for instance, 9 is nine ones, but until Hindu mathematicians succeeded in defining zero as (1 - 1), it seemed to be outside the system of other numerals. Thanks to this development, mathematicians incorporated zero into their written calculations.

The symbol for zero developed in India made it possible to write down all numbers accurately, and it thus became possible to consistently and precisely record the steps of a calculation, not just the result. Hindu mathematicians also used zero as a number in its own right, instead of just being a placeholder. This led to new discoveries: that zero added to, or subtracted from, a number is equal to that number, and that a number multiplied by zero is equal to zero.

The most challenging concept was division by zero, which is not easily solved because a number divided by zero is not equal either to that number, or to zero. Nor is a number divided by zero equal to infinity, as some mathematicians suggested, because if infinity were multiplied by zero, the result would not be a number other than zero. Therefore, 1 divided by zero cannot be equal to infinity, since infinity multiplied by zero cannot be equal to 1. Even zero divided by zero has no solution, or rather it has an infinite number of solutions, because any number multiplied by zero is zero. In fact, the solutions to these problems did not prove as important as the act of searching for them. By exploring the relationships involved in calculating with zero, mathematicians became more and more interested in studying the rules of calculation, and this influenced the development of algebra. (See essay "Playing with Numbers" in this chapter).

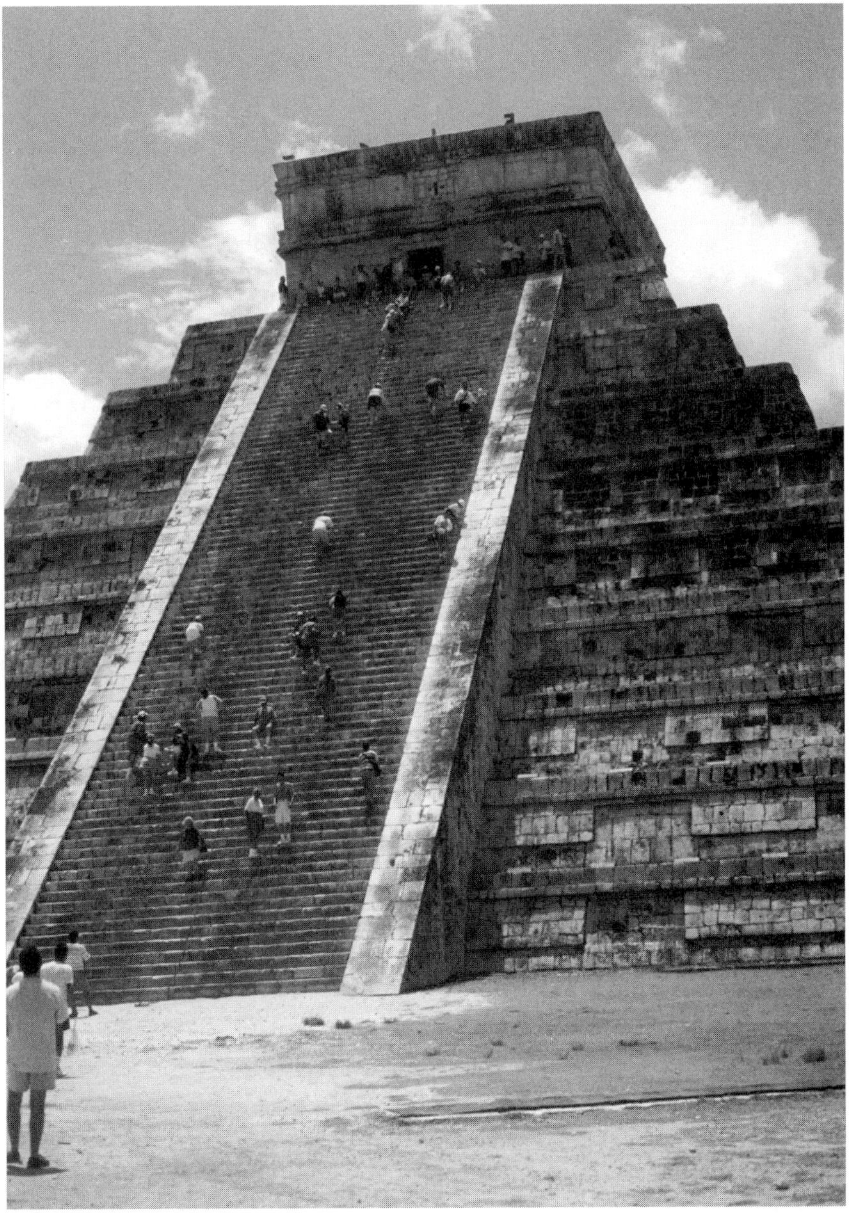

The Temple of Kulkulkan at Chichen Itza, Yucatan, Mexico. Explorers dismissed the Mayan culture as primitive despite the fact that it was highly organized, with written language, a well developed number system, and a legacy of elaborate architectural monuments. **(Reproduced by permission of Lyndi Schrecengost.)**

Other mathematical symbols

Even after Europeans adopted the Hindu-Arabic numerals, including zero, they still lacked most of the symbols, such as the plus or minus sign, commonly used in mathematics today. In this, too, they were influenced by the Muslim world, but the development of most such symbols actually arose within Europe itself.

As is often the case with any form of progress, necessity was the mother of invention. With the rise of trade in Europe during the late Middle Ages (c. 500–c. 1500) and Renaissance (c. 1350–1600), commercial arithmetic or business math became extremely important. This highlighted the problem of using words instead of symbols to indicate operations such as addition and subtraction. The word for "plus," for instance, differed from language to language, but the symbol + was universal.

Innovations of the 1400s and 1500s

German mathematician Johannes Widman (c. 1462–c. 1498) introduced the plus (+) and minus (−) signs in a 1489 work, an astounding breakthrough at a time when even the most advanced mathematical scholars in Europe were studying multiplication and division. In 1557, English mathematician Robert Recorde (1510–1558) helped to popularize the plus and minus signs in an influential work entitled *Whetstone of Witte,* which also included the first use of the equals sign (=).

Fibonacci himself, though he was long dead, spurred on the development of new mathematical symbols. His work, which had exerted considerable impact during his lifetime, had fallen into disuse, but its rediscovery in the 1500s helped inspire the development of notation that would make the use of the Hindu-Arabic numerals easier. Among the men influenced by Fibonacci's work was French mathematician François Viète (1540–1603), who introduced the use of letters such as *x* to represent unknown quantities. Viète was also one of the first Europeans to use decimal fractions (for example, 0.25).

Notation in the 1600s and 1700s

French philosopher and mathematician **René Descartes** (1596–1650; see biography in this chapter) popularized the practice of using letters at the beginning of the alphabet to represent known quantities, and ones near the end of the alphabet for unknown quantities.

Also during the 1600s, English mathematician William Oughtred (1574–1660) was the first to use "x" as a sign for multiplication, but the division symbol (÷) did not make its appearance until the 1660s. In 1706 another English mathematician, William Jones, was the first to use the Greek letter π to represent pi, or the ratio of the circumference (distance around) a circle to its diameter (distance across). **Leonhard Euler** (1707–1783; see biography in this chapter) later influenced the general adoption of this symbol.

Each of these men, by introducing or influencing the use of one symbol or another, helped to further the development of mathematical study. By simplifying the writing of math problems, and the recording of the

General Arithmetic and Algebra		Differential Calculus and Integral Calculus	
Symbol	Meaning	Symbol	Meaning
$+$	Plus (also indicates positive sign)	$\int x$	Integral of x
$-$	Minus (also indicates negative sign)	$f(x)$ or $\Phi(x)$	Function of x
$\pm$	Plus or minus	dx	Differential of x
$\times$ or $\cdot$ or $*$	Multiplied by (also called times)	dx/dy or x'	First derivative of x with respect to y
$/$ or $\div$	Divided by	$d^n x/dy^n$	n^{th} derivative of x with respect to y
$:$	Ratio	$\partial x/\partial y$	Partial derivative of x with respect to y
$=$	Equal to	$\dot{x}$	Partial derivative of x with respect to time
$\neq$	Does not equal	Δx	Increment of x
$\approx$ or $\doteq$	Approximately to	$\Gamma(n)$	Gamma function of n
$::$ or α	Proportional to		
$\sim$	Similar to		
$\cong$	Congruent to (also means defines)		
$\Rightarrow$	Implies		
$\rightarrow$	Approches		
$<$	Less than		
$<<$	Much less than		
$>$	Greater than		
$>>$	Much greater than		
$\leq$	Less than or equal to		
$\geq$	Greater than or equal to		
$\sqrt{x}$	Square root of x		
$\sqrt[n]{x}$	n^{th} root of x		
Σ	Summation of		
Π	Product of		
$!$	Factorial (e.g., $3!=3*2*1$)		
$\|x\|$	Absolute value of x (e.g., $\|-3\| =3$)		
∞	Infinity		
i	Imaginary number		
$\{\ \}$	Set		
$\%$	Percent		

A table of common mathematical symbols. **(Reproduced by permission of Hans J. Neuhart, Electronic Illustrators.)**

steps involved, these symbols made it easier for mathematicians to perform their work. They also made communication between mathematicians simpler, reduced confusion, and enabled the spread of ideas across cultural and language barriers.

GEOMETRY AND THE GREAT UNSOLVED PROBLEMS

Because he was the first true philosopher, mathematician, *and* scientist of Western civilization, Thales of Miletus (THAY-leez; c. 625–c. 547 B.C.E.) assumed larger-than-life status in the eyes of the Greeks after his death. Traditionally he is credited with bringing geometry to Greece from Egypt,

Words to Know

applied mathematics: The use of mathematics for a specific purpose, as in business or engineering. This is in contrast to "pure" mathematics.

circumference: The distance around a circle.

conic section: The cross-section of a cone when cut by a plane.

cube root: The cube root of a given number is a number that, when multiplied by itself twice, will produce that number. Thus $2 \times 2 \times 2 = 8$, and 2 is the cube root of 8.

diameter: The distance across a circle, as drawn along a path that passes through the center of that circle.

Euclidean geometry: Geometry based on the principles laid down by Euclid (c. 330–260 B.C.E.) in his *Elements*, which is concerned primarily with flat, two-dimensional space in which nonparallel lines eventually converge.

geometry: The branch of mathematics concerned with the properties and relationships of points, lines, angles, surfaces, and shapes.

inscribe: In geometry, to draw a figure inside another one in such a way that it touches, but does not overlap, the boundaries of the larger figure.

irrational number: A number that cannot be expressed as the ratio of any two whole numbers because in decimal form, irrational numbers such as pi (π) neither terminate (come to an end) nor fall into a repeating pattern.

logic: A system of reasoning, closely related to mathematics, for reaching valid conclusions about concepts, and for assessing the validity of a conclusion that has been reached.

but some of the stories regarding his extraordinary proofs of geometric principles may be more legendary than truthful.

In any case, Greece became the home of geometry, the branch of mathematics concerned with the properties and relationships of points, lines, angles, surfaces, and shapes. This influence on geometry began in about 550 B.C.E., and continued for the next three hundred years, even as

non-Euclidean geometry: A form of geometry, developed in the 1800s, that is concerned primarily with curved (and sometimes three-dimensional) space, in which it is possible that nonparallel lines do not converge.

pi: The ratio between the circumference of a circle and its diameter. Pronounced "pie" and represented by the Greek letter π, pi has a value of 3.14159265+. This is its value to eight decimal places; in fact, pi is an irrational number.

plane method: The technique of performing geometric work using only a compass and an unmarked straightedge.

polygon: A closed shape with three or more sides, all straight.

postulate: A basic principle or established rule. Sometimes called an axiom.

proof: A step-by-step process of proving certain ideas in geometry by referring to already established propositions.

pure mathematics: Mathematics for its own sake, rather than for a specific application. Compare with applied mathematics.

ratio: The relationship between two numbers or values. All fractions are ratios, but some ratios such as π (pi, the relationship between the circumference and diameter of a circle) cannot be expressed as fractions.

square: The square of a number is that number multiplied by itself. Thus 25, for instance, is the square of 5, since $5 \times 5 = 25$.

theorem: A proposition based on one or more postulates.

Greek civilization spread from Greece to other lands. Thus about 300 B.C.E., the leading center of Greek civilization, and of studies in geometry, was Alexandria, Egypt, founded and largely populated by Greeks.

The Greeks did not invent geometry, which had its origins in Babylonia and other civilizations more ancient than that of Greece. Babylonian geometry flourished about a thousand years before the Greeks took up the study, yet it

The Library of Alexandria

Scholars reading scrolls at the Library of Alexandria. (The Bettmann Archive. Reproduced by permission of the Corbis Corporation.)

It was smaller than the public library of a medium-sized American city, yet the Library of Alexandria served as the intellectual center of the Western world for many centuries. It housed works of mathematics and science, as well as literature, religion, history, and geography—the collected knowledge of Mediterranean society.

Alexandria was named after Alexander the Great (356–323 B.C.E.), who founded it during his conquest of Egypt, and it soon became the leading center of Hellenistic, or Greek-influenced, culture. The library itself was founded by Demetrius of Phaleron, a student of **Aristotle** (384–322 B.C.E.; see biography in Life Science chapter), in 297 B.C.E., and in the years that followed, the institution became a great trea-

was the Greeks who saw in geometry something more than any earlier civilization had. The Greeks were the first people to appreciate the study of mathematics in general for its own sake (see essay "The Greeks' New Approach to Mathematics" in this chapter), and this was particularly the case with geometry. Instead of simply trying to figure out angles in order to build a building, for instance, the mathematicians of Greece were fascinated with geometry as a pursuit unto itself—pure mathematics as opposed to applied mathematics.

In addition, the Greeks believed that studying geometry taught a person to see deeply into a problem, and to work out ideas consistently and thoroughly. Thus the philosopher Plato (428–348 B.C.E.) wrote in his *Republic* that the study of geometry was essential to the education of a future ruler.

sure-trove of knowledge. Figures associated with it included **Euclid** (c. 330–c. 260 B.C.E.; see biography in this chapter), **Eratosthenes** (276–c. 194 B.C.E.; see biography in this chapter), and Hypatia (c. 370–415), the remarkable female philosopher and mathematician.

In its heyday, the library boasted some 700,000 scrolls, and it added new works each year, thanks to a city law whereby ships entering Alexandria's harbor were forced to surrender all manuscripts for copying. Among the many great works to emerge from the library was the Septuagint, the first translation of the Old Testament into a European language, and the centuries that followed saw many other achievements.

Yet the library was always vulnerable to the uncertainties that plagued ancient life. It is said that troops under Julius Caesar (102–44 B.C.E.) tried to torch it, but it survived and flourished until about 400 C.E., when it came under attack by locals as a center of pagan Greek thought. The Christianized Roman emperor Theodosius allowed it to be burned in 391. After that, the library hobbled along until the 600s, when another religious group, the Arab Muslims, destroyed it completely. Thirteen centuries later, in the 1990s, the Egyptian government announced plans to rebuild the library in cooperation with the United Nations Educational, Scientific, and Cultural Organization (UNESCO).

The "game" of geometry

It is perhaps fitting that the Greeks, who gave the world a formal system of logic (see essay "The Greeks' New Approach to Mathematics" in this chapter), made their greatest mathematical advances in geometry. No branch of mathematics is as closely related to logic as geometry: both approach problem solving in the same way and are extremely methodical. Yet for all their seriousness, both areas of study can be compared to a game.

The study of logic, for instance, offers an opportunity to grapple with intriguing brain-teasers such as Zeno's paradoxes (see essay "The Greeks' New Approach to Mathematics" in this chapter). Likewise there is something almost sporting in the way that the Greeks approached what came to be known as the three great unsolved problems of geometry.

The three unsolved problems

These problems were the squaring of the circle, or creating a square with the same dimensions as a given circle; trisecting an angle (dividing an angle into three smaller angles of equal measurement); and doubling a cube. All of these can be done using various tools and techniques, but the Greeks made the "game" much harder by applying the rule that the solutions could be obtained using only an unmarked straightedge and a compass. This means of constructing geometric figures is known as the plane method.

The plane method worked for most problems in Greek geometry, but not these three. This, however, did not stop mathematicians from trying. One might ask why they continued to try, especially when it became clear that the problems could be solved by other methods. This can be explained by an analogy to sports. Suppose there were a mountain that had never been climbed, though many mountaineers had tried it. Would one of those mountaineers be content to simply ride a helicopter to the top, and then brag that he or she had conquered the mountain? Of course not. The mountaineers' goal, in this situation, is not simply to get to the top of the mountain, but to do so by a particular method. By the same token, Greek mathematicians continued to insist on trying to solve the problems using the tools available at the time they were first developed.

Indeed, efforts to solve these problems continued well into modern times. Attempts have involved the greatest mathematicians in history, as well as numerous amateurs. Each attempt had one thing in common: it failed to yield a solution. Today the impossibility of solving these problems with the plane method has been mathematically proven; nonetheless, the attempts to solve the unsolvable over the years led to important advances in many areas of mathematics.

Squaring the circle

The task of creating a square the same size as a given circle is easy if one uses pi, symbolized by the Greek letter π. Suppose a circle has a radius of 2 units (radius is the distance from a point in the center of a circle to a point on the edge of the circle). The number 2 must be squared (multiplied by itself) and multiplied by pi (about 3.14) to yield a result of about 12.56, the area of the circle. To create a square the same size, one need only obtain the square root of 12.56 (3.544), which is the length of each side on the square. But this result was not obtained using the plane method, and therefore does not really solve the problem the Greeks put to themselves.

The best attempts at a plane-method solution, beginning with the Greek mathematician Antiphon (480–411 B.C.E.), involved the use of a straightedge to inscribe polygons (closed shapes with straight sides) inside the circle. To inscribe a figure inside a circle means to draw a polygon, such as a square, so that the corners just touch the inside of the circle. By adding sides to the polygon, its area becomes closer to that of the circle—yet never equal to it, because no matter how many sides the polygon has, its area is still smaller than the circle's.

Mathematicians called this "the method of exhaustion," and by this they were not referring to physical or mental exhaustion; rather, they used the word in the same sense as "exhaust all possibilities." Actually, either meaning of exhaustion would be apt in the situation, because hundreds of thinkers over the centuries tried and failed to square the circle using the plane method.

Among these were the some of the greatest minds in science and technology, as well as mathematics: **Archimedes** (287–212 B.C.E.; see biography in Technology chapter); **Leonardo da Vinci** (1452–1519; see biography in Technology chapter); **Isaac Newton** (1642–1727; see biography in Physical Science chapter); **Gottfried Wilhelm von Leibniz** (1646–1716; see biography in this chapter); Carl Friedrich Gauss (1777-1855); and **Leonhard Euler** (1707–1783; see biography in this chapter). Along the way, the methods changed, and these men developed a number of useful ideas in their efforts to solve the problem, yet it still remained unsolved.

By the 1700s, the leading scientific institutions of Europe had received so many attempted solutions to the squaring of the circle that they ceased to review them. At one point, the quest became such an obsession that the British mathematician Augustus De Morgan (1806–1871) coined the term *morbus cyclometricus,* or "circle-squaring disease." Finally, German mathematician Ferdinand von Lindemann (1852–1939) proved that because of the irrational quality of pi, a solution to the problem using the plane method was impossible. This, however, still did not stop unconvinced amateurs from continuing to seek a solution.

Trisecting an angle

Though not as well-known as the squaring of the circle, the problem of trisecting an angle likewise attracted the attention of mathematicians and thinkers for thousands of years. Bisecting (dividing into two equal parts) an angle with the tools of the plane method is easy; so too is trisecting for angles of certain sizes, such as a 90-degree angle. But a method of trisecting *any* angle using the plane method would consume the energies of mathematical minds from Hippocrates of Chios (c. 470–c. 410 B.C.E.) onward.

Hippocrates, who is not to be confused with the great physician of the same name, is famous for his work on each of the three unsolved problems. In the case of the angle-trisection problem, he did what many other mathematicians did in approaching these challenges: produced a workable technique, but not one that used the plane method. In the process, however, he developed new curves and shapes that would prove useful to mathematicians in later studies, yet another example of the benefits gained by the seemingly impractical "game" of the three problems.

The impossibility of the trisection problem

The later history of the trisection problem was similar to that of the circle-squaring one. Attempts at its solution involved great minds such as **René Descartes** (1596–1650; see biography in this chapter), as well as a host of amateurs and cranks, and by 1775 the Paris Academy of Sciences refused to review any more angle trisection methods submitted by the public.

In 1837, French mathematician Pierre Wantzel (1814–1848) ended the futile efforts by showing that trisecting an angle is essentially the same as solving a cubic equation, or an equation involving a power of three. Just as cubic equations cannot be solved using a straightedge and compass, Wantzel showed, it is impossible to do this with only the tools of the plane method.

Doubling the cube

One of the most important religious centers in Greece was at Delos, home of an oracle—someone, usually a woman, whom people consulted for wisdom from the gods. It is said that during a time of plague (an epidemic disease), the people of Athens went to the oracle, who told them that they would win favor with the gods, and thus end the plague, if they doubled the size of a certain cube-shaped altar.

To the men of Athens, this seemed easy: supposing the altar was two units long on each side, they simply doubled this to four units all around. This, however, did not double the size of the altar, but made it eight times larger: $2^3 = 8$, whereas $4^3 = 64$. The plague therefore continued, and for this reason, the problem of doubling a cube is often called the Delian problem.

Plato later said that the gods' command was actually a reproach for neglecting the study of geometry. If that was the case, the Greeks more than made up for past failings with a series of efforts to solve the problem using the plane method. Plato himself, as well as **Eratosthenes** (276–c. 194 B.C.E.; see biography in this chapter) and others, developed solutions using mechanical devices, but by the rules of the "game," these did not count.

Solving the problem with an equation

For that matter, it is easy enough to solve the problem using a simple equation, though such an equation would not have been as simple with the primitive notation used by the Greeks. In any case, one would merely need to measure one side of a cube, then multiply that number by itself twice (that is, cube it).

The result would be the area of the original cube, a figure that would need to be doubled to find the dimensions of the second one. Supposing the first cube had sides of 2 units in length, its total volume would be 8, meaning that the second cube would need to have a volume of 16.

To find the length of each side on the second cube, one would have to obtain the cube root of 16, something that would require the use of a special calculator; but still, it could be done with relative ease. Yet this is not a solution by the plane method.

Conic sections

Once again, efforts at finding a solution to doubling the cube involved figures that ranged from Hippocrates of Chios to Persian mathematician and poet Omar Khayyam (1048–1131) more than a thousand years later. And once again, no one succeeded, though they made a number of innovations in geometry along the way. Among these was the discovery of conic sections by the Greek mathematician Menaechmus (c. 380–c. 320 B.C.E.), an idea furthered by Apollonius of Perga (c. 262 B.C.E.–c. 190 B.C.E.).

Conic sections, the shapes obtained by slicing a cone with a plane, yielded the curves known as the parabola and hyperbola, the study of which would eventually help make rocket science possible, because the path of a rocket in flight is similar to a parabola. Yet for all their benefits, conic sections still did not offer a means of doubling the cube by plane methods. As with the trisection problem, Wantzel in 1837 furnished proof that a solution to the problem by the plane method alone is impossible.

Euclid writes the *Elements*

The figure most associated with geometry is **Euclid** (c. 330–c. 260 B.C.E.; see biography in this chapter), who taught at the library of Alexandria, Egypt. The library itself was a center of Greek culture that became legendary, even in its own time, because it contained the vast collected knowledge and literature of the ancient world's most advanced civilization. Thus Euclid had exposure to numerous earlier writings on mathematics, which he used as source material in writing his masterwork, *Elements of Geometry.*

The *Elements* would become the most influential textbook in history, serving as a mathematics text for nearly twenty-two hundred years, virtually up to the beginning of the twentieth century. At one time it rivaled only the Bible in its wide distribution throughout the Western world, and its impact went far beyond math, into the realms of the sciences and philosophy.

This was not due to the originality of Euclid's ideas: he simply summed up the learning of the great mathematicians who preceded him. What made the *Elements* so popular and therefore so effective, in fact, was the clear and concise way that Euclid presented the fundamentals of geometry, or what would become known as Euclidean geometry.

The structure of Euclid's writing

Euclid's writing followed an orderly pattern modeled on the principles of logic (see essay "The Greeks' New Approach to Mathematics" in this chapter). First he began with "common notions," which are self-evident truths. For example, the first "common notion" states that if two things are equal to a third, they are equal to each other. In modern symbolic language, this would be expressed thus: If $a = c$ and $b = c$, then $a = b$.

Next, Euclid presented five postulates, sometimes called axioms, of geometry. The first four postulates are straightforward, easily accepted concepts. For instance, the first postulate states that any two points can be joined by a line. The fifth or parallel postulate, on the other hand, is much more complex. As stated by Euclid and later reformulated by other mathematicians, its essential message is this: lines that are not perfectly parallel will eventually converge or meet in space.

Euclid then went on to develop a series of several hundred theorems, derived from the postulates, and used the postulates to prove the theorems. However, he tended to apply the parallel postulate much less frequently than the other four, and this would eventually lead mathematicians to suspect that the postulate was unnecessary, and certainly not self-evident like the other four. Over the centuries that followed, hundreds of great minds set themselves to the task of proving the parallel postulate, and each failed, though many of them failed brilliantly.

The impact of Euclidean geometry

As the years passed, the *Elements* influenced and inspired some of the greatest thinkers in history, beginning with Greeks such as **Archimedes** (c. 287–212 B.C.E.; see biography in Technology chapter) and Eratosthenes (276–c. 194 B.C.E.), who used Euclidean geometry and trigonometry to calculate the size of Earth (see sidebar in the "Angles, Curves, and Surfaces" essay in this chapter).

In later centuries, the *Elements* became so successful that it completely overshadowed the more ancient texts from which Euclid had drawn in writing it. Many of these older works were lost forever in the wars that took place during the rise and fall of the Roman Empire during the period from about 200 B.C.E. to 500 C.E. But the *Elements*, which by then had been copied and recopied many times, remained in use.

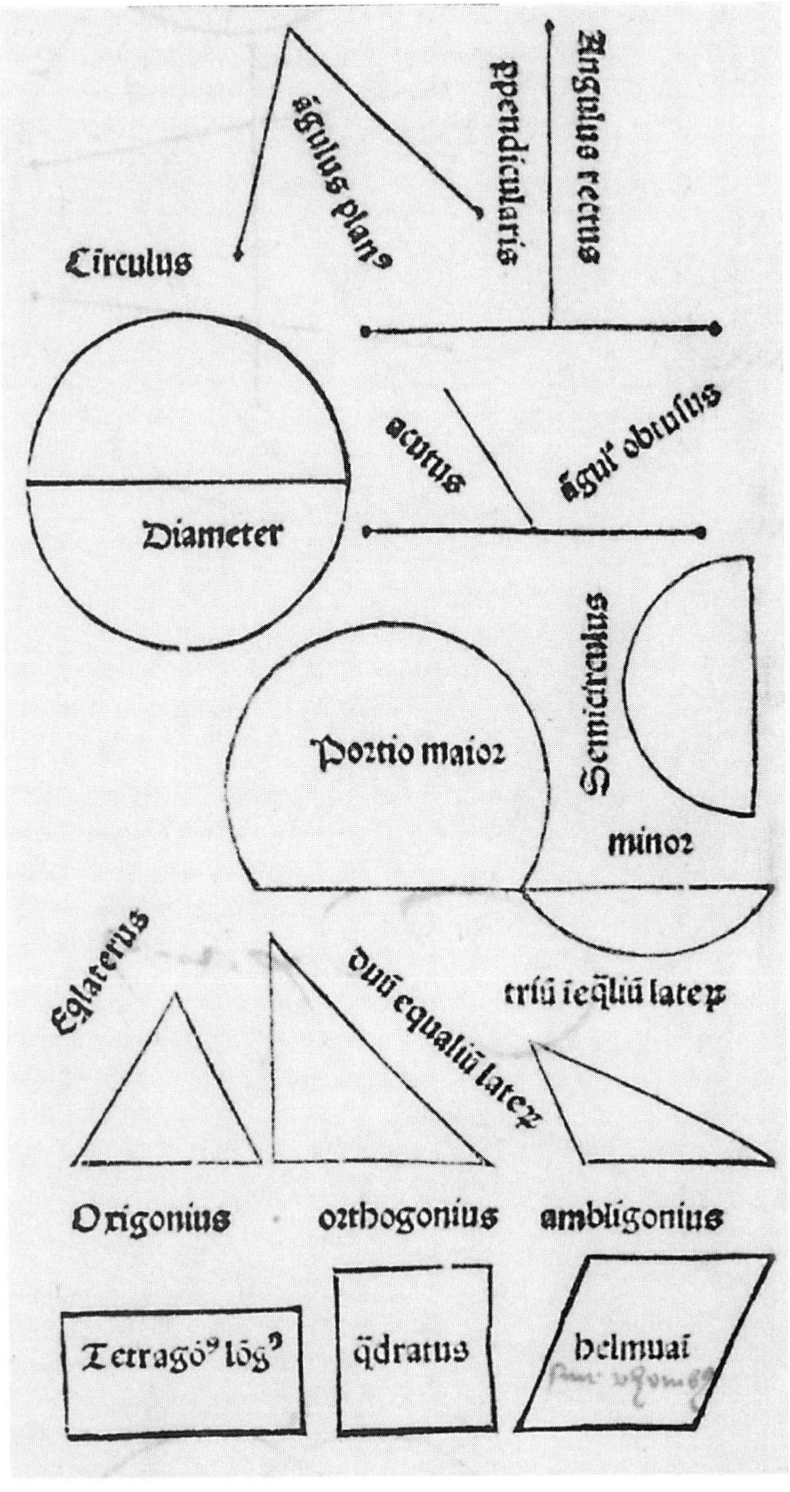

A page from Euclid's Elements. (Reproduced courtesy of the Library of Congress.)

The Arab discovery of Euclid

During the 600s, the Muslim empire that originated in Arabia took the place of Rome as the dominant power in the Mediterranean region. The Muslim world underwent a vast cultural and intellectual transformation, and one of the main forces behind this was the rediscovery and translation of ancient Greek texts—including the *Elements*—by Arab and Persian scholars.

The impact of the *Elements* can be seen in the work of the Muslim world's two greatest mathematicians, **al-Khwarizmi** (c. 780–c. 850) and Omar Khayyam (1048–1131). Al-Khwarizmi, who introduced the West to algebra and the Hindu-Arabic numerals (see essay "Hindu-Arabic Numerals and Mathematical Symbolism" in this chapter), adopted Euclid's axiomatic style; that is, his proof-oriented, point-by-point method of presenting his ideas.

Omar Khayyam, who is well known in the English-speaking world for his poetry, was also a notable mathematician. His achievements include solving cubic equations and attempting to prove Euclid's parallel postulate using quadrilateral figures. (Corbis-Bettmann. Reproduced by permission of the Corbis Corporation.)

Omar Khayyam tried to prove the parallel postulate using a four-sided figure called a quadrilateral, of which squares and rectangles are examples. Though he never succeeded in this effort, he set a pattern for later mathematicians, who from then on discussed the parallel postulate in terms of the quadrilateral.

Euclid's text reaches western Europe

Practical forms of geometry had remained alive, at least to a limited extent, in Europe during the Middle Ages (c. 500–c. 1500). This was particularly true among surveyors, whose work involved measuring areas of land. In the surveyor's work, it was very important to be precise, since land was the principal means of generating wealth, much as business ownership (or ownership of shares in a business through the purchase of stock) is today. Aside from this practical application, however, Europeans had little interest in, or understanding of, geometry.

This situation began to change with the translation of the *Elements* into Latin, which was the work of Italian scholar Gerard of Cremona (1114–1187). In the years that followed, the *Elements* had an impact on Europe far beyond the realm of mathematics. For instance, the geometry of the *Elements* helped the German monk Dietrich von Freiberg (c. 1266–1308) in his work on the reflection and refraction, or bending, of light in raindrops, and led to the first scientific theory regarding how rainbows are formed.

In addition, the *Elements* established the format for the writing of mathematical and scientific works, as well as books of philosophy. Like al-Khwarizmi before them, Western scholars followed the steps outlined by Euclid in making his points: a general statement of a principle, followed by a complete step-by-step demonstration, and a conclusion restating the original idea. This was the format used by Isaac Newton (1642–1727) in his groundbreaking work of physics, the *Principia*, and it remains the preferred model for any sort of writing or speech intended to present and prove an idea.

Challenging the parallel postulate

Precisely because the *Elements* exerted such an impact on Western thinking, the problem raised by the parallel postulate remained a subject of heated debate among European mathematicians. In the 1700s, two thousand years after Euclid's death, mathematicians were still attempting to prove the parallel postulate or to restate it in such a way that it could be proved; and some even considered the possibility of geometry without the parallel postulate.

German-born physicist Albert Einstein. Einstein's theories challenged many well-established ideas in science and mathematics, including Euclidean geometry. **(Reproduced courtesy of the Library of Congress.)**

The great German mathematician Carl Friedrich Gauss (1777–1855) suggested this idea, and during the 1800s, he and Russian mathematician Nikolai Ivanovich Lobachevsky (1793–1856), as well as Hungarian mathematician Janos Bolyai (1802–1860), independently developed non-Euclidean geometry. This in turn led to a questioning of the idea that mathematics represents a grand body of established truths. If Euclid could be challenged successfully, what was next? Could someone propose an entirely new set of rules for the universe?

In fact, that is exactly what happened. During the early years of the twentieth century, German-born physicist Albert Einstein (1879–1955) developed the theory of relativity. Einstein's work, along with the new field of quantum mechanics, completely changed the world's understanding of gravity, motion, energy, and other fundamental aspects of the physical world, as established by Newton in the *Principia*. (See essay "The Scientific Revolution" in the Physical Science chapter.) The use of non-Euclidean geometry played a significant role in the development of Einstein's model, which raised the possibility that space is curved rather than flat and neat as Euclid had imagined it.

PLAYING WITH NUMBERS

In discussing the concept of numbers, it is important to distinguish between the symbols that represent them (discussed in the essays "Early Number Systems" and "Hindu-Arabic Numerals and Mathematical Symbolism" in this chapter) and the numbers themselves. A particular number can be designated as 2, II, two, *dos* (Spanish), *deux* (French), or *zwei* (German), yet there is something beyond all these names: there is the number itself, which has a meaning separate from any symbol used to represent it. Regardless of what it is called, 2 will always have certain properties, such as being the smallest prime number.

This may sound almost magical or mystical, and indeed, thinkers such as **Pythagoras** (c. 580–c. 500 B.C.E.; see biography in this chapter) taught that numbers reveal a deep underlying order or meaning in the universe. Whether that order has any spiritual significance, as Pythagoras claimed, is a matter of opinion. Yet it is clear that such an order exists, and this becomes clear when one "plays with numbers" as mathematicians do.

Mathematics often deals with far-fetched ideas that sometimes yield surprising applications of great usefulness. Such is the case with prime numbers, along with the entire field of number theory (see sidebar to the essay "The Greeks' New Approach to Mathematics" in this chapter). Algebra, which at first seems highly abstract, turns out to be a sort of game with numbers that can often have practical applications. And even logarithms, which made possible complex mathematical processes in the days before calculators, were discovered by a mathematician "playing with numbers."

Prime numbers

Mathematicians have known about prime numbers, a number that can only be divided by itself and 1, since ancient times. Indeed, one of the greatest advances in the study of primes came with the work of the Greek mathematician **Eratosthenes** (276–c. 194 B.C.E.; see biography in this chapter), who developed a method, known as the "sieve of Eratosthenes," for finding primes. (A sieve is a metal pan with holes through which water can drain.)

To use the sieve of Eratosthenes, one begins with the set of all whole numbers above 1: 2, 3, and so on. The next step is to start from the 2, eliminating every other number, since 2 is the only even prime. Then, start from the 3 and eliminate every third number, each of which is a multiple of 3. Thus, on the way up to 20, one would eliminate 4, 6, 8, 9, 10, 12, 14, 15, 16, and 18, leaving the prime numbers 5, 7, 11, 13, 17, and 19.

Words to Know

abacus: An early form of hand-operated calculator that used movable beads strung along parallel wires inside a frame.

algebra: A branch of mathematics in which arithmetic operations (for example, addition or multiplication) are generalized. In algebraic equations, symbols represent numbers of unknown value, and the equations themselves are used to find these values.

logarithm: The power to which a given number, called a base, must be raised to yield a given product. For instance, $10^2 = 100$, and in logarithmic terms, this would be expressed thus: $\log_{10}100 = 2$.

prime number: A number that can be divided only by itself and 1.

The sieve of Eratosthenes proved highly effective, but it is rather tedious, and it cannot easily be used to determine whether a given number is prime. For this reason, thinkers throughout the centuries—among them French mathematicians Marin Mersenne (1588–1648) and **Pierre de Fermat** (1601–1665; see biography in this chapter)—have attempted to develop formulas for finding large prime numbers. Today computers have made it possible to find *extremely* large primes: the largest known prime number as of the year 2001 has 420,291 digits, enough to fill more than thirty pages in a book. A team of mathematicians discovered it in the 1990s.

Prime numbers in cryptography

Prime numbers can be fascinating and they are also useful. During the 1980s, mathematicians working in the field of cryptography—the writing and decoding of secret messages—found that primes could be used to create computer encryption codes. Today these are used by banks, military forces, and companies that do business on the Internet, to protect against hackers working their way into these institutions' computer systems.

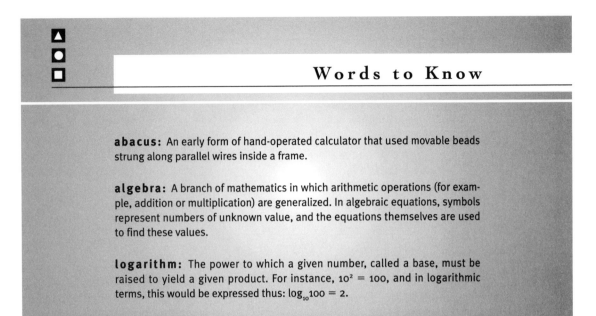

All numbers are either prime or composite. Composite numbers are formed by multiplying primes; for instance, 210 is the product of the first four primes: $2 \times 3 \times 5 \times 7$. Some composite numbers, however, involve more than one of a particular prime; thus 420 would use 2 twice. These numbers are still fairly easy to break into the primes that make them up, but the process is not so easy for very, very large numbers such as 384,119,982,448,028.

If one happened to know that this number is also 358^{143}, then the job would be fairly easy. It would be necessary to break 358 into its constituent primes, then multiply each prime by itself 142 times. This would be a time-consuming process, of course, and it would result in an extremely long string of prime numbers, but it could be done. Suppose, however, that one did not know that the large number above was 358^{143}, and had to break it down piece-by-piece. The fact that the number is even, ending in an 8, indicates that 2 is a factor, but how many twos? And how many of the other primes?

Therefore cryptographers attach very large numbers such as these as a "key" to deciphering a computerized transaction. Authorized personnel would have code sheets listing the prime factors, but if a hacker wanted to crack the code, he or she would have to break down the number into its constituent prime factors. To perform this operation would take millions of calculations and require a number of years, even with the fastest computers known.

Algebra

Suppose the owner of a coffee shop wanted to reduce the number of coins she and her customers had to use in making transactions. To achieve this, she would price each item in such a way that, with sales tax, it would come out to an even dollar amount. She determines that the price of a latte, for instance, should come out to $3.00 after 6 percent sales tax is added. To determine the price of the latte before tax, she would set up an algebraic formula, in which x stands for the unknown before-tax price: $x + 0.06x = 3$. This simplifies to $0.94x = 3$, and by "solving for x," as she learned to do in high-school algebra, she discovers that the listed price for a latte should be $2.82.

Whereas geometry, trigonometry, and even calculus (see essay "Angles, Curves, and Surfaces" in this chapter) are concerned with shapes, algebra addresses pure numbers. In fact, algebra is usually defined as a generalization of arithmetic, a way of letting symbols represent numbers to find an unknown value. These symbols are usually shown as x, y, and z. Primarily the creation of Muslim mathematicians, most notably **al-Khwarizmi** (c. 780–c. 850; see biography in this chapter), algebra constituted a great leap beyond the Greeks' geometry and trigonometry. Instead of having to treat every mathematical problem by means of a diagram, algebra made it possible for mathematicians to work out problems directly, in the form of equations.

A Sample Algebra Problem

The following example of the ways that algebra can be used comes from a Greek collection of mathematical puzzles that appeared in the 500s. Describing the great mathematician Diophantus (210–290; see sidebar in the essay "The Greeks' New Approach to Mathematics" in this chapter), the brain teaser posed the following problem: "...his boyhood lasted one-sixth of his life; he married after one-seventh more; his beard grew after one-twelfth more; and his son was born five years later. The son lived to half his father's age, and the father died four years after the son."

To solve the problem of Diophantus's life span, represented as x, the problem would be written thus in modern notation: $(1/6)x + (1/7)x + (1/12)x + 5 + (1/2)x + 4 = x$. The equation would then be restated, first by putting all the xs on the same side of the equals sign. Moving a positive number to the other side of the equation turns it into a negative, and vice versa, so the problem would become: $(1/6)x + (1/7)x + (1/12)x - (1/2)x = -9$. Using their lowest common denominator, which is 84, the fractions could be added, ultimately revealing the answer $(9/84)x = 9$. X is therefore equal to 84, meaning that Diophantus was considered a man at fourteen; married at twenty-six; grew his beard at thirty-three; became a father at thirty-eight; then at age eighty, lost his forty-two-year-old son.

Early ideas of algebra

Despite the fact that a good example of an algebra problem comes from a Greek text, the Greeks had little interest in algebra. Indeed, the subject of the problem, Diophantus (210–290)—who in his *Arithmetica* introduced the practice of using letters to represent unknown values—was one of the few Greek mathematicians to address the subject at all.

Long before Diophantus's time, the Babylonians were the first people to use special symbols for unknown quantities, and the Egyptians used a rudimentary form of algebra to solve the types of equations that high-school students today encounter in the first few weeks of an algebra class. The first thinker to directly approach what would become known as algebra was the Hindu mathematician Brahmagupta (598–670), whose work greatly influenced that of medieval Arab scholars.

The birth of algebra in the Middle East

Most notable among the Arabic writings on algebra was al-Khwarizmi's *Kitab al-jabr wa al-muqabala* (The compendious book on calculation by completing and balancing). In it, he described a method he called *al-jabr*—from which the word *algebra* is derived—for finding the value of an unknown quantity by rearranging terms in an equation. The *Kitab al-jabr* was translated into Latin in 1145 by Robert of Chester, an English scholar living in Islamic Spain.

Persian poet and mathematician Omar Khayyam (1048–1131) advanced the study of algebra by solving cubic equations, or equations in which the highest exponent is 3; for example, $x^3 + 2x^2 + x = 0$. In his work on cubic equations, Omar brought together Greek geometry, Babylonian and Hindu arithmetic, and Islamic algebra. His work greatly influenced future Islamic mathematicians, and through them the mathematicians of Renaissance Europe. (The Renaissance was a period of artistic and intellectual rebirth, lasting roughly from 1350 to 1600, that marked the end of the Middle Ages.)

Algebra in Europe

It appears that Omar had little direct impact on European mathematics. When Italian scholars in competition with one another developed their own method for solving cubic equations in the 1500s, they and the audiences who took a great interest in their competition (see sidebar, "The Tartaglia–Cardano 'Grudge Match'" on page 261) assumed that no such solution had been found previously.

Among Europeans, algebra emerged as a separate mathematical discipline only very slowly. The reason was that scholars took as their model **Euclid**'s *Elements*, and algebra bore little relation to Euclidean geometry (see essay "Geometry and the Great Unsolved Problems" in this chapter). Thus in order for algebra to gain full acceptance in the ranks of mathematical disciplines, someone had to sell the idea to the European intellectual community.

That someone was French mathematician François Viète (1540–1603), who worked to fit algebra into the categories of mathematics as outlined by the Greek philosopher and mathematician Geminus (c. 130–c. 70 B.C.E.). The efforts of Viète required nothing less than a redefinition and expansion of Geminus's categories, which had long been accepted with the same reverence given to Euclid's *Elements*. Viète would later be overshadowed in the emerging world of algebra by two vastly more influential countrymen,

René Descartes (1596–1650; see biography in this chapter) and **Pierre de Fermat** (1601–1665; see biography in this chapter), yet the new discipline owed a great deal to the unsung French mathematician who made algebra acceptable to European scholars.

Logarithms

If a person today needs the answer to a question involving the multiplication or division of large numbers, it is only necessary to punch a few buttons on a calculator. But calculators have been widely available only since the 1980s, and as recently as the 1970s, scientists and science students typically relied on slide rules to perform difficult calculations. Some people still use slide rules, maintaining that they offer benefits unavailable from a calculator.

François Viète led the effort to convince European mathematicians to accept algebra. **(Reproduced courtesy of the Library of Congress.)**

The slide rule was an essential tool for the astronauts aboard the *Apollo* Moon missions in the late 1960s and 1970s. These men depended on slide rules to provide them with answers to the many calculations necessary in the course of space flight. (An example of this can be seen in the 1995 film *Apollo 13.*) Invented in 1622 by English mathematician William Oughtred (1574–1660), the slide rule put to practical use the results of an amazing discovery by one of the most brilliant mathematicians of all time.

The man who discovered logarithms

The fact that John Napier (1550–1617) was an amateur, never formally trained in mathematics, only adds to the magnificence of his achievement. A Scottish lord, Napier dabbled in an astonishing number of pursuits, for instance designing early versions of the tank, submarine, and machine gun. His wide-ranging genius and eccentric ways attracted so much attention that enemies spread rumors that he practiced black magic and kept a black rooster possessed by a demon.

Yet Napier was far more than just a curious and interesting figure from history. In fact, his discovery of logarithms was by far the most important step forward in computer science between the Babylonians' invention of the abacus in about 2400 B.C.E. and the development of computers after World War II (1939–45). Napier first conceived the idea of logarithms from his work as an amateur astronomer, and astronomers were among the first to benefit from his discovery.

To analyze the movement of an object in the sky, an astronomer had to perform a number of relatively sophisticated calculations, many of which took hours. Thanks to Napier and his logarithms, the astronomer could simply look up the logarithms of each factor, add these together, then consult the tables again to find the number for which this sum was the logarithm.

How logarithms work

A *logarithm* is the power to which a given number, called a base, must be raised to yield a given product. For instance, $10^2 = 100$, and in logarithmic terms, this would be expressed thus: $\log_{10}100 = 2$. This in itself is not particularly interesting, but consider what happens when two logarithms are added together; for instance, $\log_2 2 + \log_2 3$. By adding the logarithms $(2 + 3)$, one obtains a result of 5, or to put it in logarithmic terms, $\log_2 2 + \log_2 3 = \log_2 5$. This is another way of saying that 2^2 (4) multiplied by 2^3 (8) equals 2^5 (32), but note that in the logarithmic equation, the logarithms or exponents are added rather than multiplied.

The same principle can be used for division, in which case logarithms are subtracted rather than added. Thus, to divide 32 by 8, one would write the equation as $\log_2 5 - \log_2 3 = \log_2 2$; in other words, $32 \div 8 = 4$. What made Napier's breakthrough so important, especially coming as it did, at a time when mathematicians were still struggling with problems of multiplication and division, was the fact that it made possible the quick multiplication and division of *any* two numbers. While anyone who has learned his or her multiplication tables in school can easily multiply 4 by 8, or divide 32 by 8, logarithms can be used to multiply and divide much more difficult numbers. More often, the logarithms involved are not whole numbers such as 2, 3, or 5, nor do the calculations usually include numbers that can be easily multiplied and divided in the way that 4, 8, and 32 can be. Yet for each base and its product, there is a logarithm, and these logarithms can be subtracted or added as needed to greatly simplify problems of long division and multiplication.

To make these calculations, it is necessary to consult a table of logarithms, a form of which appears on the surface of a slide rule. Napier and British mathematician Henry Briggs (1561–1630) spent twenty years compiling the first table of logarithms, which they published in 1614. Unlike many another innovations in math or science, this one met with immediate success, probably because scholars were eager for relief from the mind-numbing and time-consuming work of performing computations by hand.

A man sits at the rear of the Eniac computer, the first multipurpose computer, developed in the 1940s. John Napier's logarithms were an important early innovation in the development of computer science. (© Bettmann/Corbis. Reproduced by permission of the Corbis Corporation.)

Uses for logarithms

Napier's work helped lead to the discovery of *e*, the basis for what is called natural logarithms. The number *e*, like *pi*, is irrational, meaning that it is a decimal number that neither terminates nor repeats; presented in a form correct to the first nine places, it is 2.718281828. (The fact that the "1828" repeats in these first few numbers is purely coincidental, and not part of any pattern.) A variety of endeavors use *e*, a feature common to numerous equations for processes of growth or decay. For instance, financial institutions use *e* for calculating compound interest, which includes interest not only on the principal, or original amount of money, but also interest on the interest. In a very different application, nuclear scientists use *e* to determine rates of radioactive decay.

Aircraft, internal combustion engines, electrical generators, and petroleum refineries are designed with the use of logarithms, which are also involved in calculations regarding television and radio broadcast reception. Two important scales in science, the pH scale for measuring acidity and the decibel scale for measuring volume, are logarithmic. This means that every increase of 10 decibels (dB) indicates a sound ten times as loud, a fact that has very serious implications. The maximum decibel level that a human ear can endure without experiencing permanent damage is 120 dB, but some rock bands have been known to produce noise levels of 125 dB in concert. That extra 5 dB does not represent an increase of 5/120, or 0.04 percent— it is an increase of 500 percent, and represents a serious danger.

PATTERNS AND POSSIBILITIES

There is something deeply fascinating about the way that numbers work together. Indeed, many early thinkers believed that numbers possessed special significance of a spiritual nature. For that matter, many people today have such beliefs, for instance with regard to the "unlucky" number 13. These ideas have roots that go back at least as far as **Pythagoras** (c. 580–c. 500 B.C.E.; see biography in this chapter), and often such notions venture far outside the realm of mathematics and into the quasi-spiritual field of numerology.

On the other hand, research into the relationships between numbers, and between numbers and events in the real world, has often yielded practical results. In the study of statistics, probability theory, and combinatorics, one can see a remnant of the early belief that numbers can unlock deep secrets in the universe, and in a sense they can. It may not be possible to use numbers alone to predict the future, or to find deep, hidden truths, as numerologists believe; yet by properly using numbers, mathematicians have indeed found surprising patterns, and have gone on to make accurate predictions of future possibilities.

Statistics and probability theory

It is a fact of life that some things happen, but many other things that could happen do not. A man could walk out of his office on his way to lunch, for instance, be hit by a truck, and die. Or he could bump into a woman he has never seen, start a conversation, and eventually fall in love, marry, and start a family. In all likelihood, however, neither of these dramatic things is likely to happen—but they could happen.

Words to Know

combinatorics: The study of combining objects by various rules to create new arrangements of objects.

magic square: A square set of boxes—the number must always be a square number such as 9, 16, or 25—containing different numbers. In a magic square, the sum of the numbers in each row, column, or diagonal is the same.

numerology: The belief that numbers have special meanings of a spiritual nature, and can be used to predict the future.

probability theory: A branch of mathematics devoted to predicting the likelihood that a particular event will occur. Such predictions are typically based on statistical data.

statistics: A branch of mathematics concerned with the collection and analysis of numerical data.

The ultimate answer to questions regarding why things happen, whether those things are good or bad, is the territory of religion and philosophy, while science addresses how things happen; for instance, the truck had more mass, and therefore more force, than the man, and it crushed him. On the other hand, the question of what things could and might happen, and the likelihood that they will, is a part of mathematics, specifically, the fields of statistics and probability theory.

Statistics is the branch of mathematics concerned with the collection and analysis of numerical data relating to particular topics, and probability theory is devoted to predicting the likelihood that a particular event will occur. The two are closely related, because a proper statistical database is necessary before probabilities can be accurately calculated.

Gambling gives birth to a mathematical discipline

Consider the following problem, related to an area in which statistics and probability theory both play a significant role: gambling. Suppose that in ninety-nine consecutive coin tosses, a quarter comes up heads; what, then, will be the likelihood that it comes up tails on the one hundredth toss? One hundred to one? A person who bet on this might well be disappointed, since the probability of a coin coming up heads or tails is the same on the millionth toss as it is on the first: just two-to-one. On the other hand, consider the chances of pulling a red queen at random from a deck of fifty-two cards. Initially the chances are one in twenty-six (since there are two red queens), but as more cards are removed, and none is a red queen, the likelihood increases.

A fascination with dice and games of chance led to the first important work in probability theory and statistics, by French mathematicians **Blaise Pascal** (1623–1662; see biography in this chapter) and **Pierre de Fermat** (1601–1665; see biography in this chapter). Actually, Italian mathematician Girolamo Cardano (1501–1576) performed the first probability study a century earlier, but his work was neglected, and therefore Pascal and Fermat are regarded as the true ground breakers in these fields. The two disciplines remained closely linked until the end of the 1700s, by which time statistics emerged as an independent discipline, though one closely allied with probability theory.

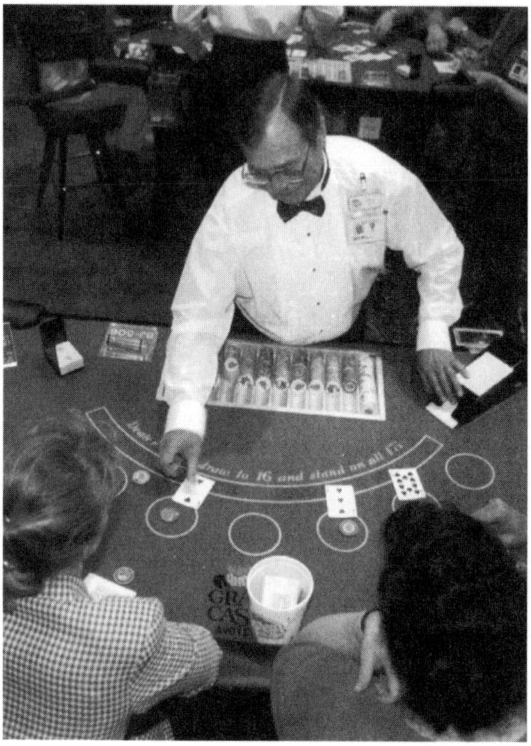

A blackjack dealer deals out cards to players. As more cards are dealt from a deck the likelihood of certain cards appearing increases. **(Reproduced by permission of AP/Wide World Photos, Inc.)**

Uses for statistics and probability theory in science

By the beginning of the twentieth century, several factors contributed to growing respect for probability theory and statistics. In physics and chemistry, quantum mechanics, which maintains that atoms have specific energy levels governed by the distance between the electron and the nucleus, became the prevailing theory of matter. Since quantum mechanics also holds that it is impossible to predict the location of an electron with certainty, probability calculations became necessary to the work of physicists and chemists.

The early twentieth century also saw the rise of the social sciences, which rely heavily on statistical research. In order to earn a graduate degree today, a prospective psychologist or sociologist must undergo an intensive course of study in statistics and calculus. These aid in the interpretation of patterns involving complex variables; for instance, the relationship between schoolchildren's diet and their test scores, or between the age at which a person marries and his or her income.

Statistics and probability theory in the insurance industry

Another factor in the growing importance of probability and statistics was the emergence of the insurance industry. Insurance is an essential element of economically advanced societies such as those of North America, western Europe, and east Asia. These economies could not survive (in a financial sense) if individuals and businesses had no way of protecting themselves against potential losses, such as from theft and natural disasters.

In the world of insurance, statistics and probability theory are so important that an entire field of study, known as actuarial science, is devoted to analyzing things that could or might happen. Without actuarial analysis, an insurance company could not make a profit while charging reasonable prices for coverage.

If everyone collected on his or her insurance policy, insurance companies would go out of business. The fortunate fact (for the customers as well as the company!) is that most people will not collect, except in the case of life insurance, in which case an individual's survivors receive an insurance settlement. Even in that situation, however, insurance companies naturally prefer to insure people who will stay alive, and keep making insurance payments, for a long time.

Insurance companies therefore charge more to insure people who are statistically most likely to collect on policies. Thus the cost of automobile insurance is high for young males, who, statistics show, tend to be the most aggressive and reckless drivers. Similarly, life and health insurance costs are high for cigarette smokers, who are statistically likely to get sick and die after a long, expensive hospitalization.

Other uses for statistics and probability theory

Statistics and probability theory also apply in areas such as political polling. It would be impossible to interview every voter in the country regarding his or her views on a particular issue or candidate, and in any case it is unnecessary. Through the use of statistics, pollsters can select a small sample group that reflects the composition of the population as a whole. For example, African Americans make up about 12 percent of the U.S. population, so a sample group of 1,000 people should include about 120 African Americans. Polling of such a group, and the application of probability calculations, make it possible for pollsters and news organizations to predict the results of an election with sometimes amazing accuracy.

Engineering uses a branch of statistics and probability theory called probabilistic risk assessment (PRA). In this field, a complex piece of machinery, whether it be an automobile or the space shuttle, is examined in order to determine the probability that a particular part will fail. Then, engineers assess all the components that will be affected if that part fails,

Numerology and Religion

Numerology is the belief that numbers have special spiritual meanings and can be used to predict the future. It is often traced back to the teachings of **Pythagoras** (c. 580–c. 500 B.C.E.; see biography in this chapter) and his followers, who claimed that the entire universe could be explained in terms of numbers. Pythagoras at least attempted to merge his spiritual ideas with mathematical ones; on the other hand, numerology of a purely religious nature probably dates back at least to the early Babylonian civilization of about 3000 B.C.E.

Ideas akin to numerology are often associated with the Bible and other Jewish scriptures. Like a number of ancient cultures, the people of Israel believed that each number had a specific character; therefore the number 7 is usually linked with God, and 6 with man's sinful nature, or even with the devil. Three, in biblical terms, implies completion; hence the number of the Antichrist, the embodiment of evil, is given in the Book of Revelation as 666.

The fact that there were thirteen men at the Last Supper, and one of them, Judas, betrayed Jesus, is the source of the superstition surrounding the

and then they assess all the things that affected components could in turn cause to fail. So it goes, until the engineers have analyzed (and presumably corrected) all risky elements.

Combinatorics

The roots of probability theory, and specialized fields such as PRA, lie in combinatorics, the study of combining objects by various rules to create new arrangements. Combinatorics play a part in the magic square, an array of numbers in which the rows, columns, and diagonals all add up to the same sum.

Magic squares first appeared in the Chinese *I Ching* or Book of Changes, which dates from the 1100s B.C.E. The *I Ching* is not a math book at all, but a work of philosophy and mysticism, and its use of numbers is an example of numerology—the belief that numbers have special spiritual meanings and can be used to predict the future.

"unlucky" number 13. This is an example of how some ridiculous numerological ideas have started with the claim that the Bible supports them, when in fact the Bible never states that thirteen is unlucky. Nor does it offer a great deal of interpretation with regard to the meaning of 666; yet throughout the ages, numerologists have tried to associate the number with public figures they wanted to discredit. (Some interpretations of Revelation, incidentally, show the number of the Antichrist as 616. On the other hand, 666 is interesting because it involves six of the seven basic Roman numerals, in order and without repetition: DCLXVI.)

Not all forms of numerology are based in the Christian or Jewish religions, of course. Eastern varieties exist as well, and numerology is perhaps most at home today in the "New Age" movement. Numerology is often used in a manner much like astrology, for instance to determine certain traits about a person based on the date of his or her birth. Yet at least astrology, in ancient times, served as the forerunner of scientific astronomy; numerology, on the other hand, appears to be completely lacking in mathematical value.

Combinatorics in the Middle Ages

Magic squares, numerology, and related concepts fascinated medieval scholars, especially those of the Jewish community in Spain and the Middle East. A number of these thinkers took an interest in the *cabala,* a mystical system for interpreting the Scriptures based on the belief that every word and punctuation mark contains a secret message. For instance, Levi ben Gerson (1288–1344) of France—one of the few Jews who came to prominence in Christian Europe, where the Jewish people were persecuted during the Middle Ages—involved himself not only in mathematics and science, but in mystical pursuits as well.

In India, whose culture also attached a religious significance to science and mathematics, combinatorics had long attracted the attention of scholars and mystics alike. For instance, the spiritual sect known as the Jains studied what they called *vikalpa,* or the possibilities of various com-

Many cultures associate special meanings with numbers. The fact that there were thirteen men at the Last Supper, and one of them, Judas, betrayed Jesus, is the source of the superstition surrounding the "unlucky" number 13. **(Reproduced by permission of The Granger Collection, New York.)**

binations, and the great Hindu mathematician Bhaskara (c. 1114– c.1185) addressed combinatorial problems in his book *Lilivati* ("The Graceful," said to be named for his daughter).

An interesting example of combinatorics appears in what came to be known as "Pascal's triangle." Yet Pascal was not the first to use the concept, most likely first developed by the Chinese mathematician Yang Hui (c. 1238–c. 1298). Whatever the case, Pascal's triangle provides a useful means of determining the number of possible combinations within a given set, thus suggesting the probability that any particular combination will occur.

Combinatorial problems have often been associated with games and puzzles such as the "rabbit problem" of Italian mathematician **Leonardo Fibonacci** (c. 1170–c. 1240; see biography in this chapter). Fibonacci's problem depicted a pair of rabbits producing a pair of offspring a month, and each pair of offspring producing a pair of their own after reaching maturity at two months. The number of rabbit pairs in any given month could be found in what came to be known as the Fibonacci sequence, wherein each number is the sum of the previous two: 1, 1, 2, 3, 5, 8, and so on.

The Königsberg bridge problem

One of the greatest combinatorial puzzles of all time did not directly involve numbers, but rather points on a graph—the other major area of combinatorics. The Königsberg bridge problem originated from a seemingly trivial matter, but would have enormous implications for areas such as business supply-chain flow, computer networking, and the design of roads and highways.

It all began when the great Swiss mathematician **Leonhard Euler** (1707–1783; see biography in this chapter) learned of a brainteaser that had long perplexed the citizens of Königsberg, Germany (now Kaliningrad, Russia), a river town on two islands. Four bridges connected the mainland with the first island, and an additional two bridges connected the second island with the shore, while a seventh bridge joined the two islands. The puzzle was this: could a person start from a particular point and walk along a route that would allow him or her to cross each bridge once and only once?

To solve the problem, Euler drew it in the form of a graph, but not a graph in the sense that the word is typically used. Euler's graph was more like a schematic drawing such as an electrician would make for the wiring of a house. Indeed, such drawings ultimately owe their existence to Euler's work. On the other hand, his graph was more than just a map; instead, it represented the four land masses (the two islands and the two sides of the river) as points, with segments between them representing paths.

After rendering the problem in this schematic form, Euler rephrased the bridge problem, asking himself if it was possible to trace over each segment without lifting the pencil. He did not simply approach it by trial and error, however; rather, he addressed it as a mathematician, looking for a general principle that would provide him with a solution. Ultimately he showed that, in order to cross each bridge only once, each landmass would have to have an even number of bridges connected to it. Therefore it was impossible to the cross all seven Königsberg bridges only once.

Modern graph theory

With the Königsberg bridge problem, Euler inaugurated the mathematical field of graph theory, as well as the larger discipline of topology, which is concerned with the properties of geometric figures when these are stretched or compressed. The implications of his work went far, far beyond mathematics, however. As noted, graph theory provided the basis for schematic drawings, not only in construction and engineering, but also in physics and chemistry.

Today, graph theory is used in designing telephone switching systems and computer networks that link cities and countries, and it also helps businesses use their resources most efficiently. For instance, a company that regularly delivers products to different locations would utilize graph theory to ensure that its drivers do a minimum of backtracking and "deadheading," or driving from one place to another without a load.

ANGLES, CURVES, AND SURFACES

The history of mathematics has been the story of applied mathematics vs. pure mathematics, that is, math with a definite purpose, as opposed to math for its own sake. Mathematics began with applied forms, such as the business and engineering calculations made by the Sumerians and Egyptians of about 3000 B.C.E., whereas pure mathematics did not appear until several thousand years later, in Greece.

Yet something funny has happened over the years. The further researchers go from the ordinary study of numbers and shapes, the more their ideas become applicable in real-world situations. Such is the case with several areas devoted to the study of angles, curves, and surfaces: trigonometry, advanced geometry, and calculus. Each of these goes beyond the world of ancient Greek geometry, and each is successively harder to grasp. Yet all three have, and have had, numerous practical applications.

Trigonometry, for instance, helped make possible the great sailing expeditions of the 1500s, and advanced geometry has been applied in everything from mapmaking to warfare. As for calculus, it quite literally opened the way for the monumental scientific advances that began in the 1700s, and have continued through the present day.

Trigonometry: An angle on the world

Trigonometry is the study of the properties of triangles—in particular, the relationships between the various sides of a right triangle—as well as the properties of points on a circle. It is one of the most practical branches of mathematics, finding uses in engineering, surveying, and various sciences, most notably astronomy. Indeed, trigonometry is so practical that the ancients did not even think of it as a branch of mathematics.

The origins of trigonometry date back to ancient Egypt, where examples of crude trigonometry appeared as early as 1850 B.C.E. The Babylonians aided the emerging discipline by developing a system of 360-degree circles, but trigonometry only came into its own with the work of Greek mathematicians and astronomers. Using trigonometry to analyze the angles between Earth, the Sun, and the Moon, the astronomer Aristarchus of Samos (c. 320–c. 250 B.C.E.) calculated that the distance from Earth to the Sun as about twenty times that from Earth to the Moon.

The Greeks measure space

Actually, Aristarchus—notable for suggesting, some eighteen hundred years before **Nicolaus Copernicus**, (1473–1543; see biography in the Physical Sciences chapter) that the Sun and not Earth is at the center of the universe—was wrong on this count. In fact, the ratio between the distances is more like forty to one. Nonetheless, Aristarchus showed that trigonometry could be used to measure something that men could not possibly measure in the traditional way, as one would find the dimensions of a room.

Words to Know

calculus: The branch of mathematics that deals with rates of change and motion.

Cartesian coordinate system: A method for identifying points on a plane by assigning to each point a unique set of numbers indicating its location. In the Cartesian system, values of *x* and *y* respectively indicate horizontal and vertical distance from the center, designated as (0,0). Cartesian graphs may also be three-dimensional, with a *z*-axis perpendicular (at a right angle to) both *x* and *y*.

conic section: The cross-section of a cone when cut by a plane.

geometry: The branch of mathematics concerned with the properties and relationships of points, lines, angles, surfaces, and shapes.

hypotenuse: The longest side of a right triangle.

ratio: The relationship between two numbers or values. All fractions are ratios, but some ratios such as π (pi, the relationship between the circumference and diameter of a circle) cannot be expressed as whole number fractions.

right triangle: A triangle with one right angle, or 90° angle. (Since the total measurement of the three angles in a triangle is 180°, no triangle can have more than one right angle.)

trigonometry: The study of the properties of triangles—in particular, the relationships between the various sides of a right triangle—as well as the properties of points on a circle.

A century later, **Eratosthenes** of Cyrene (air-uh-TAHS-thuh-neez; 276–c. 194 B.C.E.; see biography in this chapter) used trigonometry to estimate Earth's size. In this, one of the great intellectual feats of the Greek world, Eratosthenes established the field of geodesy, or the study of the shape and size of Earth. His work resulted in an amazingly accurate measurement, one that has only been improved upon in modern times. Unfortunately, however, the influential astronomer **Ptolemy** (c. 100–170; see biography in Physical Science chapter) rejected Eratosthenes's findings, and instead used figures that made the planet seem much smaller than it really is.

Despite the achievements of Aristarchus and Eratosthenes, the astronomer Hipparchus (flourished 146–127 B.C.E.) is regarded as the father of trigonometry. Hipparchus introduced to Greece the Babylonian practice of measuring angles and parts of circles in degrees, and created the first sine table. A sine for an angle in a right triangle is the ratio between the length of the opposite side and that of the hypotenuse, or longest side. Though triangles may differ in size, the value of sine for a given angle does not change.

Later, Ptolemy applied trigonometry for the measurement of distances between heavenly bodies, and for the prediction of the positions of the Sun and other celestial objects at various times. He recorded these observations in a book that came to be known by its Arabic title of *al-Majisti* (The Greatest), translated into Latin as *Almagest*—a book that defined astronomy in the West until about 1500.

Trigonometry in the East

During Ptolemy's time, knowledge of trigonometry passed to India, which at that time had regular contact with the Roman Empire. The Hindu *Paitammaha siddhanta,* written early in the 400s, used a word in the Sanskrit language that would eventually be translated as "sine." Still later, Hindu and Greek writings on trigonometry made their way into the Muslim world, where astronomers greatly refined the discipline.

Among the most important Muslim pioneers of trigonometry was the Persian astronomer Abu'l-Wefa (940–998). Along with other Muslim mathematicians, Abu'l-Wefa combined the Greek concepts of trigonometry and geometry with the superior numbering system of Hindu mathematics (see essay "Hindu-Arabic Numerals and Mathematical Symbolism" in this chapter) to create the form of trigonometry known today.

He also constructed a detailed sine table, which was an incredibly tedious and mind-numbing task. Today anyone can obtain sine values for any angle with the push of a few buttons on a calculator, but this was not the case a thousand years ago, and Abu'l-Wefa's work proved to be of enormous value for astronomers and mathematicians of his own time, and for future generations.

Abu'l-Wefa also introduced such trigonometric functions as the tangent, the ratio between the opposite side and the adjacent side of a triangle, and the secant and cosecant. The secant is the reciprocal of sine, or 1 divided by sine for a given angle, and the cosecant is the reciprocal of cosine (abbreviated *cos*), the ratio between the length of the adjacent side and that of the hypotenuse.

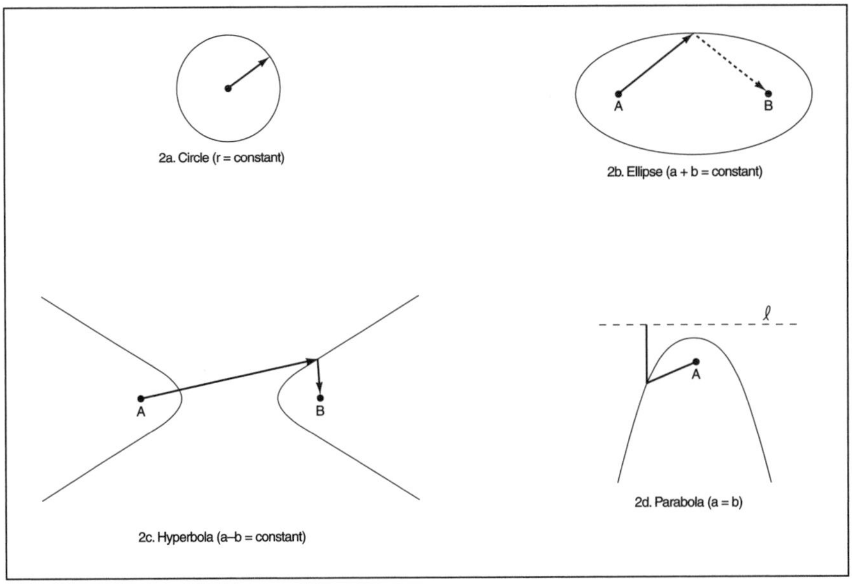

A diagram of a circle, ellipse, hyperbola, and parabola.
Illustration by Hans and Cassidy. Reproduced by permission of the Gale Group.

Later developments in trigonometry

Modern uses of trigonometry include applications of which Abu'l-Wefa and others could hardly have conceived: the design of rotating camshafts in an engine; the analysis of the buckling patterns a bridge undergoes in an earthquake; and even the study of the patterns made by an electron as it moves around the nucleus of an atom. Yet even at the time, the value of trigonometry for uses such as mapmaking, navigation, astronomy, and surveying was apparent.

Only in the late Middle Ages and early Renaissance was trigonometry finally separated, as a mathematical discipline, from its many applications. By that point, the appearance of Greek and Arab mathematical texts had inspired the work of Europeans such as German astronomer Regiomontanus or Johann Müller (1436–1476), who helped separate plane or flat trigonometry from spherical trigonometry.

As Europeans embarked on their voyages of exploration in the 1450s, trigonometry played a significant part by aiding in navigation at sea. During the centuries that followed, when the seas had been explored and Europe established trade routes with the rest of the world, simple trigonometry advanced sail designs and allowed for the design, placement, and use of heavy weaponry such as cannons.

New frontiers of geometry

During the 1700s, mathematicians increasingly employed the curves and shapes generated from conic sections to advance the study of geometry, and to gain new understanding of practical matters from geography to the use of artillery in battle. A conic section is the cross-section of a cone when cut by a plane, and the shapes that result from it include various curves such as the hyperbola and parabola. (A parabola, in very simple terms, is shaped like a deep bowl, and a hyperbola is like two parabolas with their bottoms facing one another.)

Discovery of these shapes resulted from attempts at doubling the cube in ancient Greece and later (see essay "Geometry and the Great Unsolved Problems" in this chapter), but the Greeks only thought of these curves in geometric terms. Thanks to French mathematicians **René Descartes** (1594–1650) and **Pierre de Fermat** (1601–1665; see biographies in this chapter), however, it became possible to develop formulas for describing the shapes in terms of algebra. Combined with the later discoveries of **Isaac Newton** (1642–1727; see biography in Physical Science chapter) concerning the laws of motion and gravity, the use of these algebraic functions made it possible to calculate the movements of the planets with accuracy.

Coordinate systems

Another factor that made such calculations easier was the development of coordinate systems, a method for identifying points on a plane by assigning to each point a unique set of numbers indicating its location. The most well-known of these is the Cartesian (kar-TEE-zhun) coordinate system, which students today apply in advanced algebra, trigonometry, and calculus classes. Though attributed to Descartes (Cartesian refers to his name), in fact the development of the Cartesian system was as much the work of Fermat.

Later, Newton and Swiss mathematician Jakob Bernoulli (1654–1750), working independently, introduced the idea of polar coordinates. These made it possible to map a point on a curved surface, the elliptical (egg-shaped) paths of planetary orbits, for instance, or the surface of earth.

OPPOSITE PAGE A map by Gerardus Mercator. Mercator eventually solved the problem of presenting the curved surface of Earth on a flat map with a method called Mercator projection. **(Reproduced courtesy of the American Geographical Society.)**

The two-dimensional Cartesian system could represent width, or the distance along the x-axis, and height, or the distance along the y-axis. It was not, however, capable of demonstrating three-dimensional space. Then Jakob's brother Johann Bernoulli (1667–1748) created a three-dimensional version of the Cartesian coordinate system, with a z-axis to represent depth.

Adjusting surfaces and orientations

Later, German mathematician **Leonhard Euler** (1707–1783; see biography in this chapter) established a general procedure for changing the orientation of a three-dimensional coordinate system. The specifics of this are highly complex, but in a very simplified form, Euler's system is rather like the process of mental adjustment that a person makes when looking in the mirror. If one raises one's right hand, one's reflection raises its left hand,

and in order to interpret this image correctly, one has to mentally adjust for the change of orientation created by the mirror. Euler's method formed the basis for the physical study of rotating bodies, including planets, spacecraft, gyroscopes, molecules, and atoms.

Euler and French mathematician Gaspard Monge (1746–1818) worked independently on the problem of representing a curved surface on a flat one. This had long perplexed mapmakers attempting to translate points from the curved surface of Earth to the flat plane of a map. Though it sounds easy, it is not: a straight line between two points on a map would appear as a curved line on a globe, and a straight line on a globe looks like a curved line on a map.

In 1579, mapmaker Gerardus Mercator (1512–1594) had offered a fairly workable solution by creating a map known as the Mercator projection. A Mercator projection shows the parallel lines of latitude closer together at the Equator, and further apart at the Poles. Therefore Greenland, for instance, appears larger than the continental United States, though in fact the United States is about four times as large as Greenland. The Mercator projection has been improved many times over the years, but it still looks rather distorted, as do other types of map projections.

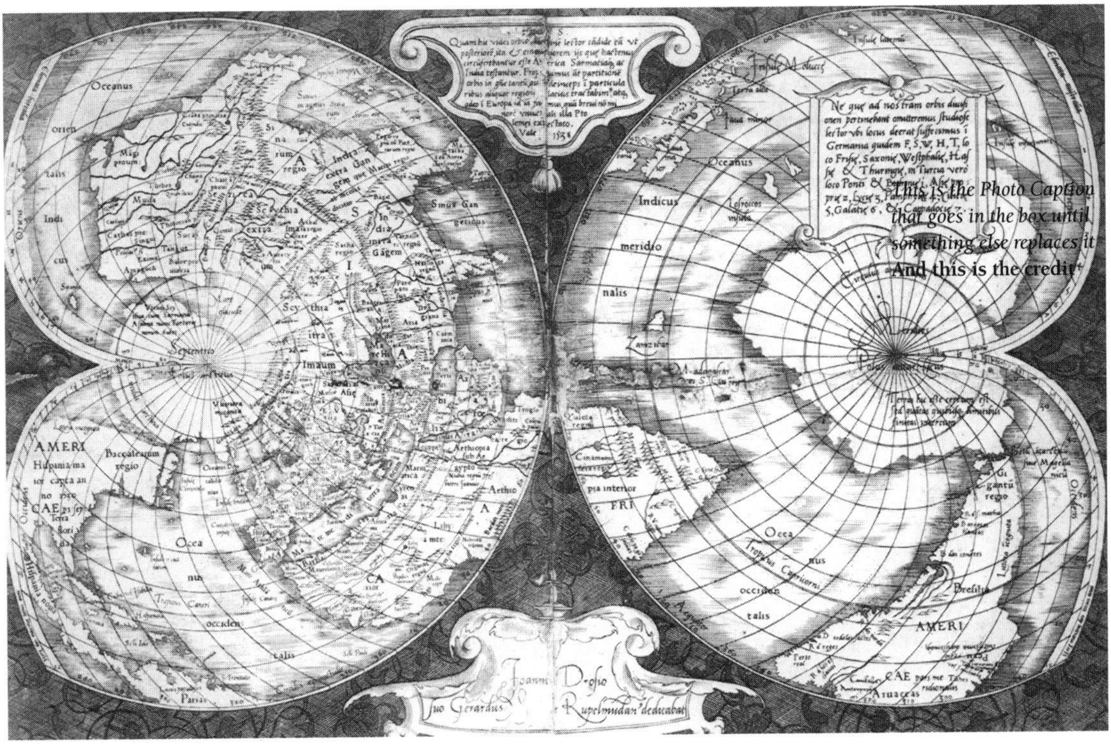

This is the Photo Caption that goes in the box until something else replaces it
And this is the credit

Projective geometry

In 1794, five years after the French Revolution began in 1789, Monge became a member of the Commission of Public Works, set up by the government to establish an institution of higher education for engineers. The school would become the Ecole Polytechnique (School of Technology), which would attract many of the best mathematical minds of the time to its faculty. There, Monge taught descriptive or projective geometry, based on a concept he had developed some time earlier.

Mathematics has always played a significant part in the operation of military artillery, or heavy guns such as cannons. In order to aim and fire them properly, artillery officers have to make detailed computations regarding the size and weight of the cannonballs, the distance they would travel before falling to earth, the best possible method of gun placement, and other specifics. Monge's development of projective geometry, the representation of three-dimensional objects through a combination of top and side views, greatly reduced the amount of time required for such calculations, and the French government considered his technique so valuable that they treated it as a military secret for many years.

In the civilian world, Monge's technique became the basis for mechanical drawing. Today, combined with Euler's method of rotating shapes, it is applied in computer-aided design (CAD), used by architects and engineers. CAD makes it possible to design a structure or piece of machinery without building expensive models, and to view the interior or exterior from various angles long before the structure is built.

Calculus

Of all the mathematical disciplines a student is likely to encounter before college, calculus is by far the most intimidating. If the student gets to calculus at all, it will be as a senior, after four years of study that include algebra, geometry, algebra II, and trigonometry.

Calculus is the branch of mathematics that deals with rates of change and motion. It is divided into two parts, differential calculus and integral calculus. Differential calculus is concerned with finding the instantaneous rate at which one quantity, called a derivative, changes with respect to another. Integral calculus deals with the inverse or opposite of a derivative.

For example, if a car is going around a curve, differential calculus would be used to determine its rate of change (that is, its speed) at any given point, but if the car's speed were already known, then integral calculus could be used to show its position at any given time. Imagine any object following a curved path: this is the territory of calculus, which measures very small changes.

The ancient roots of calculus

No single individual developed geometry, and though Hipparchus and **al-Khwarizmi** (c. 780–c. 850; see biography in this chapter) are recognized as the fathers of trigonometry and algebra (see essay "Playing with Numbers" in this chapter) respectively, both disciplines are actually the result of contributions by numerous figures. By contrast, calculus had a definite beginning in the late 1600s, and its creation was the work of two brilliant men, Isaac Newton and German philosopher and mathematician **Gottfried Wilhelm von Leibniz** (1646–1716; see biography in this chapter).

It should be noted, however, that the roots of calculus also go back to ancient Greece, specifically, to Zeno's paradoxes (see essay "The Greeks' New Approach to Mathematics" in this chapter) and the problem of squaring the circle (see essay "Geometry and the Great Unsolved Problems" in this chapter). The paradoxes raised the question of whether space and time could be subdivided infinitely. Squaring of the circle introduced the "method of exhaustion," which involved infinitely subdividing the area just inside the rim of a circle in what turned out to be a fruitless attempt to create a straight-sided figure of a size equal to that of the circle.

British physicist and mathematician Isaac Newton. He and Gottfried Wilhelm von Leibniz are both credited with developing calculus. **(Reproduced courtesy of the Library of Congress.)**

Studies of motion

Mathematics, physics, and astronomy have long been closely linked, a fact illustrated by medieval (of the Middle Ages, c. 500–c. 1500) and Renaissance (c. 1350–1600) developments in what would become known as calculus. During the late Middle Ages, the French mathematician Nicole d'Oresme (1323–1382) advanced the study of motion, or kinematics, with his work on uniform acceleration. The best example of uniform acceleration occurs when a falling body experiences a steady increase of speed, or velocity, under the force of gravity.

However, the world did not understand gravity until the Italian astronomer and physicist **Galileo** (1564–1642; see biography in Physical Science chapter), building on the work of Oresme, proved that falling bodies experience uniform acceleration. This in turn paved the way for Newton's own studies of gravity and motion, which profoundly affected the future of science. (For much more on this subject, see essay "The Scientific Revolution" in the Physical Sciences chapter.) Also influential to the development of calculus was the work of Descartes and Fermat who, as noted, devised a means of representing curves mathematically, by algebraic expressions.

Newton or Leibniz?

One of the great controversies in the history of mathematics is the question of whether Newton or Leibniz deserves credit for the creation of calculus. In fact both developed it independently, and though it appears that Newton finished his work first, in 1669, Leibniz was the first to publish his, in 1684. Over the years that followed, mathematicians and scientists would take sides along national lines: British scholars tended to support Newton's claims, and those of Germany and central Europe backed Leibniz. Even today, European mathematicians emphasize the form of calculus developed by Leibniz.

German philosopher and mathematician Gottfried Wilhelm von Leibniz. Liebniz and Isaac Newton independently developed two forms of calculus. **(Reproduced courtesy of the Library of Congress.)**

In general, Newton's work emphasized differentials and Leibniz's integrals, differences that resulted from each man's purposes and interests. As a physicist, Newton required calculus to help him explain the rates of change experienced by an accelerating object. Leibniz, on the other hand, was a philosopher, and therefore his motivations are much harder to explain scientifically. To put it in greatly simplified terms, Leibniz believed that the idea of space between objects is actually an illusion, and therefore he set out to show that physical space is actually filled with an infinite set of infinitely small objects. He was not entirely wrong, of course, since scientists now know that all matter is made up of atoms.

Calculus in the 1700s

In the years that followed, mathematicians would debate not only the subject of Newton's and Leibniz's roles in developing calculus, but also the very basis of calculus itself. As Zeno's paradoxes had revealed, the human mind is not entirely comfortable with the idea that time and space can be divided into incredibly small units, and critics of calculus such as the Irish philosopher George Berkeley (1685–1753) claimed that the discipline was based on fundamental errors. Interestingly, critiques by Berkeley and others, which forced mathematicians to develop a firmer foundation for calculus, actually strengthened it as a field of study.

The Man Who Measured the Earth

The Greeks knew that Earth was round, basing their understanding partly on the fact that the Sun's rays hit the planet at different angles depending on the location. If Earth were flat, on the other hand, the rays would always be at the same angle. From his reading, the Greek mathematician **Eratosthenes** (air-uh-TAHS-thuh-neez; 276–c. 194 B.C.E.; see biography in this chapter) discovered that at noon on the summer solstice, or June 21, at Syene (near modern Aswan, Egypt), the Sun shone directly into a deep well, and upright pillars cast no shadow. By contrast, in his hometown of Alexandria, Egypt, on the same day, the noon Sun cast a definite shadow.

This led him to the idea that, if he could determine the difference in angles between the Sun's rays in both locations, as well as the distance between the two towns, he could calculate Earth's circumference. According to legend, he paid a runner to pace off the distance to Syene, which he determined was about 500 miles (805 km). He also calculated the difference in angle of the Sun's rays, which he determined was about 7°. Then he divided 360 (the number of degrees in a circle) by 7, multiplied this by the distance between Alexandria and Syene, and estimated Earth's circumference at about 24,662 miles (39,459 km). This figure is amazingly close to the one used today: 24,901.55 miles (39,842.48 kilometers) at the Equator.

Eratosthenes published his results in his *Geography,* the first known use of the term, which means "writing about the Earth." His work sparked interest in the study of Earth, and helped promote the idea that the relative temperature of a location relates to its distance from the Equator. This idea, commonly accepted today, was revolutionary at the time.

Unfortunately, the astronomer Ptolemy (c. 100–170), one of the most influential figures of the ancient scientific world, rejected Eratosthenes's calculations and performed his own, based on faulty information. The result was a wildly inaccurate estimate of Earth's circumference at16,000 miles (25,600 km). Yet in a sense, this may have been for the best: if Christopher Columbus had known just how far it was to Asia from Europe, he might never have embarked on his celebrated voyage in 1492.

At the same time, calculus began to gain wide application in physics, astronomy, and engineering, a fact illustrated in the work of the Bernoulli family. Influenced by Leibniz, Jakob Bernoulli applied calculus to probability and statistics, and ultimately to physics, while Johann Bernoulli appears to have supplied much of the material in the first calculus textbook by French mathematician Guillaume de L'Hôpital (1661–1704). Johann's sons all made contributions to calculus. Most notable among them was Daniel Bernoulli (1700–1782), who applied it in developing the principles of fluid dynamics, an area of physics that later made possible the invention of the airplane.

Euler, who was Daniel Bernoulli's friend and Johann's student, developed variational calculus, which enables the determination of the shortest distance between two points on a curved surface. Applying the idea of a minimum, a concept in calculus, Euler advanced the principle of least action, formulated by French physicist Pierre de Maupertuis (1698–1759), which states that natural systems avoid unnecessary expenditures of energy.

Later developments in calculus

Euler and French mathematician Jean Le Rond d'Alembert (1717–1783) used calculus in the study of wave motion, which, along with the related phenomenon of oscillation (back-and-forth motion), is among the most important areas of study in physics. Not only does sound travel on waves; so do radio and TV signals, microwaves, visible light, infrared and ultraviolet light, and X rays. Except for sound, all these types of waves are part of the electromagnetic spectrum, emitted by the Sun and other sources of electromagnetic energy. The work of Euler and d'Alembert paved the way for studies by Scottish physicist James Clerk Maxwell (1831–1879), who in 1865 discovered that electricity and magnetism are aspects of the same force.

French mathematician Joseph-Louis Lagrange (1736–1813) also published important works on the principle of least action. In addition, his research addressed matters ranging from fluid mechanics (the study of gases and liquids at rest and in motion) to the orbital motions of Jupiter and Saturn. Another French mathematician, Pierre Simon de Laplace (1749–1827), analyzed the movements of planets, particularly the small differences between Newton's predictions and their actual paths.

Today calculus helps rocket scientists predict the trajectory, or path, of a rocket when it is fired. Nuclear scientists use calculus in designing the shape of a particle accelerator, a machine for speeding up atoms to split them and produce nuclear energy. They also use calculus in studying the behavior of electrons, though in the case of these subatomic particles, it is impossible to know their speed and their position at the same time. Calculus has also been used to test scientific theories regarding the origins of the universe and the formation of tornadoes and hurricanes. Outside the scientific world, businesses use calculus to increase efficiency by maximizing production while minimizing costs.

BIOGRAPHIES

ARYABHATA (476–550)

Indian mathematician and astronomer

The *Aryabhatiya* (499) of Aryabhata was among the most important mathematical texts ever written, and introduced a number of important concepts. Most notably, it was the first major book to discuss the Hindu-Arabic numerals that would eventually revolutionize mathematics. Yet Aryabhata, like a number of early mathematicians, was an astronomer first, and placed greater value on the study of the stars than he did on the study of numbers.

In the 500s, the fall of the Roman Empire had brought about a long age of intellectual stagnation in western Europe. At the same time, the Middle East was still several centuries away from taking the forefront in mathematics and science. Yet learning thrived in India. The city of Ujjain had become a center of astronomical study. Aryabhata, however, lived far from Ujjain in the eastern Indian city of Pataliputra. Once the capital of India, Pataliputra had long since crumbled into ruins, and the priests who dominated what was left of Pataliputra encouraged superstitious beliefs—the idea that Earth was flat, for instance, and that space was inhabited by demons.

The *Aryabhatiya*

These limitations in his environment made Aryabhata's achievements all the more impressive. Bringing together teachings from ancient Greek and Indian astronomers, as well as new ideas of his own, his *Aryabhatiya* introduced a number of concepts. Not only did it explain the Hindu-Arabic numerals in a manner more thorough and significant than that of any preceding text, but it was also one of the first books to discuss the idea of number position or place value.

The *Aryabhatiya* contained various rules for arithmetic and trigonometric calculations, and included one of the first recorded uses of algebra. It also presented the idea of inversion, or starting with a solution and working backward to the original problem. These and other concepts in the book, most of all, the Hindu numerals, would prove highly influential in later centuries, when they moved westward to the Muslim world, and still later to Europe.

In addition, Aryabhata calculated the most accurate number for pi (π, the ratio of circle's circumference to its diameter) up to that point in history, and in his poem *Ganita,* he correctly stated the formula for finding the area of a triangle. As an astronomer, he suggested that the reason the stars and planets seem to move around Earth is that Earth is in fact rotating on its axis as it moves around the Sun. It would be nearly a thousand years before a Western astronomer, **Nicolaus Copernicus** (1473–1543; see biography in Physical Science chapter), recognized the same fact.

René Descartes
(Reproduced courtesy of the Library of Congress.)

RENÉ DESCARTES (1596–1650)

French philosopher and mathematician

Often regarded as the father of modern philosophy, René Descartes (day-KART) contributed to understanding of mathematics and the sciences as well. He associated with a number of noted French mathematicians, among them Marin Mersenne (1588–1648), **Pierre de Fermat** (1601–1665; see biography in this chapter), and **Blaise Pascal** (1623–1662; see biography in this chapter), and his work with Fermat helped break down the barriers between algebra and geometry. As a philosopher, he commented on a number of scientific matters, in particular human physiology and the relationship of the brain to the body.

Born in La Haye (now Descartes), France, Descartes came from a wealthy family. His father, Joachim, owned farms and houses, and had a role in the local parliament. Descartes's mother died when he was only a year old. Later, the father remarried and moved away, and Descartes went to live with his mother's mother and other relatives in Le Haye. While studying at the Jesuit college in the French town of La Flèche, which he entered at age eight in 1604, he began to suffer from health problems, and therefore adopted a lifelong habit of sleeping till 11:00 in the morning.

After spending some time in Paris, Descartes in 1614 entered the University of Poitiers, where he received a law degree two years later. He then studied at a military school in The Netherlands, and went on to serve a stint in the army of Bavaria, a region in what is now Germany. The years from 1620 to 1628 found him traveling throughout Europe, but in 1628 he decided to settle in Holland, where he would remain for the next twenty years.

Writings on physics and mathematics

The period that followed was the most fruitful in Descartes's life. Soon after moving to Holland, he completed a work on physics, *Le monde* (The World), but then he heard that **Galileo Galilei** (1564–1642; see biography in this chapter) had come under attack by the Roman Catholic Church for showing that Earth revolves around the Sun, an idea that went against approved teachings. Therefore he decided not to publish the book, which finally appeared (and then only partial form) after his death.

In 1637, Descartes published his famous *Discourse on Method,* a work of philosophy and science significant for a number of reasons. It was perhaps the first major philosophical text written in an everyday European language, French, rather than in Latin, which had been the language of scholarly communication up to that time. Wide-ranging in the topics it approached, the book marks the first attempt to treat the subject of weather, or meteorology, from a scientific standpoint.

Discourse also discussed geometry, showing how algebra could be used to treat geometric problems in the form of an equation. Descartes is also credited with developing the Cartesian (kar-TEE-zhun) coordinate system, a means of visually representing the values obtained from algebraic equations with points on a graph. Though it is named after him—"Cartesian" is an adjectival form of "Descartes"—it is likely Fermat had more to do with creating the system.

Philosophical and physiological ideas

In *Meditations on First Philosophy* (1641) and *Principia philosophiae* (1644), Descartes presented the essentials of his philosophical ideas. He began by calling into question all the things that people think they know, and decided that only one thing was certain: *Cogito, ergo sum* (I think, therefore I am). From this basis, he pioneered a school of philosophy called rationalism, which maintained that certain ideas, including the concept of God, are innate or native to the human mind.

Thus Descartes's philosophical interests led him into the exploration of human physiology and the activities of the human brain. Among his publications in the life sciences was *L'Homme, et un traité de la formation du foetus* (Man, and a Treatise on the Formation of the Fetus, 1664). Although Descartes argued that animals are purely mechanical and had no soul, he described human beings as being a combination of mind and body. These two parts of the human being, he believed, interacted in the pineal gland of the brain. (For more about Descartes's contributions in these areas, see essay "The Human Machine" in the Life Science chapter.)

Due to religious reactions against his ideas in Holland, as well as in France, Descartes decided to move farther from the center of Catholic influence. Therefore in 1649, he sought refuge with Queen Christina (ruled 1632–54) of Sweden, a land that had adopted Protestantism. Christina insisted that he give her philosophy lessons at 5:00 every morning, and this wore down his health. Descartes contracted pneumonia, and died in the Swedish capital of Stockholm in February 1650.

ERATOSTHENES (c. 276–c. 194 B.C.E.)

Greek mathematician, astronomer, and geographer

Eratosthenes (air-uh-TAHS-thuh-neez) is most noted for his contributions to mathematics, including an incredibly accurate measurement of Earth's circumference, as well as the development of a method for finding prime numbers that remained in use until modern times. Yet Eratosthenes excelled in a wide range of areas, from astronomy to philosophy to poetry. As head of the renowned Library of Alexandria, Egypt (see sidebar in the essay "Geometry and the Great Unsolved Problems" in this chapter), he had exposure to the collected knowledge of the ancient world.

Born into the Greek community of Cyrene, now part of Libya, Eratosthenes studied under various learned men in Alexandria, a great center of Greek civilization. He then traveled across the Mediterranean to receive further schooling at the center of that civilization, Athens. His poetic writings attracted the attention of Ptolemy III Euergetes (reigned 246–221 B.C.E.), Greek ruler of Egypt, who invited him to Alexandria to serve as tutor to the crown prince. Soon afterward, Ptolemy appointed Eratosthenes director of the city's famed library.

During his fruitful career, Eratosthenes contributed to mathematical knowledge with a technique for finding prime numbers that came to be known as the sieve of Eratosthenes. A sieve is a metal pan with holes through which water can drain, leaving solid material such as sand behind. In Eratosthenes's case, the "solid material" was prime numbers, or numbers that can only be divided by themselves and 1. To use the sieve of Eratosthenes, one begins with the set of all whole numbers above 1: 2, 3, and so on. The next step is to start from the 2, eliminating every other number, since 2 is the only even prime. Then, start from the 3 and eliminate every third number, each of which is a multiple of 3. Thus, on the way up to 20, one would eliminate 4, 6, 8, 9, 10, 12, 14, 15, 16, and 18, leaving the prime numbers 5, 7, 11, 13, 17, and 19.

Measuring Earth

Eratosthenes also contributed to the study of the Delian problem, or doubling the cube (see essay "Geometry and the Great Unsolved Problems" in this chapter), but his greatest contribution lay in his measurement of Earth. This he did by measuring the distance from Alexandria to the city of Syene in the south, and calculating the difference in the angle of the Sun's rays on both cities. He arrived at a figure of 24,662 miles (39,459 km) for Earth's circumference, which is amazingly close to the actual distance around the planet, as measured at the Equator: 24,901.55 miles (39,842.48 km).

The idea that Earth was round had become firmly established in Greek thought prior to Eratosthenes, and his work might have opened up new frontiers of exploration by revealing the planet's vast size. Unfortunately, however, the Greek astronomer **Ptolemy** (c. 100–170 C.E.; see biography in Physical Science chapter) rejected Eratosthenes's figure in favor of a smaller one, thus influencing misconceptions regarding the planet's size. Because of this, when Christopher Columbus (1451–1506) landed in the Americas, he was certain he had reached Asia.

Eratosthenes may also have developed the calendar that remained in use throughout the Greco–Roman world until the time of Julius Caesar (102–44 B.C.E.) Certainly he established the first reliable method of dating events, by reference to the years of the Olympic festivals. In his later years, he went blind, and perhaps in despair over the fact that he could no longer read any of the scrolls from his beloved library, he starved himself to death.

EUCLID (c. 330–c. 260 B.C.E.)

Greek mathematician

Euclid (YOO-klid) wrote the most successful textbook of all time, *Elements,* which remained the principal geometry text for about two thousand years. His writing is notable not for its original ideas—the *Elements* merely sums up the collected geometric knowledge of ancient Greece—but for the clear, concise way in which he explained them.

Given his great influence as a mathematician, it is ironic that very little is known about Euclid's life. For years, historians disputed his dates, and some even suggested that "Euclid" was actually the name for a group of men who composed the *Elements.* Mathematicians today, however, accept the idea that there was a single individual named Euclid, who spent most of his career in Alexandria, Egypt, a great center of Greek learning at the time.

The place of Euclid's birth remains a matter of dispute, but he apparently studied in Athens before moving to Alexandria. There he became involved with the city's famous library as its first teacher of mathematics. During those years, he wrote a number of books on mathematics, many of which have been lost. In any case, none of these could possibly compare, in terms of historical significance, with the *Elements*.

The structure of the *Elements*

Euclid's great geometry text consists of thirteen books, or sections. Book I begins with the definition of points, lines, planes, angles, circles, triangles, quadrilaterals, and parallel lines. A quadrilateral is a four-sided, closed figure such as a square or rectangle, and in Book II he discussed these shapes further. Book III is concerned with circles and Book IV with polygons, closed shapes with three or more straight sides.

Euclid. (Reproduced courtesy of the Library of Congress.)

In Book V, Euclid discussed proportion and area, and in Book VI he applied these ideas to the topic of plane geometry, or the geometry of flat areas. Book VII covers arithmetic, Book VIII irrational numbers (numbers such as pi that cannot be expressed as a fraction), and Book IX rational numbers. The remaining four books are devoted to three-dimensional, or solid, geometry.

The influence of Euclid's work

Among Euclid's original contributions was a new proof of the Pythagorean theorem (see essay "The Greeks' New Approach to Mathematics" in this chapter for an explanation of this theorem), along with a proof of the existence of irrational numbers. He also developed a means of showing that the number of primes (numbers divisible only by themselves and 1) is infinite. Yet his most important contribution lay in the clear, logical method he used for teaching geometry, beginning with five postulates or basic ideas and using these to derive several hundred theorems.

Thanks to his step-by-step approach, which involved proofs of each theorem, Euclid made geometry highly understandable to readers. Yet one aspect of his work troubled mathematicians for years to come: the fifth, or parallel, postulate. The fifth postulate stated, in effect, that lines which are not parallel must eventually cross. Because the fifth postulate did not seem clearly related to the four that preceded it, it came under increasing challenge from mathematicians in later centuries. This controversy would lead to the development of non-Euclidean geometry in the nineteenth century. (For more on this subject, see essay "Geometry and the Great Unsolved Problems." in this chapter)

LEONHARD EULER (1707–1783)

Swiss mathematician

A number of great mathematicians of the past, including **Eratosthenes** (c. 276–c. 194 B.C.E. and **René Descartes** (1596–1650; see biographies in this chapter), distinguished themselves in a variety of fields. Leonhard Euler, on the other hand, is known almost entirely for his achievements in mathematics, but his work touched on virtually every mathematical discipline.

Leonhard Euler. **(Reproduced by permission of Photo Researchers, Inc.)**

Most famous among his achievements was the solving of the Königsberg bridge problem. The town of Königsberg included two islands in the middle of a river connected to the mainland, and to each other, by a total of seven bridges. The question was whether it was possible to cross all seven bridges without backtracking or crossing a bridge twice. Euler's resolution was an important contribution to the field of combinatorics, or the arrangement of items in various sequences. This led to the development of graph theory and topology, two mathematical disciplines with wide applications. Euler also worked in areas ranging from number theory to calculus, leaving behind a body of work with enormous applications to the sciences and technology. Nearly nine hundred books and papers are attributed to him, a particularly impressive feat given the fact that he was blind in one eye for the last thirty-one years of his life, and completely blind for the final seventeen.

An unpromising start to a great career

Born in Basel, Switzerland, on April 17, 1707, Euler was the son of a Calvinist pastor who intended for him to follow in the ministry. However, after the family moved to the town of Reichen, Euler went to study under the Swiss mathematicians Jakob (1654–1705) and Johann (1667–1748) Bernoulli. The Bernoulli brothers convinced Paul Euler that God had called his son to work as a mathematician, and the father reluctantly allowed him to follow that path.

Despite the fact that the Bernoullis recognized his talent, Euler's career did not get off to a promising start. He failed to win a contest for designing the placement of masts on sailing ships, but this probably had more to do with the fact that he came from landlocked Switzerland (and had never seen a ship) than from any lack of ability. In later years, he would accumulate a dozen awards from the French Royal Academy of Sciences, which sponsored the contest.

Rejected by the University of Basel, where he had applied for a professorship, Euler was thrilled when Johann's son Daniel Bernoulli (1700–1782) offered to help him obtain a position teaching medicine at the St. Petersburg Academy in Russia. By 1733, six years after Euler arrived in St. Petersburg, Bernoulli returned to Switzerland, and Euler took his place as director of the mathematics department at St. Petersburg.

Euler's life and work in the 1730s

Also in 1733, Euler married Catharina Gsell, the daughter of a Swiss painter who served in the court of Czar Peter the Great (ruled 1682–1725). Eventually the couple had thirteen children, of whom three sons and two daughters survived. In 1735, Euler lost the sight in his right eye, probably while studying the Sun in another contest put forth by the French Royal Academy.

In the 1730s, Euler distinguished himself by solving a number of practical problems on matters such as weights and measures for the Russian government. Less practical, but most noteworthy, was his solution to the famous Königsberg bridge problem, which involved an attempt to cross seven bridges without backtracking. (See essay "Patterns and Possibilities" in this chapter.) Also during this period, Euler wrote one of his most important works, *Mechanica* (1736–37), in which he became the first to mathematically analyze the laws of physics discovered by **Isaac Newton** (1642–1727; see biography in the Physical Science chapter).

To Germany and back again to Russia

Peter the Great, eager to modernize his country, had actively recruited scientists and mathematicians from western Europe, yet Russia was not the most pleasant place to work. Aside from the bitterly cold weather, the country suffered under a repressive political system, and by 1740 Euler was ready to leave. He therefore accepted an appointment by King Frederick the Great of Prussia (ruled 1740–86) to Germany's Berlin Academy.

He would remain in the service of the German king for nearly a quarter-century, again assisting with practical matters such as pension plans and the water supply system. It was during this time that Euler produced his proof of **Pierre de Fermat**'s (1601–1665; see biography in this chapter) famous Last Theorem, which involves proving that the equation $x^n + y^n = z^n$ has no whole-number solution if n is greater than 2. Though in fact his proof contained an error, Euler's work on the problem helped make possible the development of a successful proof more than two hundred years later.

After a falling-out with Frederick, Euler returned to St. Petersburg in 1766, to serve under Catherine the Great (ruled 1762–96), who presented him with an estate and servants. During this last phase of his life, Euler produced some of his most important work in calculus. In 1776, his wife died and Euler remarried the following year. He continued to work on a number of problems related to astronomy right up to the time of his death. Euler died of a stroke while playing with his grandson on September 18, 1783.

PIERRE DE FERMAT (1601–1665)

French mathematician

Pierre de Fermat. (Corbis-Bettmann. Reproduced by permission of the Corbis Corporation.)

Pierre de Fermat was the classic example of a talented amateur, someone who excels in an area for which he has received no formal training. He outshone many of the leading professional mathematicians of his day, and proved himself the equal of his two most outstanding contemporaries, French mathematicians **René Descartes** (1596–1650) and **Blaise Pascal** (1623–1662; see biographies in this chapter). Fermat, who was never shy about his talents, managed to make plenty of enemies, including Descartes. He also pioneered in probability theory, along with Pascal; laid down the fundamentals for the branch of calculus known as differential calculus; and left behind a problem that confounded mathematicians for more than 325 years.

The son of a wealthy leather merchant, Fermat later added the "de" to his name, which made it sound as though he came from the French nobility when in fact he did not. In 1631, he married his fourth cousin, Louise de Long, with whom he had five children. By then he had studied at a number of institutions before earning his law degree from the University of Orléans. In the years that followed, he progressed through the legal profession, but mathematics was his favorite form of relaxation.

Stepping on other mathematicians' toes

In the 1630s, Fermat became part of the mathematical circle that gathered around Marin Mersenne (1588–1648) and which included a number of distinguished figures, including Descartes and Blaise Pascal's father. However, Fermat's behavior won him few friends among the other mathematicians, who became increasingly irritated by his habit of presenting them with incredibly difficult problems. In time they began to suspect that Fermat did not know how to answer such questions himself, and started requesting proof that he had reached a solution.

Fermat and Descartes independently developed analytic or coordinate geometry, a mathematical discipline that incorporates algebraic equations, which are represented with graphs. These graphs are plotted along what is known as the Cartesian coordinate system (the term Cartesian refers to Descartes), though in fact Fermat seems to have been more responsible for it. His role in creating analytic geometry helped spark a rivalry with Descartes, who had discovered the concepts first, but Fermat was the first to present the ideas of analytic geometry to Mersenne's Paris circle.

Mersenne himself is primarily remembered for his work on prime numbers, and here again Fermat managed to encroach, by developing his own theory of primes. He also laid the groundwork for differential calculus, yet professional concerns (along with an outbreak of plague, or epidemic disease) brought his mathematical studies to a halt during the period from 1643 to 1654. In 1654, Pascal sent him a letter requesting help in solving a problem involving dice and games of chance, and this led to a lively interchange that resulted in the creation of probability theory. (See essay "Patterns and Probabilities" in this chapter.)

Fermat's Last Theorem

In addition, Fermat took an interest in number theory, or the properties and relationships of numbers, and this would lead to his most intriguing—though perhaps not his most significant—legacy. While reading a Latin translation of *Arithmetic* by the Greek mathematician Diophantus (210–290), Fermat jotted down a note in the margin, indicating that the equation $x^n + y^n = z^n$ has no whole-number solution if n is greater than 2. This would become known as Fermat's Last Theorem, and while it seemed to be true, mathematicians over the centuries found themselves unable to prove it.

Among the distinguished figures who tried and failed to furnish a proof was **Leonhard Euler**, (1707–1783; see biography in this chapter) and the man who finally did prove it, English mathematician Andrew Wiles (1953–), devoted much of his career to the quest. Given the complexity of Wiles's proof, which he presented in 1994, some mathematicians—rather like Fermat's old rivals in the Mersenne circle—have questioned whether Fermat himself was able to prove the theorem.

In his later years, Fermat had been weakened by the plague, and he died on January 12, 1665. In answer to the mathematicians over the centuries who would labor over the proof of his Last Theorem, he left only a note in the Diophantus book: "I have discovered a truly remarkable proof which this margin is too small to contain."

LEONARDO FIBONACCI (c. 1170–c. 1240)

Italian mathematician

Leonardo Fibonacci. (Reproduced by permission of the Granger Collection.)

Sometimes known as Leonardo of Pisa, Leonardo Fibonacci was, without a doubt, the most important European figure in the history of mathematics for at least a thousand years. He is credited with introducing the Hindu-Arabic numeral system (0, 1, 2... 9) to Europe, an effort that ultimately led to the abandonment of the cumbersome Roman numeral system. Fibonacci also created what became known as the Fibonacci sequence, a combination of numbers that greatly enhanced understanding of several mathematical disciplines.

He was born in the Italian city of Pisa, a great trading center, and when Fibonacci was a boy, his father received an appointment as director of a warehouse in the North African port city of Bugia. There Fibonacci trained under a Moorish (North African Arab) instructor, who used the system of numerals developed centuries earlier in India and later adopted throughout the Arab world. The Hindu-Arabic numerals intrigued Fibonacci, who, like all Europeans of his day, had been raised with Roman numerals. The Roman numeral system had no expression for zero or any concept of place value, and was so difficult to use that calculations involving large numbers had to be performed on a counting-board or abacus. (See essay "Early Number Systems" in this chapter.)

Liber abaci

After traveling through the Mediterranean, Fibonacci returned to Italy, where in 1202 he produced *Liber abaci* (Book of Calculations.) The book explained the fundamentals of reading and using Hindu-Arabic numerals, and went on to a discussion of fractions, squares, and cube roots before addressing more challenging applications in geometry and algebra. Fibonacci, himself trained in business mathematics, also included chapters on the practical uses of the numeral system.

The publication of *Practicae geometriae* (1220), which examined a number of algebraic, geometric, and trigonometric questions, added to Fibonacci's growing reputation. Soon he attracted the attention of Holy Roman emperor Frederick II (1194–1250), who in 1225 visited Pisa and held a mathematical competition to test Fibonacci's talents. Fibonacci managed to solve the equations put forward by Johannes of Palermo, a mathematician working for the emperor, and the other competitors withdrew without providing a single solution.

The Fibonacci sequence

Later in 1225, Fibonacci wrote *Liber quadratorum,* a work dedicated to the emperor, which discussed the problems used in the competition. In 1228, he wrote a revised edition of *Liber abaci,* which contained the famous Fibonacci sequence, which developed from a problem involving a pair of rabbits who produce offspring at the rate of one pair a month, beginning in the second month.

Supposing that each pair will reproduce at the same rate, and no rabbits will die, the problem addressed the question of how many pairs of rabbits would be produced over a given period. The number of rabbit pairs at the end of each month was the Fibonacci sequence: 1, 1, 2, 3, 5, 8, 13, 21, and so on. Each number is the sum of the two numbers that precede it: $1 + 1 = 2$, $1 + 2 = 3$, and so forth. This is known as a recursive series, or one in which the relationship between successive terms can be expressed by means of a formula. Today computers use a number of recursive series, which also appear in everyday operations such as interest calculations.

Fibonacci's sequence laid the foundations for later studies in areas that include number theory, or the relationships and properties of numbers, as well as combinatorics, or the arrangement of items in a sequence. Fibonacci died in about 1250, during a war between Pisa and the Italian city of Genoa, and for a few centuries after his death, his work was largely ignored. Rediscovered in the 1400s, it helped spur the full-scale adoption of Hindu-Arabic numerals by European society.

AL-KHWARIZMI (c. 780–c. 850)

Arab mathematician and astronomer

Two words in the vocabulary of mathematicians reflect the influence of al-Khwarizmi. One is *algorithm,* derived from his name, which describes any systematic procedure for obtaining a mathematical result. The other is *algebra,* the European version of his term *al-jabr,* or "balancing"—the name he gave to the mathematical discipline he pioneered. In addition, he deserves credit, along with **Leonardo Fibonacci** (c. 1170–c. 1240; see biography in this chapter), for introducing the Hindu-Arabic numeral system to the West.

He probably came from what is now Iraq, whose capital city, Baghdad, was then the capital of the Muslim empire that controlled much of the Middle East and north Africa. The caliph, or ruler, al-Ma'mum (ruled 813–833) had established a center for scholarship called the House of Wisdom, and al-Khwarizmi was among the scholars invited to join this early think-tank.

al-Khwarizmi
(Reproduced by permission of Keith Bauman, TNA Associates, Franklin, Michigan.)

Writings on algebra and numeral system

Al-Khwarizmi's first important mathematical text was *Kitab al-jabr wa al-muqabala* (The Compendious Book on Calculation by Completing and Balancing), probably written in the period from 825 to 830. The book addressed matters of practical mathematics, offering solutions to problems involving unknown quantities by using what al-Khwarizmi called *al-jabr,* "restoration" or "balancing."

In his second major mathematical work, whose title is translated as *Treatise on Calculation with the Hindu Numerals,* al-Khwarizmi provided a guide for the use of the numerals 0 through 9. Up to that time, the Muslim world had generally used an alphabetic numbering system, which, like the Roman numerals used by Europeans of the same era, lacked the valuable concept of place value. Thus calculations were extremely difficult, and would become much easier through the application of the number system developed in India.

The book had little direct impact on Muslim mathematicians, yet in the centuries that followed, the Muslim world largely adopted the Hindu numeral system. By the 1100s, al-Khwarizmi's work had appeared in translations in Europe, where it exerted an enormous influence. Since Europeans had little access to Hindu mathematical texts, they mistakenly referred to the numerals discussed by al-Khwarizmi as "Arabic numerals."

Al-Khwarizmi also wrote books on geography, providing information on the latitude and longitude of various Muslim cities. In addition, he produced, among others, astronomical works that amplified concepts developed earlier by Indian scientists; a commentary on the Jewish calendar; and a history of the Islamic world during the early 800s.

GOTTFRIED WILHELM VON LEIBNIZ (1646–1716)

German mathematician and philosopher

His development of calculus, around the same time that British physicist **Isaac Newton** (1642–1727; see biography in Physical Science chapter) introduced his own version of the discipline, was the most well-known of Gottfried Wilhelm von Leibniz's contributions. Yet he also created a philosophical system that placed him on a level with the two most prominent figures of the rationalist school, **René Descartes** (1596–1650; see biography in this chapter) and Benedict Spinoza (1632–1677). Additionally, he commented on areas ranging from physics to religion to what would now be called computer science.

Gottfried Wilhelm von Leibniz. (Reproduced courtesy of the Library of Congress.)

Born in Leipzig, in the German state of Saxony, on July 1, 1646, Leibniz (LYB-nitz) was the son of Friedrich and Catherina Schmuck Leibnütz. He later altered his last name and added a term meaning "of" (in his case, the German *von*), which made him sound like an aristocrat. By the time he was twelve, Leibniz, whose father had died when he was six, had proven something of a boy wonder: he could read Latin, and he had begun work on a vast encyclopedia.

Meetings with remarkable men

At age fifteen, Leibniz entered the University of Leipzig, where he earned his bachelor's degree two years later. By 1664, the eighteen-year-old had received a master's degree and performed the work necessary to receive his doctorate in law, but the university refused to award the degree because of his age. He therefore moved to the University of Altdorf in Nuremberg, where he received his doctorate at age twenty.

After holding several jobs, Leibniz went to work for the Elector of Mainz, a powerful nobleman of the Holy Roman Empire that controlled most of what is now Germany. In the years that followed, his work for the Elector gave him considerable opportunities for travel, during which he met most of the leading scientific, mathematical, and philosophical figures of the day:

Descartes; **Blaise Pascal** (1623–1662; see biography in this chapter); British chemist Robert Boyle (1627–1691); British microscopist Robert Hooke (1635–1703); Spinoza; Dutch microscopists Jan Swammerdam (1637–1680) and **Anton van Leeuwenhoek** (1632–1723; see biography in Life Science chapter); and many others. At the same time, Leibniz produced vast quantities of writings, and composed more than fifteen thousand letters.

Calculus and other contributions

Leibniz introduced his differential calculus in a 1684 paper and unveiled what was known as integral calculus two years later. (See essay "Angles, Curves, and Surfaces" in this chapter for more about calculus.) In 1689, Newton published his own work, and eventually it became apparent that the two men had developed more or less the same method from quite different approaches. There would follow a heated debate as to who should be credited for developing calculus, and whose method was better. Even the two great men themselves became drawn into the squabbling. Supporting Newton was the British scientific and mathematical community, while their European counterparts backed Leibniz.

In addition to calculus, Leibniz made a number of other contributions to mathematics. Among these was his idea for a calculating machine to perform arithmetic functions, a prototype for the computer. In his philosophical writings, he suggested the existence of monads, an entity in which the total structure is contained in every part. The concept seemed preposterous until the late twentieth century, when it became apparent that the structure of human brain cells, as well as that of holographic images, resembles Leibniz's monads.

Leibniz enjoyed some honors during his lifetime, including election to Britain's prestigious Royal Society in 1673, as well as the Royal Academy of Sciences in Paris. He was even elected president of the Berlin Academy, the German equivalent of these distinguished institutions, when it was founded in 1700. Yet Leibniz was largely forgotten by the time of his death on November 14, 1716. He was buried in an unmarked grave, and neither the Royal Society nor even the Berlin Academy considered his passing important enough to warrant an obituary.

BLAISE PASCAL (1623–1662)

French mathematician and philosopher

A mathematical prodigy who first made a name for himself at age sixteen, Blaise Pascal had a meteoric career that concluded before he was forty. His work was further cut short by his interest in a religious sect, which took much of his attention during the latter part of his life. Yet during his brief years of fruitful work, he helped develop the foundations of projective geometry with fellow French mathematician Girard Desargues (1591–1661); established probability theory with **Pierre de Fermat** (1601–1665; see biography in this chapter); and created a number of inventions, including the syringe, the hydraulic press, and the world's first mechanical calculator.

Today the French town of Clermont-Ferrand, known simply as Clermont in Pascal's day, is famous as the birthplace of three things: Michelin tires, the Crusades (Pope Urban II preached the sermon initiating the First Crusade there in 1095), and Pascal. Son of mathematician and civil servant Etienne Pascal (1588–1651), Pascal came from a tightly knit family. His mother died when he was three, and this only drew him closer to sisters Gilberte and Jacqueline, as well as to his father.

Blaise Pascal
(Reproduced courtesy of the Library of Congress.)

Develops core ideas of projective geometry

When Pascal was eight, the family moved to Paris, and there he began to excel as a student of mathematics and ancient languages. He and his father also became associated with the discussion group that centered around Marin Mersenne (1588–1648), and included such leading figures as **René Descartes** (1596–1650; see biography in this chapter) and Fermat. The family moved to the French town of Rouen in 1639, but Pascal and his father continued to visit Paris, and in the following year the sixteen-year-old presented a paper on mathematics that impressed Descartes himself.

The title of the paper was *Essai sur les coniques,* and Pascal's purpose in writing it was to clarify ideas Desargues had presented, using highly complex and confusing terminology, in a recent publication. As he continued work on it, however, the youth went far beyond Desargues's original point, and his ideas, combined with those of Desargues, helped form the basis for projective geometry. Developed further by Gaspard Monge (1746–1818), projective geometry made it possible for the French army to calculate the proper locations of artillery guns when building a fort, and today is used in computer-aided design (CAD). (See essay "Angles, Curves, and Surfaces" in this chapter for more on projective geometry.)

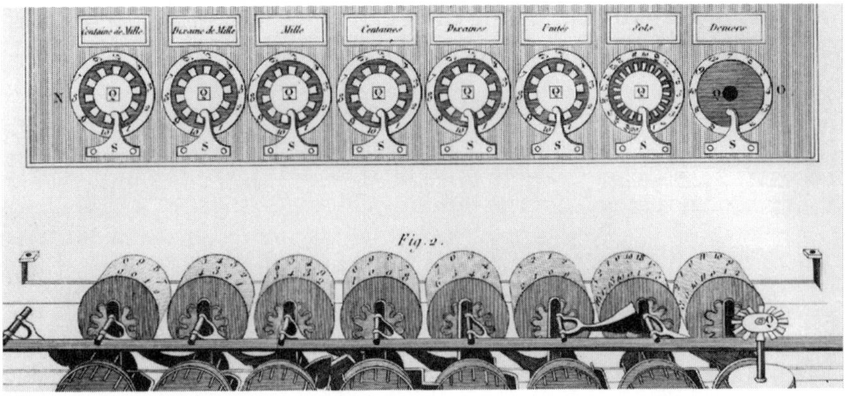

Blaise Pascal's calculating machine. (Reproduced courtesy of the Library of Congress.)

Pascal's inventions

Despite health problems in the 1640s, Pascal developed his calculator, which used cogged wheels to perform its computations, and in 1649 received permission from the French king to become its exclusive manufacturer. As it turned out, costs of production were prohibitively high, but when mechanical calculators did finally appear in later centuries, many were modeled on Pascal's design.

From the age of twenty, Pascal became increasingly involved with the Jansenists, a religious group that believed in predestination, the idea that God has chosen in advance who will go to heaven and who will go to hell. Despite his growing preoccupation with spiritual matters, Pascal during this period conducted a number of experiments to measure atmospheric pressure, and used the information he gathered to invent the syringe and the hydraulic press. The hydraulic press was one of the most important pre-industrial machines and is still used in car jacks and other applications.

The early end of a brilliant career

In 1647, the family returned to Paris, and Pascal's father died three years later. Seven years later, Pascal had a horse-riding accident that nearly took his life, and as a result decided to join his sister Jacqueline at the Jansenist convent of Port-Royal. After that, his scientific work tapered off, while his writings in religious philosophy increased.

However, just before this happened, an exchange of letters with Fermat regarding a game of dice led to the development of probability theory. (See "Patterns and Possibilities" in this chapter for more on probability theory.) Long interested in matters relating to combinatorics, or the arrangement of items in a sequence, Pascal is also credited with creating Pascal's triangle, though in fact the idea first appeared in China centuries earlier. Pascal's triangle, a group of numbers arranged in a triangular shape, makes it possible to determine the number of possible combinations within a given set.

Pascal had always been sickly, and time was running out. In 1662, he devoted himself to designing a public transportation system of carriages for Paris, but before the system became operational, he died on August 19 of a malignant stomach ulcer at his sister Gilberte's home.

PYTHAGORAS (c. 580–c. 500 B.C.E.)

Greek philosopher and mathematician

Pythagoras. (Corbis-Bettmann. Reproduced by permission of the Corbis Corporation.)

Despite the fact that he is associated with the Pythagorean theorem for finding the length of a right triangle's sides—a formula actually developed thousands of years earlier in Babylonia—Pythagoras did not see himself primarily as a mathematician. Nor did the members of the society he founded, whose principles addressed non-scientific subjects such as reincarnation. Yet Pythagoras and his followers, the Pythagoreans, were the first thinkers to view numbers as abstract entities; that is, to think of 2 itself, as opposed to two fingers, two rocks, or some other set of two things. Thus the Pythagoreans virtually established the serious study of mathematics in the West.

The son of a merchant from Tyre, now in Lebanon, Pythagoras grew up in Samos, on the west coast of what is now Turkey. His father's profession gave him reason to travel widely, and apparently the boy accompanied him on trips as far away as Italy. During his youth, Pythagoras fell under the influence of several great teachers, most notably Thales (THAY-leez; c. 625– c. 547 B.C.E.), who was the first Western philosopher, scientist, and mathematician.

A mystical education

Around the year 535 B.C.E., Pythagoras visited Egypt, where he became interested in various mystical practices while studying at the temple of Diospolis. Following the invasion of Egypt in 525 B.C.E. by the Persians, he was taken to the city of Babylon, in what is now Iraq, as a prisoner. This placed him in contact with a number of the ancient world's great civilizations: not only Babylonia and Persia (modern Iran), but also Israel;

most Israelites were captives in Babylon at the same time. The Israelites ultimately adopted several ideas, including the concept of Satan, from the Persian religion of Zoroastrianism, and likewise Pythagoras came under the influence of Zoroastrianism and the much older religion of the Magi.

By 520 B.C.E., Pythagoras had made his way back to Samos, where he founded a school to teach the mystical wisdom he had learned in Egypt and Babylonia. Few students in his hometown were interested in his rather strange ideas, and by 518 B.C.E. he had settled in Croton on the southern tip of Italy. There he established the Pythagorean society, a group that lived communally (they shared everything), practiced vegetarianism, and took vows of secrecy and loyalty.

The world of the *mathematikoi*

The Pythagoreans, who called themselves *mathematikoi,* believed that mathematics was at the heart of reality, and that mathematical symbols possessed a mystical significance that made humans closer to the gods. Aside from all their other unusual qualities, they stood apart from much of the ancient world by allowing women to enjoy full participation in their society as the intellectual equals of men.

The Pythagoreans investigated the relationships between mathematics and music, and between both of these and astronomy. To them, all ideas could be expressed in terms of whole numbers, and they rejected untidy figures, including those that were too large (infinite) or too small (infinitesimal). Particularly abhorrent to the Pythagoreans were irrational numbers, or ones that cannot be expressed as a fraction, yet it was one of the *mathematikoi,* Hippasus (flourished about 500 B.C.E.), who discovered irrational numbers. According to legend, the other Pythagoreans reacted so violently to the idea of irrational numbers that they ordered him to leave the group, and possibly even killed him.

By the time of Hippasus, however, the Pythagorean community was under threat from something a great deal more dangerous than irrational numbers: a rich and powerful enemy. This was a local nobleman named Cylon, who in 508 B.C.E. tried to force his way into the society. Pythagoras rejected him because he did not regard Cylon as having a pure interest in mathematics for its own sake, so Cylon set out to destroy the society. Pythagoras fled to the Italian city of Metapontum, where according to some accounts he committed suicide rather than allow Cylon to take over the society he had founded. In later years, the Pythagoreans became a powerful force in southern Italy, so much so that in the mid-400s B.C.E. they came under severe attack from political foes, and had to return to Greece.

BRIEF BIOGRAPHIES

MARIA GAËTANA AGNESI (1718–1799)

Agnesi was an Italian algebraist and geometer who, as part of her effort to teach mathematics to her younger brothers and sisters, wrote a textbook in 1748. Among the topics it discussed was a curve that came to be known as the "Witch of Agnesi."

AHMES (c. 1680–c. 1620 B.C.E.)

Ahmes was an Egyptian scribe credited with writing down the material in what later became known as the Rhind Papyrus. He was a secretary rather than an author, and his job was to record information from a mathematical work written as early as 2000 B.C.E. The Rhind Papyrus contains eighty-seven problems in basic arithmetic and illustrates simple fractions.

APOLLONIUS OF PERGA (c. 262–c. 190 B.C.E.)

Apollonius was a Greek mathematician, known as "The Great Geometer" for his contributions to that discipline. With his *Conics,* he pioneered the study of conic sections, the shapes made when a cone is cut by a plane. Thus he laid the foundations for rocketry, space science, and ballistics (the study of projectile action, as when a bullet is fired) centuries later.

ARCHIMEDES (c. 287–212 B.C.E.)

One of the greatest minds of the ancient world, the Greek scientist Archimedes (see full biography in Technology and Invention chapter) contributed to understanding of physics, technology, and mathematics. He is best known for his numerous discoveries, such as the principle of buoyancy; and for his inventions or improvements, including pulley systems and the catapult. In attempting to square the circle, he developed the first reliable figure for *pi,* and conducted studies of curved surfaces that foreshadowed the calculus of **Isaac Newton** (1642–1727; see biography in Physical Science chapter) and **Gottfried Wilhelm von Leibniz** (1646–1716; see biography in this chapter)

ARCHYTAS OF TARENTUM (c. 428–c. 350 B.C.E.)

A Greek mathematician, Archytas was the first thinker to systematically combine mathematics with the area of physics known as mechanics. This he did by using mathematical principles to explain the workings of the pulley and the screw. Influenced by **Pythagoras**, (c. 580–c. 500 B.C.E.; see biography in this chapter) Archytas was particularly interested in the application of mathematics to music, and discussed numerical ratios between notes. He also worked on the problem of doubling the cube, and was noted for his achievements as a statesman and military leader. Archytas literally changed history by saving the great philosopher Plato (427–347 B.C.E.) from execution at the hands of the tyrant Dionysius the Younger. He was widely admired for his nobility and kindness, which he displayed with his gentle treatment of slaves and his fondness for babies and small children. His inventions included a flying mechanical pigeon and a rattle for amusing babies.

JAKOB BERNOULLI (1645–1705)

Bernoulli was a Swiss mathematician, and the first member of his distinguished family to attain international notoriety. Eventually there would be a half a dozen Bernoullis prominent in the world of mathematics and science, the most famous among them being Jakob's nephew Daniel. Jakob maintained a long correspondence with **Gottfried Wilhelm von Leibniz,** (1646–1716; see biography in this chapter) and was one of the first scholars to fully understand calculus. (See sidebar on his younger brother Johann Bernoulli on page 258.)

BHASKARA (1114–1185)

Bhaskara was an Indian mathematician and astronomer who became the first to comment on the challenging problem of dividing by zero. He was also the first to analyze and identify the products that result when negative and positive numbers are multiplied or divided. In about 1150, Bhaskara also made one of the first descriptions of a machine for perpetual motion—a machine that would produce more output than the input required to run it—an idea that turned out to be an impossible dream.

BOETHIUS (c. 480–524)

Boethius (boh-EETH-ee-us) was a Roman philosopher and scholar whose writings on mathematics served as the principal authority on the subject for Europeans during the early medieval period. In addition to his *Arithmetic,* he translated several works of Greek mathematics. He was not a mathematician, but at a time when progress in mathematical learning had come to a halt in western Europe, his work assumed a prominence it might not otherwise have had. Boethius's most famous book, however, was the *The Consolation of Philosophy,* written while he was in prison awaiting his death at the hands of the Ostrogoth chieftain Theodoric (c. 454–526). The gloomy, resigned spirit of *Consolation* set the tone for nearly a thousand years of European history.

BRAHMAGUPTA (598–670)

Brahmagupta was an Indian astronomer and mathematician who, in a work translated as *The Opening of the Universe* (628), defined zero as the result obtained when a number is subtracted from itself, by far the best definition of zero up to that time. He also provided rules for "fortunes" and "debts" (positive and negative numbers), and used a place-value system much like that which exists today. *The Opening of the Universe* also used rudimentary forms of algebraic notation.

CH'IN CHIU-SHAO (c. 1202–c. 1261)

Ch'in Chiu-shao, or Qin Jiushao, was a Chinese mathematician whose *Shu-shu chiu chang* (1247) discussed algebra equations and other subjects. Variously translated as *Mathematical Treatise in Nine Sections* and *The Nine Sections of Mathematics,* the book's title honored that of an ancient Chinese textbook, *Nine Chapters on Mathematical Procedures.* As was typical of Chinese mathematical books, the *Nine Sections* was heavily concerned with practical applications crucial to government administration, including matters relating to calendars and finances.

CHU SHIH-CHIEH (c. 1280–c. 1303)

Chu Shih-chieh, or Zhu Shiejie, was a Chinese mathematician whose written works greatly influenced mathematical studies in east Asia for centuries. His *Introduction to Mathematical Studies* (1299) disappeared from China some time after his death, but spread to Japan and Korea, where it came into wide use as a textbook beginning in the 1400s. The most significant of his works was *Precious Mirror of the Four Elements* (1303), in which he introduced a technique of solving equations that became known as the Ruffini–Horner procedure after European mathematicians Paolo Ruffini (1765–1822) and William George Horner (1786–1837) "discovered" it six centuries later. The book also discussed what came to be known as Pascal's triangle after **Blaise Pascal** (1623–1662; see biography in this chapter) though it had actually been discovered earlier by other Chinese mathematicians.

THE MARQUIS DE CONDORCET (1743–1794)

The Marquis de Condorcet (mar-KEE; KAHN-dohr-say), a French nobleman whose real name was Marie-Jean-Antoine-Nicholas de Caritat, used mathematics to study social problems. He is therefore often regarded as one of the founding fathers of the modern social sciences. In his *Essay on the Application of Analysis to the Probability of Majority Decisions* (1785), he presented what became known as the Condorcet Paradox: if the majori-

Johann Bernoulli and His Family Rivalries

Johann Bernoulli (1667–1748) was among the most prominent members of a distinguished family of Swiss mathematicians and physicists. Younger brother of Jakob Bernoulli (1645–1705), he was the father of Daniel Bernoulli (1700–1782; see biography in the Technology and Invention chapter), whose work on fluid mechanics made him the most influential Bernoulli of all. As for Johann, he is noted as much for his bitter rivalries with family members as he is for his contributions to mathematics, which were many and varied. (See essay "Angles, Curves, and Surfaces" in this essay.)

Like Jakob, Johann was a friend and associate of **Gottfried Wilhelm von Leibniz** (1646–1716; see biography in this chapter) and helped influence acceptance of calculus throughout Europe. He proved much more loyal to Leibniz and others than he did to family members, however. After quarreling with Jakob over the solutions to several complex problems, he took a position at the University of Gröningen in The Netherlands, knowing that Jakob would keep him off the faculty at his own University of Basel in Switzerland. Following Jakob's death in 1705, however, Johann took his place as professor of mathematics at Basel.

By then, Johann had a new rival: his son Daniel. Though he had other sons destined to make names for themselves in the European scientific community, Johann must have rightly sensed that only Daniel would outshine him. Therefore he discouraged his son from studying the sciences, and when Daniel presented his famous work concerning fluid pressure (the Bernoulli's principle, discussed in "Fluids, Pressure, and Heat" in the Technology and Invention chapter), Johann attempted to present it as his own. He even published a book on the subject, with the date of publication altered to make it appear as though his had come out first.

ty of the population prefers option A over option B and option B over option C, it is still possible for a majority to prefer option C over option A. (The reason is that option C may have aspects that make it seem worse than option B, yet other aspects may make it seem better than option A.) A political liberal, Condorcet participated in the French Revolution when it broke out in 1789. Four years later, however, the radical or extremist Jacobin group launched a campaign of executions and imprisonments known as the Reign of Terror, and Condorcet was one of its victims.

JEAN LE ROND D'ALEMBERT (1717–1783)

D'Alembert (DAL-em-bayr) was a French mathematician and physicist most noted for his collaboration with Denis Diderot (DEED-uh-roh; 1713–1784) in creating the *Encyclopédie,* the first major encyclopedia of the modern Western world. A leading figure among the eighteenth-century social critics known as *philosophes,* his contributions include d'Alembert's principle, an extension of Newton's third law of motion ("for every action, there is an equal and opposite reaction.")

GIRARD DESARGUES (1591–1661)

Desargues (day-ZARZH) was a French mathematician recognized, along with **Blaise Pascal** (1623–1662; see biography in this chapter) for foundational work in the area of projective geometry. In *Traité de la section perspective* (Treatise on the Perspective Section, 1636), he challenged existing ideas of perspective, offering a new version of geometry that contrasted with that of **Euclid** (c. 330–260 B.C.E.). Scorned in his lifetime for breaking with tradition, his work paved the way for that of Gaspard Monge (1746–1818.)

DIOPHANTUS OF ALEXANDRIA (210–290)

Diophantus was a Greek mathematician who pioneered in the areas of algebra and number theory, or the properties and relationships of numbers. At a time when European scholarship was in decline, Diophantus produced one of the last great mathematical works of ancient times, the *Arithmetica.* In it, he explored the use of special symbols to represent unknown quantities, and he seems to have been the first mathematician to treat fractions as numbers. His work later influenced **Pierre de Fermat** (1601–1665; see biography in this chapter) in creating his celebrated Last Theorem.

CARL FRIEDRICH GAUSS (1777–1855)

Gauss was a German mathematician and astronomer who laid the groundwork for non-Euclidean geometry, and who contributed to numerous mathematical areas. He advanced number theory, probability theory, and topology while also contributing to understanding of astronomy. The gauss, a magnetic unit of measurement, is named after him.

GEMINUS (c. 130–c. 70 B.C.E.)

Geminus was a Greek philosopher, astronomer, and mathematician noted for his classification of mathematical disciplines, and for his efforts to define both mathematics and science. In his *Theory of Mathematics,* now lost, he attempted to define mathematics as a whole, and to classify it within the context of the sciences. Because he believed arithmetic and geometry were concerned with the greatest possible ideas, he regarded them as the highest forms of mathematics.

AL-HAJJAJ (FLOURISHED 786–833)

Al-Hajjaj was the first Arab scholar to translate the *Elements* of **Euclid** (c. 330–260 B.C.E.) and one of the first to translate the *Almagest* by **Ptolemy** (see biography in Physical Science Chapter), from Greek to Arabic. The European name *Almagest* comes from al-Hajjaj's title, *Kitab al-mijisti.*

HIPPARCHUS (FLOURISHED 146–127 B.C.E.)

Hipparchus of Rhodes was a Greek astronomer sometimes credited as the father of trigonometry. He discovered the precession of the equinoxes, or the shift in direction of Earth's axis of rotation, and produced a calculation of the year's length to within 6.5 minutes of the actual figure. Though his role as father of trigonometry is subject to some dispute, it appears that he laid the foundations for the discipline. He was also the first Greek mathematician to divide the circle into 360 degrees.

HIPPOCRATES OF CHIOS (c. 470–c. 410 B.C.E.)

Hippocrates, not to be confused with the physician of the same name, is regarded as the greatest Greek mathematician of the 400s B.C.E., the era between **Pythagoras** (c. 580–500 B.C.E.) and **Euclid** (c. 330–260 B.C.E.; see biographies in this chapter). Among the topics he addressed were the unsolved geometry problems of squaring the circle and doubling the cube. He wrote a book, the text of which has been lost, called *Elements of Geometry,* which apparently influenced Euclid's more famous work of the same name.

HYPATIA OF ALEXANDRIA (c. 370–415)

Hypatia was a Greek mathematician and philosopher, and one of the first notable female intellectual figures in history. The daughter of Theon, the last known director of Alexandria's renowned museum, she had exposure to a wide range of knowledge, and spent much of her career teaching. She apparently wrote commentaries on several leading mathematicians of pre-

The Tartaglia–Cardano "Grudge Match"

During the Renaissance (a period of artistic and intellectual rebirth, lasting roughly from 1350 to 1600, that marks the end of the Middle Ages), mathematicians often engaged in public challenges and contests. Sometimes these took place against a backdrop of powerful emotions—the sixteenth-century equivalent of a grudge match—and attracted great interest from the public. Such was the case with the controversy between Italian mathematicians Niccolò Fontana, better known as Tartaglia (1500–1557) and Girolamo Cardano (1501–1576).

The immediate cause for the ill-will between the two men was a method of solving cubic equations, or equations in which the highest exponent is 3. Actually, Persian mathematician Omar Khayyam (1048–1131) had solved cubic equations centuries before, but neither of these men knew it. Therefore when Cardano learned that Tartaglia had developed a method for solving cubic equations, Cardano pressured him to share his secret. Finally Tartaglia agreed to do so, provided that Cardano would not pass it on to anyone until Tartaglia had published it.

Tartaglia took his time publishing, to the point that Cardano realized he was going to take the secret to his grave. In the meantime, Cardano and his

ceding centuries, including Apollonius of Perga (c. 262 B.C.E.–c. 190 B.C.E.) and Diophantus (210–290). Because she advocated the old Greco–Roman pagan religion, Hypatia was brutally killed by a mob of Christians.

AL-KASHI (1380–1429)

Al-Kashi was a Persian mathematician and astronomer who made the first notable use of decimal fractions. (In contrast to a common fraction such as 1/2, a decimal fraction is rendered with the use of a decimal point, for example, 0.5.) He also calculated pi (π, the ratio of a circle's circumference to its diameter) to sixteen decimal places. This was the best estimate of π until Ludolph van Ceulen (1540–1610) calculated the number to twenty decimal places some two hundred years later.

assistant, Ludovico Ferrari (1522–1565), happened to be going through the papers of the deceased mathematician Sciopione dal Ferro (1465-1526), when they discovered that dal Ferro had solved the cubic equation two decades earlier.

As the two men learned, when he was near death, dal Ferro had explained the secret to his student, Antonio Fior. Fior had later foolishly challenged Tartaglia to a mathematical contest involving thirty problems that all required solutions to cubic equations. In danger of having his reputation damaged if he was defeated by Fior, and realizing that dal Ferro had developed a solution, Tartaglia figured out the solution, and soundly defeated Fior.

Having learned this, Cardano felt he was no longer under obligation to Tartaglia, and in 1545 published the method for solving cubic equations. Tartaglia was furious, and began conducting a fierce letter-writing campaign against Cardano. Ferrari defended his teacher at a public challenge in Milan in 1548. It so happened that Ferrari was from Milan, and because he possessed the "home-field advantage," he and his supporters forced Tartaglia to back down.

COMTE JOSEPH-LOUIS LAGRANGE (1736–1813)

Lagrange, a French–Italian mathematician and astronomer, is considered one of the most important European mathematicians of the 1700s. He established the metric standard of measurement, which went into effect in France after the revolution of 1789. In addition, Lagrange contributed to algebra, number theory, calculus, and the area of physics known as fluid mechanics.

LI YEH (1192–1279)

Li Yeh was a Chinese mathematician who in 1248 devised a system for showing negative numbers by using a cancellation mark drawn across the numerical symbol. This symbol appeared in his *Sea Mirror of Circle Mea-*

surements, which also presented 170 problems involving right triangles inscribed in circles or vice versa.

LIU HUI (FLOURISHED ABOUT 263 C.E.)

A Chinese scholar, Liu Hui is regarded as the first significant mathematician outside of Greece. He developed an early approximation of pi (π, the ratio of a circle's circumference to its diameter), and is also known for his commentary on an ancient Chinese mathematical work, the *Nine Chapters of Mathematical Art.* Liu Hui also discussed the use of counting rods, a form of calculating device developed by mathematicians in China centuries earlier.

MARIN MERSENNE (1588–1648)

Mersenne was a French mathematician who corresponded with, and brought together, some of the greatest minds of his time: **Galileo Galilei** (1564–1642; see biography in Physical Science chapter), **René Descartes** (1596–1650), **Pierre de Fermat** (1601–1665), **Blaise Pascal** (1623–1662; see biographies in this chapter), and Dutch physicist **Christiaan Huygens** (1629–1695; see biography in the Physical Science chapter). At a time when there were no scientific journals, Mersenne helped spread knowledge by writing letters to various thinkers, and by conducting weekly scientific discussions in Paris that became the basis for the French Académie Royale des Sciences. He also conducted research into finding large prime numbers, which are today called Mersenne primes.

GASPARD MONGE (1746–1818)

Monge was a French mathematician, physicist, and chemist best known for his development of descriptive or projective geometry as a means of representing three-dimensional objects in two dimensions. His technique was so valued for its military applications, particularly the placement of large artillery guns in forts, that the French government pledged him to secrecy. Monge also contributed to the adoption of the metric system of measurement, and his other work as a mathematician, physicist, and chemist took him into a variety of arenas, including the studies of sound, light, and heat.

ISAAC NEWTON (1642–1727)

A British physicist and mathematician, Newton was one of the most influential scientists—indeed, one of the most influential *individuals*—of all time. As a physicist, he identified the gravitational force between bodies, and developed a formula for calculating its magnitude. He also formulated the three laws of motion, which explain the operations of gravitational force in the universe. As a mathematician, Newton created calculus in

1669, but he did not publish his results at that time. This led to a dispute between Newton's followers and those of **Gottfried Wilhelm von Leibniz** (1646–1716; see biography in this chapter) who published his own work on calculus in 1684. (For a full biography of Newton, as well as much more about his work, see Physical Science chapter.)

OMAR KHAYYAM (1048–1131)

Omar was a Persian mathematician and astronomer who is best known to the English-speaking world through his poetry. Omar's *Rubaiyat,* published in an English-speaking translation by Edward Fitzgerald in 1859, contains two particularly famous lines: "A loaf of bread, a jug of wine, and thou..." and "The moving finger writes, and having writ, moves on...." As a mathematician, Omar developed solutions to cubic equations, or equations in which the highest exponent is 3 (see sidebar "The Tartaglia–Cardano Grudge Match" on page 261). In his work as an astronomer, Omar made an amazingly accurate calculation of the year's length: 365.24219858156 days.

NICOLE D'ORESME (1323–1382)

Nicole, sometimes referred to as Nicole Oresme or Nicholas of Oresme, was a French mathematician who developed a type of coordinate geometry nearly three centuries before his fellow French mathematician **René Descartes** (1596–1650; see biography in this chapter). He was the first European thinker to use fractional exponents, in which the denominator indicates not the power of a number, but a root. For instance, $8^{1/3}$ means the cube root of 8, or the number that, when raised to the power of 3, equals 8, in other words, 2. He also discussed a logical relationship between the calculating and graphing of values, thus paving the way for a basic form of coordinate geometry.

WILLIAM OUGHTRED (1574–1660)

Oughtred was an English mathematician who invented the slide rule and introduced the symbol $\times$ for multiplication. The multiplication symbol appeared, along with other new symbols for specialized operations, in his *Clavis mathematicae* (1631). In *The Circles of Proportion and the Horizontal Instrument* (1632), he discussed the idea of a slide rule as an instrument to aid in navigation. Though one of his students later claimed that *he* had invented it, Oughtred is generally credited with the slide rule, which he may have invented as early as 1621. The slide rule would remain an important tool of computation for some 350 years, until the appearance of hand-held calculators.

Sophie Germain

Sophie Germain
(Reproduced by permission of The Granger Collection, Ltd.)

Sophie Germain (1776–1831) was a French mathematician whose work attracted the admiration of several leading men in the world of mathematics, an impressive feat at a time when most women were forbidden to study math or science. A member of a prominent family, she was traumatized by the French Revolution, which broke out when she was thirteen years old. Instead of marrying, as her sisters did, she devoted herself to study.

Under the pseudonym Monsieur Le Blanc ("Mr. White"), Germain submitted several papers for a class taught by French mathematician Joseph-Louis Lagrange (1736–1813) at the Ecole Polytechnique in Paris. Lagrange was so impressed that he sought out the "mystery man" and, when he discovered that "Le Blanc" was a woman, encouraged her to continue her studies.

Lagrange was but one of many distinguished mathematicians who, to one degree or another, took Germain under their wings. She carried on a lengthy correspondence with German mathematician Carl Friedrich Gauss (1777–1855), and in 1806 used her family's political connections to help protect the German mathematician from French soldiers invading his homeland.

Her correspondence with French mathematician Adrien-Marie Legendre (1752-1833) led to a collaboration of sorts. Legendre in 1830 published Germain's attempt to prove the famous Last Theorem of **Pierre de Fermat** (1601–1665; see biography in this chapter). The proof, like all attempts through the early 1990s, turned out to be incorrect, but Germain nonetheless advanced understanding of the problem.

PANINI (c. 400S B.C.E.)

Panini was an Indian scholar of grammar whose system of rules for the Sanskrit language is regarded as a forerunner of modern formal language theory, used today in computer science. In his *Astadhyayi*, Panini gave some four thousand short rules for the language. Panini's rules have often been likened to mathematical functions, and it has been suggested that the Hindu number system and mathematical reasoning are linked to the structure of the Sanskrit language.

PAPPUS (c. 290–c. 350)

Pappus of Alexandria was a Greek mathematician, astronomer, and geographer whose major work was the *Synagoge* (Collection). While serving as a handbook of geometry, the *Synagoge* also incorporated the work of earlier mathematicians, in many cases providing the only existing source for these ideas. The book also contains influential work on astronomical and projective geometry, and both **René Descartes** (1596–1650; see biography in this chapter) and **Isaac Newton** (1642–1727; see biography in Physical Science chapter) were influenced by Pappus's work.

PLATO (427–347 B.C.E.)

Plato was a Greek philosopher who probably had more effect on Western thought than any individual in history other than his student **Aristotle** (384–322 B.C.E.; see biography in Life Science chapter). Though Aristotle had much more impact on the sciences than his teacher, the work of Plato influenced the philosophy and study of mathematics. In his most famous work, the *Republic,* Plato recommended mathematics as a key component in the education of future leaders. A central aspect of Plato's philosophy was the idea that reality is divided into a world of senses, of which people can only have incomplete knowledge, and the world of ideas, of which they can have true and complete knowledge. Probably the partial result of **Pythagoras**'s (c. 580–c. 500 B.C.E.; see biography in this chapter). influence on Greek thinking, these ideas led Plato to hold numbers, as well as the shapes studied in geometry, in high esteem.

PROCLUS (410–485)

Proclus was a Byzantine, or medieval Greek, philosopher whose writing has provided scholars with knowledge concerning a number of long-lost mathematical texts. He lived at a time when the pace of Greek learning had slowed dramatically, and his work represents a summing-up of past Greek achievements. Proclus wrote a variety of works, none more important than his commentary on the *Elements* of **Euclid** (c. 330–c. 260 B.C.E.; see biography in this chapter)

ROBERT RECORDE (1510–1558)

Recorde was a Welsh–English mathematician who introduced the equals symbol (=), and helped popularize the plus and minus signs. Not only was he the first to write on arithmetic, geometry, and astronomy in English rather than Latin, Recorde introduced the study of algebra to England. In *The Whetstone of Witte* (1557), Recorde presented the equals sign, using what he considered the best possible symbol of equality: two parallel lines of equal length. He also wrote an early urological treatise, *The Urinal of Physick* (1547).

TAKAKAZU SEKI KOWA (c. 1642–1708)

Takakazu Seki Kowa was one of the few notable Japanese mathematicians prior to the late modern era. At a time when his country was shut off from most of the world and controlled by military dictators called shoguns, Seki Kowa, himself a samurai under the shogunate, sparked Japanese scholars' interest in mathematics. In the course of his career, he developed his own system of notation to solve algebraic equations, along with an early form of calculus. (He and **Isaac Newton** (1642–1727; see biography in Physical Science chapter), one of two men credited for developing calculus, were born in the same year.) Seki Kowa's one notable publication was *Hatubi sanpo* (1674), written in response to the announcement of some fifteen supposedly unsolvable problems that had been put forth four years before. He solved them all; however, it was not the Japanese custom to show how one had arrived at one's solutions, and it appears that even Seki Kowa's students remained unaware of how he did it.

TSU CH'UNG-CHIH (ZU CHONGZHI; 429–500)

Tsu Ch'ung-chih was a Chinese mathematician and astronomer who developed a remarkably accurate calculation of pi (π, the ratio between the circumference and diameter of a circle). Tsu's figure of 355/113 or 3.1415926 is correct to six decimal places, and remained the most reliable approximation for many centuries.

ULUGH BEG (1394–1449)

Ulugh Beg was a Turkic central Asian ruler, astronomer, and mathematician who, in addition to gathering a number of leading scientific minds around him, made important contributions to trigonometry. A grandson of the bloodthirsty conqueror Tamerlane (1336–1405), Ulugh Beg ruled the

John Napier

Amateur Scottish mathematician John Napier (1550–1617) was not only one of the most brilliant figures in the history of mathematics; he was also one of the most unusual. As a pioneer of logarithms and an inventor of an early calculator, he helped make possible the twentieth-century computer revolution, and yet he never earned a college degree.

A member of the Scottish nobility, Napier inherited Merchiston Castle, along with the title eighth laird (lord) of Merchiston; hence his later nickname, "the Marvelous Merchiston." With his first wife, Elizabeth Stirling, he had two children, and after Elizabeth died, Napier married Agnes Chisholm, with whom he fathered ten more children.

He was equally productive in his scholarly work. While making astronomical observations, which involve detailed computations, Napier began to wonder if it might be possible to simplify the tedious calculations. It was then that he discovered the concept of a logarithm, the power to which a given number, called a base, must be raised to yield a given product. These numbers can be added or subtracted, making relatively easy work of what were once extremely time-consuming multiplication or division problems.

With English mathematician Henry Briggs (1561–1630), Napier put together the first table of logarithms, which another English mathematician, William Oughtred (1574–1660), applied in his invention, the slide rule. The slide rule remained the principal form of calculator until the development of computers in the twentieth century.

Napier himself also invented an early calculator, a set of numbered rods known as "Napier's bones". He also developed a hydraulic screw; a revolving axle for pumping water; an early submarine and tank; and a mirror for using the Sun to set enemy ships on fire. He even claimed to have created a version of what would later become known as the machine gun.

An ardent Protestant, Napier wrote a highly popular tract identifying the pope as the Antichrist. His enemies claimed that he practiced black magic and kept a black rooster as a demonic spiritual guide.

city of Samarqand in what is now Uzbekistan. There he established a school that included some of the most talented mathematicians and astronomers of the Muslim world, including al-Kashi (1380–1429) and others. He was more interested in mathematics than in ruling, however, and his son later seized the throne and had Ulugh Beg executed.

FRANÇOIS VIÈTE (1540–1603)

Viète was a French mathematician who, with *In artem analyticum isagoge* (Introduction to the Analytical Arts, 1591), established the letter notation still used in algebra. This included vowels for unknown quantities or variables, and consonants for known quantities. He introduced a number of mathematical terms, and his *Isagoge* is regarded as the first algebra textbook of the modern era. Viète is perhaps best remembered for his advocacy of algebra, which European mathematicians were reluctant to accept because its approach differed so greatly from that of geometry.

YANG HUI (c. 1238–c. 1298)

Yang Hui was a Chinese mathematician who, some four centuries before **Blaise Pascal** (1623–1662; see biography in this chapter) created an early version of what became known as Pascal's triangle. The latter is a number diagram that provides a means of determining the possible combinations within a given set, thus suggesting the probability that any particular combination will occur. Some scholars consider Yang Hui's career the high point of Chinese algebraic studies, and indeed of mathematics in China, which declined after his time.

RESEARCH AND ACTIVITY IDEAS

1. Without the abstract concept of numbers, that is, numbers themselves, rather than numbers of specific items, mathematics could never have progressed beyond the simplest ideas. Think about the ways that you use numbers every day, not just in math class, but in every aspect of your life. List as many everyday uses for numbers as you can, then group them under headings: for instance, the use of numbers involving money (at the store, for example); numbers involving time (not just hours and minutes, but years); and so on.

2. The mathematical system in use throughout most of the world is decimal, or based on 10. However, it would be possible to have a system of numerals based on any number larger than 1. Various societies and applications have used base-2, -5, -12, -20, and -60 number

systems, and it is conceivable that one could develop a system based even on a number such as 7 or 11. Choose a particular number as a base, then show how the numbers from 1 to 100 would be represented in this system. (The sidebar to in the essay "Early Number Systems" shows examples of numbers in the binary system.) When you are finished, have a teacher check your work, and discuss your various math systems as a class.

3. One of the greatest steps forward in the history of mathematics was Europeans' adoption of Hindu-Arabic numerals in place of the Roman numeral system. Thanks in large part to the great impact Europe has exerted on other nations (either directly or through European-influenced societies such as that of the United States), Hindu-Arabic numerals have spread to most of the world. Yet as familiar as these are today, they have been in use only about one-quarter the amount of time Europeans used Roman numerals. To get an idea of just how difficult mathematics was with the Roman system, take a sample page of problems in your mathematics textbook and attempt to solve them using Roman numerals instead of Hindu-Arabic numerals. Afterward, discuss this as a class. Did you find yourself *thinking* in Hindu-Arabic numerals, even though you could only write your equations in Roman numerals? Where would mathematics be today if Roman numerals were still in use?

4. One of the best sources for biographical information about mathematicians on the Internet is a site maintained by the University of St. Andrews in Scotland. Its address is http://www-groups.dcs.st-and.ac.uk/~history/BiogIndex.html. Visit the site, which allows searches of mathematicians by time period, birthplace, etc. (It also includes a special list of female mathematicians.) Choose a mathematician, and prepare a report on his or her life and work. Many of the concepts mentioned will be ones you have not yet studied in school, but you should at least make an attempt to define the ideas in very general terms. In order to do this, you may have to use other reference sources in your research.

5. Many of the most useful concepts in mathematics have emerged from seemingly trivial, or unimportant, beginnings—puzzles and brain teasers. Among these are the three great unsolved problems of Greek geometry, discussed in "Geometry and the Great Unsolved Problems," and Euler's Königsberg bridge problem, discussed in "Patterns and Possibilities." As a class, discuss these and other puzzles or game-like concepts mentioned in this chapter, for example

Zeno's paradoxes and magic squares, with regard to the contributions they have made to the study of mathematics. The discussion might be further enhanced by examining some of the problems in a book or Web site devoted to math brain teasers; for example, *Cool-Math* (http://www.coolmath.com/) or *Interactive Mathematics Miscellany and Puzzles* (http://www.cut-the-knot.com/content.html).

⑥ Think about and discuss the ways that studying mathematics helps a person in later life. One of the challenges most students have in learning math is that it appears to be something they will never use, and this makes it seem boring. Most people, of course, will seldom have any reason to directly apply algebra or geometry, but what do these and other mathematical disciplines (including arithmetic) teach us about problem-solving? Also, as discussed in the essays "The Greeks' New Approach to Mathematics," "Playing with numbers," and other places in this chapter, math can be viewed as a kind of game. In light of that, think about and discuss ways that learning math could be made more fun.

FOR MORE INFORMATION

Books

Anderson, Margaret J. and Karen F. Stephenson. *Scientists of the Ancient World.* Springfield, NJ: Enslow Publishers, 1999.

Caron, Lucille and Philip M. St. Jacques. *Pre-Algebra and Algebra.* Berkeley Heights, NJ: Enslow Publishers, 2000.

Caron, Lucille and Philip M. St. Jacques. *Geometry.* Berkeley Heights, NJ: Enslow Publishers, 2001.

Cavanagh, Mary C. *Math to Know: A Mathematics Handbook.* Wilmington, MA: Great Source Education Group, 2000.

Catherall, Ed. *Numbers.* Illustrated by David Anstey. Chicago: Childrens Press International, 1983.

Gay, Kathlyn. *Science in Ancient Greece.* New York: F. Watts, 1998.

Glass, Julie. *The Fly on the Ceiling: A Math Myth.* Illustrated by Richard Walz. New York: Random House, 1998.

Hoyt, Edwin Palmer. *He Freed the Minds of Men: René Descartes.* New York: Messner, 1969.

Lasky, Kathryn. *The Librarian Who Measured the Earth.* Illustrated by Kevin Hawkes. Boston: Joy Street Books, 1994.

McPherson, Joyce. *A Piece of the Mountain: The Story of Blaise Pascal.* Illustrated by Jennifer B. Robinson. Lebanon, TN: Greenleaf Press, 1995.

Moscovich, Ivan. *Probability Games.* New York: Workman, 2000.

Patilla, Peter. *Numbers.* Des Plaines, IL: Heinemann Library, 2000.

Pumfrey, Stephen et al. *Science, Culture, and Popular Belief in Renaissance Europe.* New York: Manchester University Press, 1991.

Reimer, Luetta and Wilbert Reimer. *Mathematicians Are People, Too: Stories from the Lives of Great Mathematicians.* Palo Alto, CA: Dale Seymour Publications, 1990.

Shimek, William J. *Patterns: What Are They?* Illustrated by Charles Stenson. Minneapolis: Lerner Publications, 1969.

Stewart, Melissa. *Science in Ancient India.* New York: F. Watts, 1999.

Stonaker, Frances Benson. *Famous Mathematicians.* Philadelphia, PA: Lippincott, 1966.

Valens, Evans G. *The Number of Things: Pythagoras, Geometry, and Humming Strings.* New York: Dutton, 1964.

Woods, Michael and Mary B. Woods. *Ancient Computing: From Counting to Calendars.* Minneapolis, MN: Runestone Press, 2000.

Web sites

Ancient Geometry and Insights into the History of Mathematics. http://members.aol.com/bbyars1/contents.html (accessed on April 2, 2002).

"Biographies of Women Mathematicians." *Agnes Scott College.* http://www.agnesscott.edu/lriddle/women/women.htm (accessed on April 2, 2002).

Images of Mathematicians on Postage Stamps. http://www.geocities.com/mathstamps/ (accessed on April 2, 2002).

Earliest Known Uses of Some of the Words of Mathematics. http://members.aol.com/jeff570/mathword.html (accessed on April 2, 2001).

Fernandes, Luis. *The Abacus: The Art of Calculating with Beads.* http://www.ee.ryerson.ca:8080/~elf/abacus/ (accessed on April 2, 2002).

"History of Egyptian and Mesopotamian Mathematics Page." *Baldwin-Wallace College Department of Mathematics and Computer Science.* http://www.bw.edu/~dcalvis/egypt.html (accessed on April 2, 2002).

"History of Mathematics." *Simon Fraser University.* http://www.math.sfu.ca/histmath/ (accessed on April 2, 2002).

The History of Mathematics. http://www.maths.tcd.ie/pub/HistMath/ (accessed on April 2, 2002).

Hix, Sherry. "A Timeline of Mathematical Subjects." *University of Georgia Department of Mathematics Education.* http://jwilson.coe.uga.edu/emt668/emt668.student.folders/Hix/EMT635/ Subjects.timeline.html (accessed on April 2, 2002).

"Indexes of Biographies." *School of Mathematics and Statistics, University of St. Andrews, Scotland.* http://www-groups.dcs.st-and.ac.uk/~history/BiogIndex.html (accessed on August 2, 2002).

FOR MORE INFORMATION

Interactive Mathematics Miscellany and Puzzles. http://www.cut-the-knot.com/content.html (accessed on April 2, 2002).

Joyce, David E. "History of Mathematics." *Clark University Department of Mathematics.* http://aleph0.clarku.edu/~djoyce/mathhist/mathhist.html (accessed on April 2, 2002).

Jui-ling Chao. *Welcome to a Mathematical Journey through Time.* http://nunic.nu.edu/~frosamon/history/math.html (accessed on April 2, 2002).

Lancon, Donald Jr. *An Introduction to the Works of Euclid with an Emphasis on the Elements.* http://www.obkb.com/dcljr/euclid.html (accessed on April 2, 2002).

MathPages. http://www.mathpages.com/home/index.htm (accessed on April 2, 2002).

Measure 4 Measure: Sites That Do the Work for You. http://www.wolinsky-web.com/measure.htm#science (accessed on April 2, 2002).

MegaConverter. http://www.megaconverter.com/Cv_start2.htm (accessed on April 2, 2002).

"Social and Historical Aspects Of Mathematics." *University of Wolverhampton School of Computing and Information Technology.* http://www.scit.wlv.ac.uk/~cm1993/maths/mm2217/hmmod.htm (accessed on April 2, 2002).

chapter three Physical Science

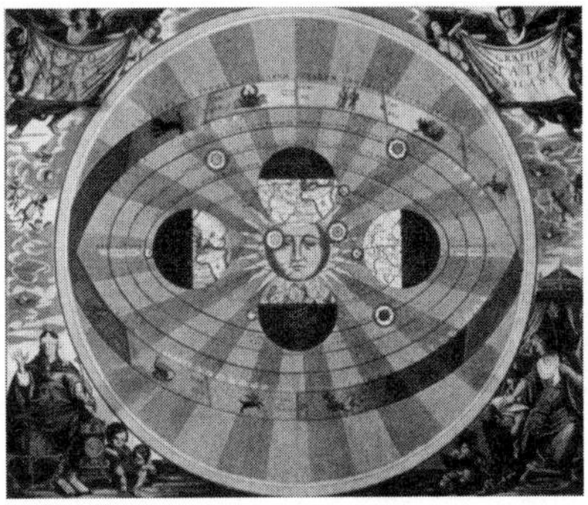

CHRONOLOGY

c. 600 B.C.E.
Thales of Miletus originates both Western philosophy and the physical sciences by stating that water is the basic substance of the universe.

c. 425 B.C.E.
Democritus, a Greek philosopher, states that all matter consists of tiny, indivisible particles called atoms.

c. 350 B.C.E.
Greek philosopher Aristotle proves that Earth is spherical and establishes principles of physics that, though incorrect, will remain influential for the next two thousand years.

c. 260 B.C.E.
Aristarchus of Samos, a Greek astronomer, states that the Sun, not Earth, is the center of the universe.

c. 150 C.E.
The Greco-Roman astronomer Ptolemy (Claudius Ptolemaeus) writes his highly influential *Almagest,* whose geocentric (Earth-centered) model of the universe will be widely accepted for the next fifteen hundred years.

c. 1000
Arab physicist Alhazen (Abu 'Ali al-Hasan Ibn al-Haytham) argues against the prevailing belief that the eye sends out a light that reflects off of objects.

1543
In his *De revolutionibus orbium coelestium* (The revolutions of the heavenly spheres), completed in 1530 but not published until the time of his death, Nicolaus Copernicus (Mikolaj Kopernik) proposes a heliocentric, or Sun-centered universe, thus initiating the Scientific Revolution.

1572
Danish astronomer Tycho Brahe observes a supernova, or exploding star, an event that puts to rest the long-held Aristotelian notion that the heavens are perfect and unchanging.

1587
Galileo Galilei begins experiments that lead to his law of falling bodies, showing that, contrary to Aristotle, the rate that a body falls is independent of its weight, and that all objects will fall at the same rate in a vacuum.

1609
Johannes Kepler introduces his laws of planetary motion.

1687
Isaac Newton publishes *Philosophiae naturalis principia mathematica,* generally considered the greatest scientific work ever written, in which he outlines his three laws of motion and offers an equation that becomes the law of universal gravitation.

The physical sciences include astronomy, the study of the planets and other bodies in space; physics, or the interaction between matter and energy; chemistry, involving substances and the transformations they undergo; and the earth sciences. The earth sciences include geology, the study of Earth's physical history; oceanography, the study of the seas; and meteorology, the study of weather.

The first of the physical sciences to take shape was astronomy, which developed in Babylonia after 2000 B.C.E. Ironically, astronomy grew out of a pursuit considered unscientific today: astrology, which is based on the idea that the position of the stars directly affects the course of events on Earth. Yet as a result of their interest in the stars and the planets, and the relationship between these heavenly objects and human destiny, the Babylonians undertook the first scientific studies of the skies. One of the results of this endeavor was the creation of a calendar, aspects of which remain in use today.

The study of the stars likewise held an interest for ancient societies in China, India, and Central America, and in each case astrology yielded scientific data, facts gleaned from physical evidence. The impact of ancient studies in astronomy is still felt today and serves as an aid to historians attempting to pinpoint the date of an event in the past. Thus for instance Chinese astronomers' observations of eclipses, which occur when one heavenly body blocks another from view, make it possible for historians to be certain concerning dates in China's history after about 840 B.C.E.

The Greeks debate the nature of Earth and the universe

Though astronomy and the calendar originated in Babylonia and other parts of the East, the physical sciences as a whole took shape in ancient Greece. The Greeks were the first to ask the most basic of scientific questions, questions that became the foundation for formal studies in astronomy, physics, chemistry, and the earth sciences: What is the basic substance that makes up the world? How are its parts arranged? And what is the place of Earth in the universe?

The first thinker to ask, let alone answer, such questions was Thales of Miletus (c. 625–c. 547 B.C.E.), who may rightly be regarded as the father of

Signs of the zodiac, in relation to the seasons. (© Corbis-Bettmann. Reproduced by permission of the Corbis Corporation.)

both the physical sciences and philosophy. Philosophy, the search for a general understanding of reality, is closely tied with the core principles of science, and in early centuries philosophy and the physical sciences were virtually inseparable. Thales said that water is the basic substance of the universe. In other words, the whole world is in a fluid state.

Single-substance theories of matter

Later, Heracleitus (c. 540–c. 480 B.C.E.) maintained that the substance of the world is akin to fire. In making this statement, Heracleitus was not necessarily identifying fire as the basic substance of the physical world. Like Thales before him, he was attempting to describe the behavior of physical substances: to Heracleitus, the physical world tended toward continual conflict and change.

Other philosophers suggested that air, and not water or fire, represented the basic structure of all existence. And all of them, including Greek philosopher Parmenides (born c. 515 B.C.E.), assumed that the entire physical universe consists of a single substance. In Parmenides's view, not only is the world all one thing, but there is no possibility of change. His student Zeno of Elea (c. 495–c. 430 B.C.E.), in trying to prove these principles, developed his famous paradoxes, which would greatly influence scientists' understanding of logic, or the system of reasoning necessary for reaching accurate conclusions. (See essay "The Greeks' New Approach to Mathematics" in Mathematics chapter.)

Atomism and the four elements

A few years after Zeno presented his theories, Democritus (c. 460–c. 370 B.C.E.) promoted a radical theory concerning the physical world: all of reality, he maintained, is made up of tiny particles called atoms. Aspects of Democritus's ideas were flawed, but the basic idea was a sound one, and today chemists and physicists know that the world is indeed made up of atoms. Despite this, atomic theory was largely ignored until the 1600s and only became influential after English chemist John Dalton (1766–1844) formulated the first modern atomic theory in about 1800.

Democritus's theory was ignored as another, much less scientific principle, became the dominant idea and remained so for about two thousand years. This was the concept of the "four elements"—earth, air, fire, and water—which, in different combinations, supposedly comprised the physical makeup of the world.

The four elements system, introduced by Greek philosopher Empedocles (c. 490–430 B.C.E.), had absolutely no basis in science. In fact there are ninety-two elements (substances that cannot be chemically broken down into other substances) that occur in nature, and none of the four supposed elements is even on that list. (See essay "Early Greek Theories of Matter: What *Is* Everything?" in this chapter.)

Aristotle's universe

Scientists do not possess a crystal ball that gives them special insight; rather, they observe the physical world, and based on their observations form a theory or model to explain what they see. In effect, they try to combine all the available facts into a sort of story, and if that story is convincing enough, other scientists accept it. In this regard, atomic theory had a number of marks against it when compared with the four-elements theory.

Atoms are so small that 250 million of them side-by-side would measure only one inch in length, and even with the most highly powered modern microscopes, no one can see them. Only their effects can be observed, and then only with precision equipment unknown to the Greeks or even to scientists a few hundred years ago. Thus it is hard to imagine ancient people accepting something they could not see; by contrast, everyone could see and experience the four elements were things that. It was a case of truth (atomism) being stranger than fiction (the four elements).

The idea of the four elements would affect not only what modern people call chemistry, but also physics and astronomy, particularly the area of astronomy known as cosmology, which is concerned with the structure of the universe. This widespread impact came largely as the result of efforts on the part of one individual, a man who greatly influenced the course of Western history: the Greek philosopher **Aristotle** (384–322 B.C.E.; see biography in Life Science chapter).

A flawed science

A student of the great philosopher Plato (c. 428–c. 348 B.C.E.), Aristotle had reacted to his teacher's mysticism by taking a scientific approach to nature and reality, observing facts and drawing conclusions from them. He therefore had an enormously positive influence on the sciences, particularly biology. Aristotle also had a profound impact on the physical sciences, but in this case his influence was not as positive.

Rejecting atomism, Aristotle embraced the theory of the four elements, and from this he developed a highly believable—if almost entirely inaccurate—explanation of the physical world. For instance, Aristotle maintained that heavy objects fall when dropped because the elements in them are seeking their natural position, and the heavier the object, the faster it falls. In fact, as people know today, objects fall because Earth exerts a gravitational pull on them, and the only reason a stone seems to fall faster than a feather is because of air resistance. In a vacuum, an area devoid of air or other matter, they would fall at the same rate.

Cosmology and Ptolemy

It is not at all obvious that a stone and a feather fall at the same speed; therefore, Aristotle's physics seemed like a convincing explanation. His idea that heavy objects always move toward the center of the Earth also seemed to explain the arrangement of the universe. Earth was obviously heavy and therefore must be at the center, whereas the stars and the planets (a term that included the Sun and the Moon) must be very light because they floated in the sky.

The theory behind atomism, which dealt with the arrangement of objects in the universe, came much closer to the truth. But atomism was rejected because it seemed too unbelievable. Likewise, the astronomer Aristarchus of Samos (flourished c. 270 B.C.E.) had suggested that the Sun, and not Earth, was the center of everything. At a time before telescopes,

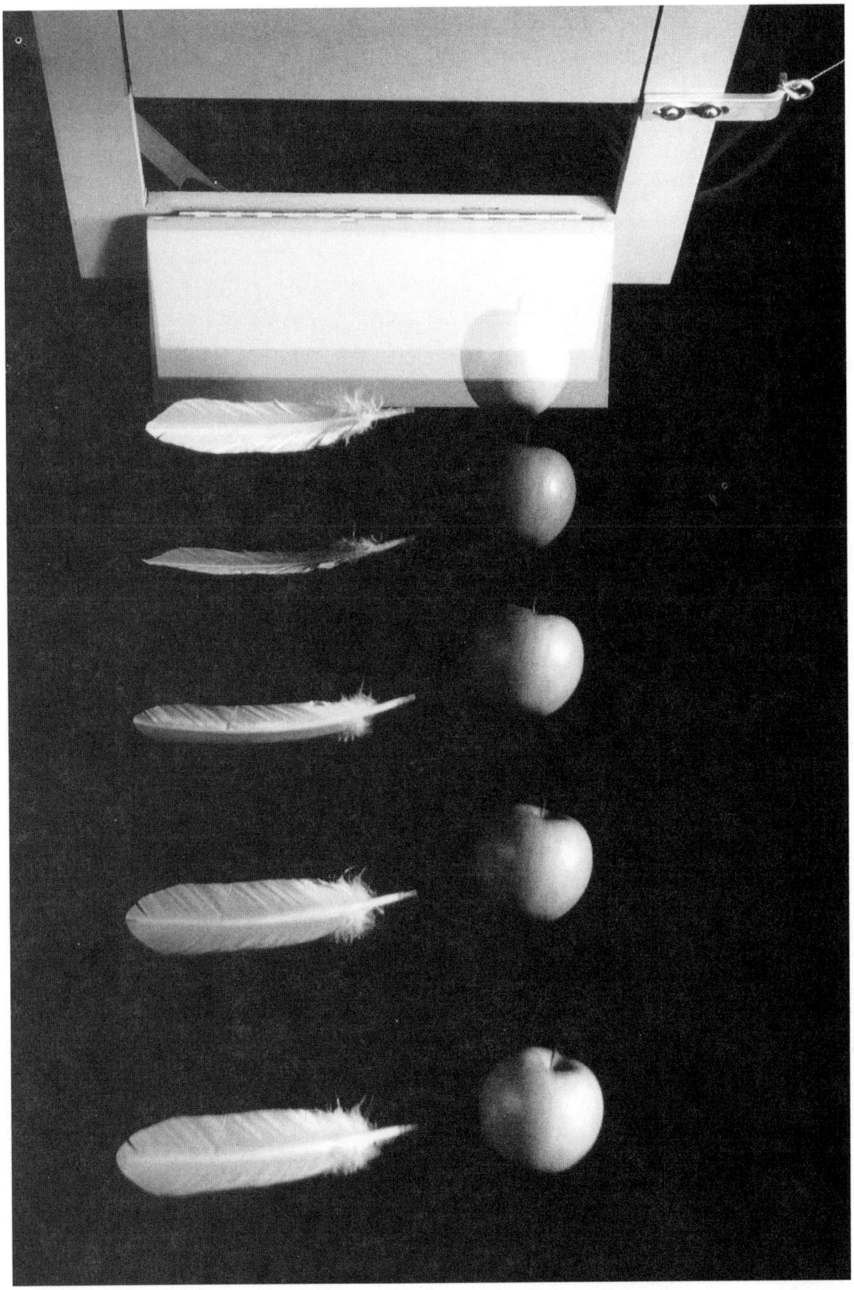

A feather and an apple falling at the same rate in a vacuum chamber. (James A. Sugar/Corbis. Reproduced by permission of the Corbis Corporation.)

when astronomers had no idea of any planets beyond Saturn, the term "universe" referred to what people now call the solar system. Yet the Greco-Roman astronomer **Ptolemy** (c. 100–c. 170; see biography in this chapter), influenced by Aristotle, built an elaborate and convincing case for a geocentric, or Earth-centered, universe. He presented this in his book the *Almagest,* which would remain the most influential astronomy text for nearly fifteen hundred years.

The state of science in the Middle Ages

For about six hundred years after Ptolemy, little of note occurred in the history of the physical sciences in the West. The sciences continued to flourish in the East, particularly in India, home to such great scientists as the astronomer **Aryabhata** (476–c. 550; see biography in Mathematics chapter), and China. China became the source of numerous technological innovations, from paper to clocks. (See essay "China's Gifts" in Technology and Invention chapter.)

Ptolemy believed Earth was at the center of the universe.

Yet in the Mediterranean world once dominated by Greece and Rome, scientific inquiry was brought to an end by political instability, primarily through the decline of the Roman Empire from about 200 to 500 C.E., along with attacks and invasions by nomadic tribes such as the Goths, a Germanic people who overran the Roman Empire in the early centuries following its decline, and the Huns, a nomadic people from central Asia who seized control of large portions of central and eastern Europe under its leader Attila around 450 C.E. And when progress in the sciences finally did resume, it was not in Europe at all, but in the Muslim world of the Middle East.

Science in the Muslim world

Beginning in about 800, Muslim scholars set about translating the classics of Greek science, which had been largely forgotten by western Europe. But these Arab and Persian (Iranian) thinkers did not simply absorb the knowledge of the Greeks; they began to develop new ideas of their own, and during the next centuries the Islamic world produced some of the most remarkable minds of the medieval period (or Middle Ages; c. 500–c. 1500 C.E.). Among these were the alchemists Geber (Jabir ibn Aflah; 1100–1160) and **Rhazes** (c. 865–c. 923); the physicist **Alhazen** (965–1039); and the physician-philosophers Avicenna (980–1037) and **Averroës** (1126–1198). (See biographies of Rhazes and Averroës in Life Science chapter, and biography of Alhazen in Physical Science chapter.)

Two of the areas in which Muslim physical scientists excelled were optics, concerned with the production and transmission of light, and astronomy. Both fields illustrate the manner in which Middle Eastern thinkers, having studied the works of the ancient Greeks, went beyond Greek ideas. In optics, Alhazen criticized the Greek belief that the eye sends out invisible rays and that this makes objects visible. At the same time, Arab astronomers, while generally accepting Ptolemy's cosmology, began to question its workability.

Europe recovers

During the period after about 1100, western Europe began to recover from the long period of intellectual and cultural stagnation that had descended on it with the decline of the Roman Empire more than seven centuries earlier. To a large extent, this recovery came about as a result of exposure to the Muslim world during the Crusades (1095–1291); a series of religious wars in which Europeans attempted to gain control of the Holy Land over the Muslims who ruled the Middle East), and other religious conflicts. These encounters introduced Europeans to Arab and Persian works of science as well as Arabic translations of long-lost texts from Greece and Rome. Just as the Muslims had benefited from the Greek influence, but gone on to develop scientific theories of their own, now Europeans such as German philosopher and scientist Albertus Magnus (c. 1200–1280) improved upon the ideas they had gathered from the Arabs.

Among the concepts that made their way westward in the wake of the Crusades was alchemy. Practiced from ancient times, alchemy is based on the belief that things can be perfected; that it is possible, for instance, to turn plain lead into gold. Like astrology, it is based in error; but just as ancient astrology influenced the legitimate field of astronomy, alchemy helped to spawn the genuine science of chemistry. It influenced the work of scientists from **Rober Bacon** (c. 1220–1292; see biography in Technology and Invention chapter) to **Robert Boyle** (1627–1691; see biography in this chapter), one of the leading figures of the Scientific Revolution, who introduced the modern era of chemistry.

The Scientific Revolution and Enlightenment

In the period from about 400 to 1300, the Catholic Church had remained the most powerful force in European society. During that time, it had preserved and fostered learning, and thanks to the influence of Albertus Magnus's famous pupil Thomas Aquinas (1225–1274), Aristotelian philosophy became blended with Catholic theology to create a powerful Christian framework for viewing the world. But during the late Middle Ages (c. 1100–1500 C.E.), as Europe's population became larger, more educated,

A woodcut illustrating the alchemical concept of the world.

more wealthy, and more independent, the balance of power shifted. This affected all aspects of life, and where the sciences were concerned, the church, once the friend of scholars, began to view emerging scientific ideas as a threat to the established order.

Aristotle's and Ptolemy's model of the universe had long since won approval from the church because it seemed to agree with the Bible; therefore church leaders perceived attempts to question these ancient scientists as a form of challenge to God's word. Yet as scholars learned more, the old geocentric model began to seem increasingly inaccurate. The astronomer Regiomontanus (Johann Müller; 1436–1476) initiated a serious critique of Ptolemy, but he did not live long enough to exert a great deal of influence. His work, however, had a great impact on the man who—quite literally—changed human understanding of the universe: **Nicolaus Copernicus** (1473–1543; see biography in this chapter).

From Copernicus to Galileo

Copernicus, who showed that the Earth is not the center of the universe, avoided serious repercussions because his work appeared to be primarily of interest to astronomers. Eventually, however, church authorities and scientists began to realize what Copernicus had done: disproved the fifteen-hundred-year-old Ptolemaic model that had come to be identified with the Bible itself. (This last fact is ironic, since Ptolemy himself was not a Christian but probably worshipped the gods of Greece and Rome.)

Half a century after Copernicus's death, when the Italian philosopher Giordano (originally Filippo) Bruno (1548–1600) endorsed the new Copernican model of the universe, he was burned at the stake. Wishing to avoid such a fate, **Galileo Galilei** (1564–1642; see biography in this chapter) publicly renounced his support of Copernican theories. He had shown that the Earth itself moves, which is true, but under threat of being silenced he announced that the Earth is standing still, as Aristotle and Ptolemy had claimed. It is said, however, that in private he protested: "*E pur si muove!*" (But it does move!).

From Galileo to Newton

Placed under house arrest by the authorities, Galileo turned his attention to an effort that would strike the fatal blow against the old model of the cosmos: a proof of the Copernican system in terms of physics. In the years that followed, he devoted himself to developing the concept of gravity, an idea that would reach its fullest expression in the work of **Isaac Newton** (1642–1727; see biography in this chapter). Even greater than the impact of his findings, however, was the importance of Galileo's approach.

Copernicus is credited with initiating the Scientific Revolution (about 1550–1700), a period of accelerated discovery that completely reshaped the world. Yet Galileo introduced something that is every bit as relevant today as it was in his time: the scientific method, a process that involves the collection of data through observation and experimentation, and the development and testing of hypotheses. Instead of accepting ideas because they merely sounded good, scientists after Galileo began subjecting principles to hard scrutiny, separating fact and falsehood.

Isaac Newton. Newton's laws of gravitation and motion revolutionized the study of physics. (© Mikki Rain. Reproduced by permission of Photo Researchers, Inc.)

This scientific approach gained influence, and became more clearly defined, through the work of great men from Galileo's time onward: astronomers Tycho Brahe (1546–1601) and **Johannes Kepler** (1571–1630; see biography in this chapter); chemist Robert Boyle; physicists **Christiaan Huygens** (1629–1695; see biography in this chapter), Robert Hooke (1635–1703), and, greatest of all, Isaac Newton. Building on the work of Copernicus, Galileo, Kepler, and others, Isaac Newton went much further than any scientist before him, introducing his law of gravitation and his three laws of motion.

Thus Newton completely destroyed the Aristotelian/Ptolemaic model, introducing a framework that would be accepted by scientists until the introduction of quantum mechanics and relativity theory in the early twentieth century. Even today, quantum principles primarily address the behavior of subatomic particles such as electrons, and have little to do with everyday life. With very rare exceptions, people still live in a Newtonian universe, one in which objects fall because of gravity, and every action produces an equal and opposite reaction. (That every action produces an equal and opposite reaction statement is Newton's third law of motion.)

Other progress in the sciences

Meanwhile Boyle separated alchemy from chemistry, setting the stage for that discipline's coming of age with **Antoine-Laurent Lavoisier** (1743–1794; see biography in this chapter) and Joseph Priestley (1733–1804). Likewise the earth sciences, first studied seriously by the Chinese and later examined by figures such as Albertus Magnus and Italian painter, architect, and scientist **Leonardo da Vinci** (1452–1519; see biography in Technology and Invention chapter), came to much greater maturity thanks to Hooke, Nicolaus Steno (1638–1686), Johann Gottlob Lehmann (1719–1767), and Abraham Gottlob Werner (1750–1817).

During the 1600s and 1700s, the physical sciences, along with a number of other scientific disciplines, saw an explosion of knowledge. Edmond Halley (1656–1742) discovered his famous comet; Daniel Gabriel Fahrenheit (1686–1736) and Anders Celsius (1701–1744) developed their respective temperature scales; **Daniel Bernoulli** (1700–1782; see biography in Technology and Invention chapter) established the principles of fluid mechanics; **Benjamin Franklin** (1706–1790; see biography in Technology and Invention chapter) and others studied electricity; and Pierre-Simon Laplace (1749–1827) suggested that the universe had developed from a cloud of gas.

Toward the end of the eighteenth century, in 1781, William Herschel (1738–1822) used the telescope, an invention popularized by Galileo, to make the first discovery of a planet, Uranus, since prehistoric times. Astronomy, first among the physical sciences, would continue to yield vast new treasures of knowledge in the years that followed, as would physics, chemistry, and the earth sciences.

ESSAYS

GAZING AT THE STARS: HOW SCIENCE BEGAN

Certain basic aspects of life unite humans of all cultures and time periods, and one of these is a fascination with objects in the sky. The Sun, the Moon, the planets, and the stars inspired in prehistoric peoples a sense of awe that ultimately led to the association of heavenly bodies with gods and goddesses. This in turn provided the basis for astrology, the study of the positions and movements of heavenly bodies in the belief that these have an effect on people's individual lives.

Today astrology has long been discredited as a pseudo- or false science, yet early astrological studies provided the basis for astronomy, a genuine science rooted in the study of those heavenly bodies' positions and movements. From the beginning, it was clear that stargazing—seemingly an activity remote from everyday life—had significant everyday uses, for instance by helping to predict the changes of season and hence the best times for planting and harvesting.

In an age when people spent a great deal of the daylight hours outside, working in fields, and when the stars were by far the brightest lights at night, the sky held much greater importance than it does today. Furthermore, amid the uncertainty of life in prehistoric and ancient times, the heavens provided a sense of permanence and stability.

The ancient skies

From an early time, humans noticed the positions of the stars relative to one another and picked out patterns, grouping them together in constellations and assigning names to them. They also noticed the regularity of some celestial events, particularly ones involving the Sun and the Moon, and began to see how this order related to occurrences in the natural world around them.

Gazing into the night sky from Earth, using the naked eye (the only instrument available to people of ancient times), it appears that the stars hold constant positions in relation to one another, and all move together in a regular manner. During each night they appear to travel together eastward across the sky, and their sunrise positions each morning are always slightly to the east of their positions the morning before. By the time a year ends, the positions of these fixed stars at sunrise seem to make a complete circle.

The behavior of other objects in the sky, however, is quite different. Their positions shift daily relative to each other and to the regular positions of the stars, and therefore the ancient Greeks called them "wanderers," or planets. The ancients recognized seven planets: the Sun, the Moon, and the five planets visible to the naked eye, namely Mercury, Venus, Mars, Jupiter, and Saturn.

The "seven planets"

Each day the Sun shifts eastward in relation to the fixed stars, so that it seems to complete an entire cycle in the course of a year. Its height in the sky also varies, and people in ancient times recognized that this motion is clearly related to the changing of the seasons, to warmth and cold, and to the proper times for planting and harvesting.

The Moon moves steadily along, close to the same path in the sky as the Sun (called the ecliptic or zodiac), and seems to overtake the Sun about thirteen times a year. During the course of a 29.5-day period, it waxes and wanes (grows more full and less full, respectively) through a series of phases. From an early stage, ancient observers likewise recognized that the Moon's phases affect events on Earth, including ocean tides.

Words to Know

astrology: The study of the positions and the movements of the stars, planets, and other heavenly bodies in the belief that these have an effect on people's individual lives.

astronomy: The scientific study of the stars and other heavenly bodies, in particular, their positions and movements.

celestial: Of the skies or heavens.

constellation: A group of stars. These groupings are not "real"—in many cases the stars involved are at incredible distances from one another—but they seem, from Earth's perspective, to form groups.

cosmology: A branch of astronomy concerned with the origin, structure, and evolution of the universe.

cosmos: The universe.

ecliptic: The great circle of the heavens, which is the apparent path of the Sun as it seems to move across the sky, or the path of Earth as seen from the Sun.

horoscope: A chart that uses the positions of planets and constellations for the purpose of creating an astrological forecast.

retrograde motion: The apparent backward movement, or reversal of direction, by outer planets in the solar system. In fact retrograde motion is simply an optical illusion, created by the fact that Earth is orbiting the Sun much faster than the outer planets are.

star catalogue: A listing of the known stars with their names, positions, and movements.

zodiac: An imaginary band in the heavens, divided into twelve constellations or astrological signs.

The planets behave somewhat differently from the Sun and the Moon. Even though they generally move in an eastward direction across the sky on paths similar to the ecliptic, they sometimes seem to reverse themselves and move westward in what is called retrograde motion before once again continuing eastward. Though their movement is quite different from that of the Sun and the Moon, the behavior of the "seven planets" seemed enough alike that ancient observers grouped them together.

Given the obvious effect that the Sun and the Moon exerted on daily life, it seemed likely that the five planets likewise influenced events on Earth. Therefore the ancients attributed godlike qualities to all seven planets. This was not a view limited to the people of one geographical area; rather, peoples in every region of the globe regarded the planets and other celestial objects as having the power of gods.

Egypt

The Egyptians made observations of the stars, drew constellation maps, and seem to have regarded the planet Venus as a god. Egyptian priests were perhaps the first to establish a link between religious beliefs and the movements of celestial objects, making them the founders of astrology.

However, the astrology practiced in Egypt was of a rather crude form in comparison to later astrological developments. There is little evidence that the Egyptians constructed any sort of horoscope, a chart that uses the positions of planets and constellations for the purpose of creating an astrological forecast.

In view of the fact that the Egyptians were not particularly advanced astrologers, it is hardly surprising that they were even less proficient with the basics of astronomy that grew out of astrology. It does not appear, for instance, that they made any regular, systematic effort to develop any method for predicting the motion of the planets.

Mesopotamia

To the east of Egypt, in what is now Iraq, were the civilizations of Mesopotamia. The first of these was Sumer, which flourished from about 3500 B.C.E. to 2000 B.C.E., approximately the same era when Egyptian power was at its height. There was also Babylonia, which came into existence in about 3000 B.C.E., reached an early high point under the king Hammurabi (died 1750 B.C.E.), and then faded before assuming its greatest power under the Chaldean or Neo-Babylonian Empire (625–539 B.C.E.).

Whereas the Egyptians excelled in the life sciences and technology, the peoples of Sumer and Babylonia are most noted for their work in the physical sciences and mathematics. Babylonian astrologers made the first charts of the zodiac, and, beginning in about 1880 B.C.E., put forward the first systematic observations, theories, and predictions concerning the movements of the stars.

Archaeologists have found clay tablets from Babylonia containing detailed calculations and lists of star and planet positions, as well as evidence that this information was used for making astrological predictions. From the time of Sumerian ruler Sargon of Akkad, history's first great conqueror and empire-builder who flourished in the twenty-fourth and twenty-third centuries B.C.E., Mesopotamian kings depended on astrological readings when planning battles or other engagements.

Babylonian astronomers recorded an eclipse as early as 1375 B.C.E., and the astrologers of Babylonia constructed the first horoscope in 410 B.C.E. By then, the Babylonian Empire, under the leadership of people from Chaldea (kal-DEE-uh), an ancient region on the Euphrates River and the Persian Gulf, had risen and fallen, yet Chaldeans remained noted for their talent in astrology. Even today, the word "Chaldean" is a synonym for "astrologer."

The Babylonians were the first to divide the zodiac into zones ruled by specific constellations, an idea later passed on to the Greeks. The Greeks eventually introduced Babylonian astrology to Egypt, which they conquered under the leadership of Alexander the Great (356–323 B.C.E.). Along with astrology came knowledge of what would now be called astronomy (the ancients did not understand any such distinction), which made it possible to predict such things as the annual flooding of the Nile River, which flows through Egypt, based on the changes of seasons.

Weeks, days, and planets

The Sumerians and the Babylonians also developed the models for timekeeping still used today, and here the term "timekeeping" refers to keeping

The pyramid of Zoser. Though the ancient Egyptians are not noted for their work as astronomers, their placement of the pyramids indicates great understanding of the ways in which the Sun and other heavenly bodies move. (© Charles & Josette Lenars/Corbis. Reproduced by permission of the Corbis Corporation.)

track of everything from years to seconds. (Mesopotamian contributions to yearly and monthly timekeeping are discussed in the Technology and Invention chapter, while the influence of the Mesopotamian base-sixty number system on the division of the day into hours, minutes, and seconds is addressed in the Mathematics chapter.)

In between a month and a day in terms of length is the division of time known as a week, and again, Mesopotamian astronomers seem to have originated this idea. They based the length of a month on a complete cycle of Moon phases, of which there are four: the new Moon (completely

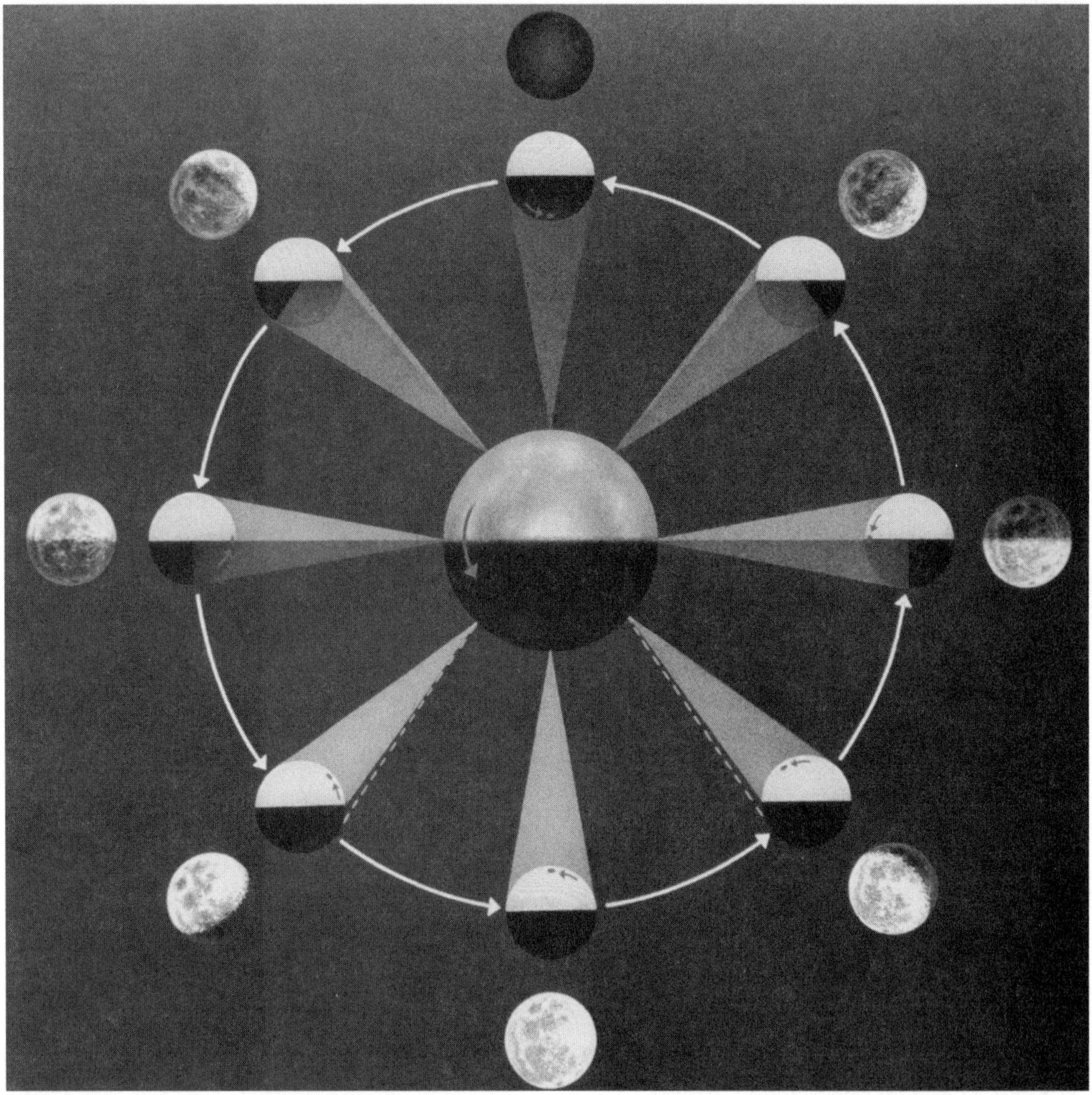

An illustration of the Moon's phases. **(Reproduced by permission of Photo Researchers, Inc.)**

dark); first quarter (lit on one side); full Moon (completely lit); and last quarter (lit on the side opposite of the first quarter).

Given these four phases, it made sense to divide the twenty-eight-day lunar month into four seven-day weeks. In addition, the Sumerians and the Babylonians established the practice of linking the days of the week with the planets and deities or gods who ruled them, a practice reflected in the modern names for the days of the week (see sidebar on page 296).

The impact of Mesopotamian astrology

Though Sumerian and Babylonian astrology might seem misguided from a modern standpoint, at the time it represented a great forward step for science. Instead of basing predictions of future events on dreams, visions, or other purely religious methods, they at least attempted to create a type of scientific forecast by studying the behavior of heavenly bodies.

In addition, they were the first to construct a cosmology, an attempt to explain the origin and the structure of the universe through astronomy. (See essay "Aristotle and Ptolemy: Wrong Ideas That Defined the World" in this chapter.) First to note the regularity of celestial events, the people of Mesopotamia clearly recognized the importance of the heavenly bodies. This emphasis on astronomy and astrology is reflected in the design of the Mesopotamian ziggurats, temple towers that seem to reach toward the heavens.

China

The work of Chinese astronomers was so precise that historians can be absolutely certain about dates in Chinese history after 840 B.C.E. Long before that time, however, the Chinese stargazers became the first to observe and record a number of events in the heavens.

The Chinese made the first recorded sighting of a comet in 2296 B.C.E. and in 240 B.C.E. were the first to observe what became known as Halley's comet. The earliest record of a solar eclipse comes from China (2134 B.C.E.), as does the first account of a sunspot (165 B.C.E.), a dark patch on the Sun's surface. In 352 B.C.E. Chinese astronomers were the first to observe a supernova, an exploding star, and fourteen hundred years later, in June 1054, Chinese and Japanese astronomers made the first detailed description of a supernova.

Heaven and government

Instead of astrology as practiced by the Babylonians and later Western civilizations, the Chinese constructed an elaborate system that linked the heavens, Earth, and China's government. By the time of the Shang Dynasty (c. 1766–c. 1027 B.C.E.), the government employed official astronomers, and it became widely accepted that all astronomical events reflected the will of the gods. Under the Chou Dynasty (c. 1027–c. 221 B.C.E.) rulers expanded this idea greatly.

The Chou leaders introduced to China the idea that a ruler held power according to the Mandate of Heaven, or the favor of the gods. This favor was reflected in the movement of the stars, in the culmination of political events, and in the forces of nature. Thus for instance a good harvest indicated that Heaven was looking down with favor on a particular ruler, as did an accurate prediction of an eclipse by the ruler's official astronomer.

If an astronomer failed to predict an eclipse, the consequences were dire. He would be executed, and the people, if not the ruler himself, usually interpreted the incorrect prediction as a sign that the ruler was losing the Mandate of Heaven. Likewise, a flood or an earthquake indicated the disfavor of the gods, while a series of natural disasters was a clear sign that an entire ruling house or dynasty had lost the Mandate of Heaven. When this happened, it was time to replace one dynasty with another.

Tian-an Men, the Gate of Heavenly Peace. Chinese astrology linked the heavens, Earth, and China's government. The leaders of the Chou dynasty introduced the notion that leaders were chosen by the Gods. (© Corbis. Reproduced by permission of the Corbis Corporation.)

India

In the minds of the ancients, astronomy and astrology were inseparable; likewise these two pursuits were impossible to separate from religion. Nowhere was this tendency more obvious than in India, where astronomers of both the Hindu and the Jain faiths recorded observations and developed elaborate cosmologies.

Jainism, based on the teachings of Vardhamana (known as Mahavira; c. 599–527 B.C.E.), is similar to another Indian religion, Buddhism, in its emphasis on achieving enlightenment and overcoming the endless cycles of reincarnation that are a cornerstone of the Hindu religion. Jain religious writings from about 350 B.C.E. show a cosmological model typical of premodern peoples, an idea of the universe similar to what Europeans still believed some fifteen hundred years later.

In the Jain cosmology, the center of the cosmos, or universe, was Mount Meru, just as in later Christian cosmology, Jerusalem (in present day Israel) was the center of the world and thus of the cosmos. Though it may have been associated with Mount Kailas in southwestern Tibet, Meru was not an actual mountain but rather a mythical place believed to form the axis of the Earth. Earth itself was motionless, surrounded by the Sun, the Moon, the planets, and the constellations.

Hindu astronomy

Early Hindu astronomers, as recorded in the scriptures known as the *Vedas*, created a lunar calendar, that is, one based on the cycles of the Moon rather than Earth's movement around the Sun. They also developed a small star catalogue, or a listing of the stars with their names, positions, and movements. Portions of the *Vedas* date back as early as 1500 B.C.E., though additions went on for many hundreds of years, and therefore it is hard to say with certainty when Hindu astronomers made some of their early advances.

It has sometimes been claimed that the Hindus preceded the Greeks in discovering the fact that Earth is a sphere, but it is more likely that observations about Earth's roundness were added later, as a result of Greek influence. In any case, it was quite common among ancient cultures to envision the cosmos or the universe as a sort of bowl suspended over Earth.

However, Hindu texts do exhibit highly advanced ideas regarding topics such as the color of the sky. They even suggest some notion of gravity, as well as an idea of the Sun as the center of the universe, or what modern people now recognize as the solar system. A group of texts called the *Vaiseshika Sutras* (dating somewhere between 100 and 500 C.E.) presents the idea that matter is composed of atoms, which may even be combined

A painting by Eugène Delacroix of a scene from Dante's Divine Comedy, *which was completed in 1321. The model of the universe Dante presented in his monumental poem was similar to the Jain model developed fifteen hundred years earlier.* (© Corbis-Bettmann. Reproduced by permission of the Corbis Corporation.)

to form something like the modern idea of molecules. (See essay "Early Greek Theories of Matter: What *Is* Everything?" in this chapter.)

Scientific astronomy

Despite the strong religious basis for Indian astronomy, by about 500 C.E. the astronomers of India had begun to develop a more scientific approach to stargazing. Just as astronomy, astrology, and religion were linked in ancient society, so astronomy and mathematics were virtually inseparable for many premodern peoples. Thus many of the greatest Indian astronomers are also remembered as much for their contributions to mathematics as to stargazing.

Such was the case with the first great Hindu astronomer and mathematician, **Aryabhata** (476–c. 550; see biography in Mathematics chapter), whose *Aryabhatiya* (499) contained an important early explanation of the Hindu-Arabic number system. (See essay "Hindu-Arabic Numerals and Mathematical Symbolism" in Mathematics chapter.) The *Aryabhatiya* was also notable for its presentation of Aryabhata's idea that Earth is not motionless, but rather rotates on its axis.

Aryabhata lived in western India, but far away in the central region of the subcontinent, the city of Ujjain had become an important center for astronomical studies. Among the astronomer-mathematicians there was Brahmagupta (598–c. 665), who made a fairly accurate estimation of Earth's circumference at 22,369 miles (35,790 kilometers). This was about ninety percent of the actual distance around the planet at the Equator. (See essay "Angles, Curves, and Surfaces" in Mathematics chapter.)

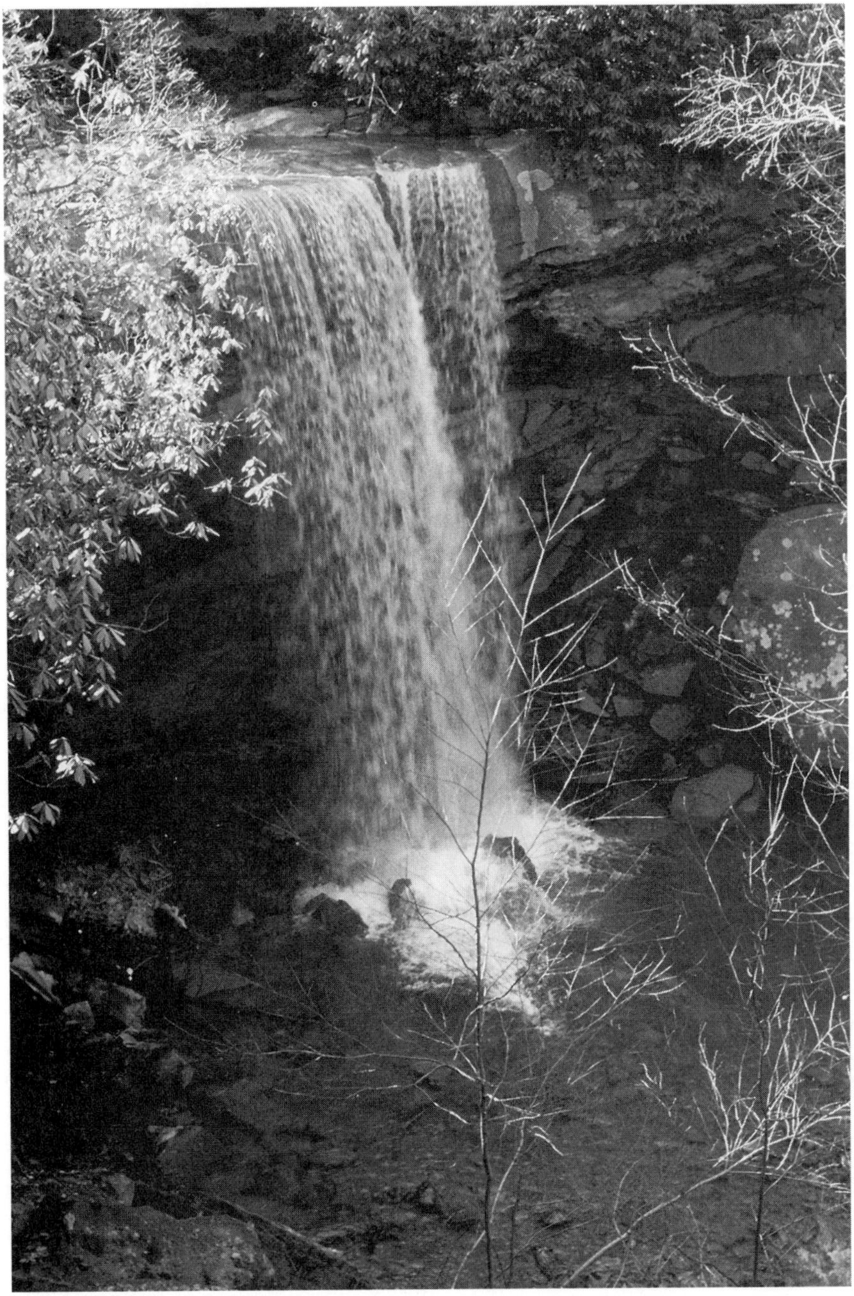

A waterfall. The idea of gravity may have been explained, in basic terms at least, in India long before Isaac Newton. **(Photograph by Robert J. Huffman. Reproduced by permission of Field Mark Publications.)**

Following the lead of an earlier astronomer, Varahamihira (505–587), Brahmagupta also developed a relatively advanced explanation of gravity: "Bodies fall toward the Earth, as it is in the nature of the Earth to attract bodies, just as it is the nature of water to flow." This was still a long way

Gods, Planets, and Days of the Week

The Babylonians established the tradition of relating the planets to gods and goddesses, and of naming days of the week after those heavenly bodies. For example, the Babylonians associated their goddess of love, Ishtar, with the second planet from the Sun, and with the day known in English as Friday. The Greeks, following the Babylonian lead, named the second planet after their love-goddess, Aphrodite. The Romans called her Venus, a name still associated with the planet itself, and, in countries that speak Romance, or Latin-based, languages, Venus is associated with the sixth day of the week, known for instance as Vendredi (French) or Viernes (Spanish).

There is a similar pattern with other deity, planet, and day names: Marduk, the chief Babylonian deity, became Zeus and later Jupiter, whose name is reflected in the Romance names for Thursday, for example, Jeudi in French, Jueves in Spanish. The reason that the names for days of the week are so different in the English-speaking world is that in English and other languages based on German, the names for the days of the week come from Norse gods and goddesses.

Both the Romance and the Germanic languages relate Sunday to the Sun, and Monday to the Moon. Likewise both equate Saturday with Saturn, father of Jupiter. In the case of Tuesday and Friday, the functions of the deities are the same in both Germanic and Romance languages: the war-gods Tiu and Mars are equated with Tuesday, and the love-goddesses Freya and Venus are related to Friday. On the other hand, the Germanic languages relate Woden, king of the gods, to Wednesday while the Romance languages equate Wednesday with Mercury. Thor (Thursday) was the most popular of the Norse gods, with no obvious Latin equivalent.

from the model established by Isaac Newton (see essay "The Scientific Revolution" in this chapter), but it came somewhat closer to the truth than the ideas established by **Aristotle** (384–322 B.C.E.; see biography in Life Science chapter) and accepted by Europeans until about 1500. (See essay "Aristotle and Ptolemy: Wrong Ideas That Defined the World" in this chapter.)

EARLY GREEK THEORIES OF MATTER: WHAT *IS* EVERYTHING?

With the emergence of philosophy and the sciences in Greece during the period after about 600 B.C.E., the character of the physical sciences changed dramatically. The other great civilizations of the ancient world had been primarily interested in astronomy, which they linked with astrology and religion; the Greeks, on the other hand, extended their interests to what would become known as chemistry and physics. But this was only the beginning of the differences between the Greek thinkers and their counterparts in other advanced societies.

Most people in the West are familiar with the biblical account of how the universe began—a story that, while compelling from a spiritual, moral, and even literary standpoint, contradicts scientifically based theory on the origins and composition of the physical world. In fact the story of Genesis, a product of ancient Israelite civilization, was quite sophisticated compared to other tales regarding the origins of the universe. For example, one Babylonian account attributes the origin of the world to a sexual encounter between the god of the waters, Enki, and the goddess of the soil, Ninhursag.

Like the Babylonians, the Greeks never distinguished between astrology and astronomy, yet they were still able to develop far more scientific theories of matter and the universe. This difference between the Greeks and all others had its roots in one of Greece's greatest legacies to the world: *philosophy,* a term derived from Greek words meaning "love of wisdom." Philosophy is the area of study that seeks to provide a general understanding of reality. This may sound like a tall order, and indeed it is, but the philosophers of ancient Greece were concerned with nothing less than answers to questions such as What *is* everything? Where did it come from? And what is the place of humanity and Earth in the middle of it all?

The Greeks may not have been the first to ask such questions, but they were the first to attempt answers based on general principles or laws, rather than on the will of God or the gods. Some of their ideas may sound a little strange to modern people, but for the world in which the Greeks lived, they represented the cutting edge of scientific thought. Thanks to the contributions of Greek thinkers between about 600 and 300 B.C.E., it became possible to begin thinking about, and attempting to explain, the very foundations of the physical world.

The two principal problems

Despite the many differences between Greek philosophers, there was an underlying belief that the universe has some kind of order that can be

Words to Know

chemistry: An area of the physical sciences concerned with the composition, structure, properties, and changes of substances, including elements, compounds, and mixtures.

cosmology: A branch of astronomy concerned with the origin, structure, and evolution of the universe.

cosmos: The universe.

element: A substance, made up of only one kind of atom, that cannot be broken down chemically into another substance. Scientists only developed this definition in about 1800; prior to that time, a number of misguided theories prevailed. Most notable among these was the Greek notion of four elements: earth, air, fire, and water.

geocentric: Earth-centered.

heliocentric: Sun-centered.

matter: Physical substance that occupies space, possesses mass, and is ultimately convertible to energy. Matter can be a gas, liquid, or solid.

philosophy: The area of study that seeks to provide a general understanding of reality.

physics: An area of the physical sciences that is concerned with matter, energy, and the interactions between them.

understood by the human mind; indeed, the word *cosmos* comes from a Greek term meaning "order." In seeking to understand this order, Greek thinkers had to confront two basic issues.

The first of these issues might be characterized as "the one and the many," and it revolved around the question of whether the universe is made of just one thing, or many things. If it is only one thing, they asked themselves, then how is it possible that so many different objects can exist? Yet if it is many things, then how can it have any unity or structure?

The second, and related, question concerned continuity and change. If an object or event is one thing, and cannot be something else, then why and how do things appear to change into other things? Yet if change is real, then how can anything have a permanent and distinct identity?

The Milesians: Single-substance theories

His name is hardly a household word, but Thales of Miletus (THAY-leez; c. 625–c. 547 B.C.E.) is regarded as the father of the physical sciences, of geometry, and of philosophy. Certain aspects of his biography may well have been mythical, but it is certain that he lived in the region of Miletus in what is now western Turkey. Furthermore, there is no reason to doubt that Thales formed the first scientific statement about the nature of the physical world: "Everything is water."

This may not sound very impressive, but in fact it was one of the most important observations in the history of science. In making it, Thales was asserting that the entire universe is in a fluid state, like that of water, and that the transformations of water—from steam to liquid to ice—serve to illustrate an underlying force for change. His was the first of several theories of matter built around a single substance, and it served as a basis for the theories of other philosophers who followed him in what became known as the Milesian (my-LEE-zhun) school.

Anaximander and Anaximenes

The Milesians studied such phenomena as earthquakes, thunderbolts, and the origin of animals, and developed a general cosmology, an explanation of the origins and the structure of the universe, that suggested that the universe grew from a single "seed." Thales's successor Anaximander (610–c. 547 B.C.E.) held that the universe is constituted out of a single, eternal material principle he called the "unbounded" (*apeiron*), which generates within itself all contraries, such as hot and cold. These in turn influence the interaction of basic elemental principles (water, air, and fire), as well as opposing powers and qualities related to them.

Today an element is defined as a substance made up of only one kind of atom, which cannot be broken down chemically into another substance. Scientists only developed this definition in about 1800. Prior to that time, a number of misguided theories prevailed. Most notable among these was the Greek notion of the four "elements"—earth, air, fire, and water—whose roots can be traced to Anaximander. Unsophisticated as this idea now seems, at the time it was a highly advanced concept, and Anaximander used the opposing qualities of the elements to explain phenomena such as wind, lightning, and thunder.

The third Milesian philosopher, Anaximenes of Miletus (an-uk-SIM-uh-neez; flourished c. 545 B.C.E.), proposed air as the universal element. In his view, air gives rise to other substances by an ongoing process of alternating condensation and rarefaction (becoming more dense and less dense, respectively). According to Anaximenes, condensed air produces water and earth, while rarefied air generates fire.

OPPOSITE PAGE
A table of twenty-four of the most common or important elements.
(Reproduced by permission of the Gale Group.)

The Pythagoreans: A world of numbers

Unlike the Milesians, the school of thought that developed around the mathematician and philosopher **Pythagoras** (c. 580–c. 500 B.C.E.; see biography in Mathematics chapter) was not concerned with the physical substance of the universe; rather, the Pythagoreans attempted to explain the cosmos spiritually. In their view, the universe was made up of numbers, which they regarded as perfect spiritual entities. (See essay "The Greeks' New Approach to Mathematics" in Mathematics chapter for more about the Pythagoreans.)

Pythagoras also taught that all nature consisted of four elements, further spurring on the development of the four-element theory. Unlike later thinkers, however, he based his idea not so much on observation as on a belief in the perfection of the number four. More useful to later scientific development was the Pythagorean approach to cosmology, the first such system that attempted to identify laws of the universe. Furthermore, the Pythagorean emphasis on numbers introduced the idea of a quantitative cosmology, or a universe that could be described in exact numerical terms rather than with imprecise qualitative ideas such as big or small.

Geocentric and heliocentric cosmologies

Adopting a geocentric (Earth-centered) model of space, Pythagoras maintained that the Sun, the Moon, and the five known planets (Mercury, Venus, Mars, Jupiter, and Saturn) all moved in perfect mathematical order around Earth. The Pythagoreans had discovered that musical harmonies could be expressed as numerical ratios or proportions, and they applied this idea to the motion of the heavens, arguing that the movements of the stars and the planets made music. (People cannot hear this music of the spheres, they explained, because they have been exposed to it since birth.)

In the 400s B.C.E., the Pythagorean astronomer Philolaus departed from the geocentric model. He suggested that both Earth and the Sun revolve around a central fire in the cosmos. To explain why this central fire was never seen from Earth, Philolaus imagined the existence of an "anti-Earth" always placed between Earth and the fire. Though this aspect of it is rather fanciful, Philolaus's idea that the center of the universe is beyond Earth or

Element	Symbol	Percent of all atoms* In the universe	In the earth's crust	In sea water	In the human body	Characteristics under ordinary room conditions
Aluminum	Al	—	6.3	—	—	A lightweight, silvery metal
Calcium	Ca	—	2.1	—	0.2	Common in minerals, seashells, and bones
Carbon	C	—	—	—	10.7	Basic in all living things
Chlorine	Cl	—	—	0.3	—	A toxic gas
Copper	Cu	—	—	—	—	The only red metal
Gold	Au	—	—	—	—	The only yellow metal
Helium	He	7.1	—	—	—	A very light gas
Hydrogen	H	92.8	2.9	66.2	60.6	The lightest of all elements; a gas
Iodine	I	—	—	—	—	A nonmetal; used as antiseptic
Iron	Fe	—	2.1	—	—	A magnetic metal; used in steel
Lead	Pb	—	—	—	—	A soft, heavy metal
Magnesium	Mg	—	2.0	—	—	A very light metal
Mercury	Hg	—	—	—	—	A liquid metal; one of the two liquid elements
Nickel	Ni	—	—	—	—	A noncorroding metal; used in coins
Nitrogen	N	—	—	—	2.4	A gas; the major component of air
Oxygen	O	—	60.1	33.1	25.7	A gas; the second major component of air
Phosphorus	P	—	—	—	0.1	A nonmetal; essential to plants
Potassium	K	—	1.1	—	—	A metal; essential to plants; commonly called "potash"
Silicon	Si	—	20.8	—	—	A semiconductor; used in electronics
Silver	Ag	—	—	—	—	A very shiny, valuable metal
Sodium	Na	—	2.2	0.3	—	A soft metal; reacts readily with water, air
Sulfur	S	—	—	—	0.1	A yellow nonmetal; flammable
Titanium	Ti	—	0.3	—	—	A light, strong, noncorroding metal used in space vehicles
Uranium	U	—	—	—	—	A very heavy metal; fuel for nuclear power

*If no number is entered, the element constitutes less than 0.1 percent.

the Sun is quite accurate. In fact, the solar system is revolving around the center of the Milky Way galaxy, which itself is far from the center, but this would not be discovered for more than two thousand years.

Xenophanes, Heraclitus, and Parmenides

The first Greek philosopher to explain the cosmos in terms completely separate from religion was Xenophanes (zen-AHF-uh-neez; c. 560–c. 478 B.C.E.) This does not mean that Xenophanes was an atheist; on the contrary, his idea of God was much more in line with Christianity than the with Greeks' religion. He criticized his own people's religious views, saying they had created gods to reflect their own weaknesses and vices, whereas Xenophanes imagined an all-powerful deity who had set the universe in motion through the sheer power of his mind.

OPPOSITE PAGE The southern Milky Way. The discovery that the solar system revolves around the center of the Milky Way supports Philolaus's ancient belief that Earth and the Sun revolve around a central cosmic fire. **(Photograph by Fred Espenak. Reproduced by permission of Photo Researchers, Inc.)**

Earth, in Xenophanes's view, was infinite in length, width, and depth; so too were the heavens above it. Because of this, he further maintained, there were infinite possibilities in the universe, and therefore the Sun that rose today was different from the Sun that rose yesterday or the one that will rise tomorrow. Though this idea was obviously incorrect, Xenophanes had a positive influence on Greek thought both by separating religion from science and by advocating the use of observation. By observing what could be seen, Xenophanes suggested, it was possible to form ideas concerning what could not be seen.

Heracleitus versus Parmenides: Change or no change?

The next two great thinkers staked out opposing positions that influenced their successors for centuries. For Heracleitus (hair-uh-KLY-tus; c. 540–c. 480 B.C.E.), nature is in a constant state of change; by contrast, Parmenides of Elea (par-MIN-uh-deez; born c. 515 B.C.E.), maintained that nature is unchangeable, and that change itself is an illusion. Parmenides' Eleatic school later produced the philosopher Zeno of Elea (c. 495–c. 430 B.C.E.), who developed his famous paradoxes in an attempt to prove the impossibility of change (see essay "The Greeks' New Approach to Mathematics" in Mathematics chapter for a discussion of Zeno's paradoxes).

Some scholars regard Xenophanes, and not Parmenides, as the founder of the Eleatic school; yet it is equally easy to see the reflection of Xenophanes's ideas in those of Heracleitus. Just as Xenophanes maintained that the same Sun never rises twice, Heracleitus, making a point about the changeable quality of nature, formulated the famous observation: "You cannot step into the same river twice, for other waters are ever flowing on." According to Heracleitus, fire is the underlying element and principle of the universe, and all things are in a process of conflict and change.

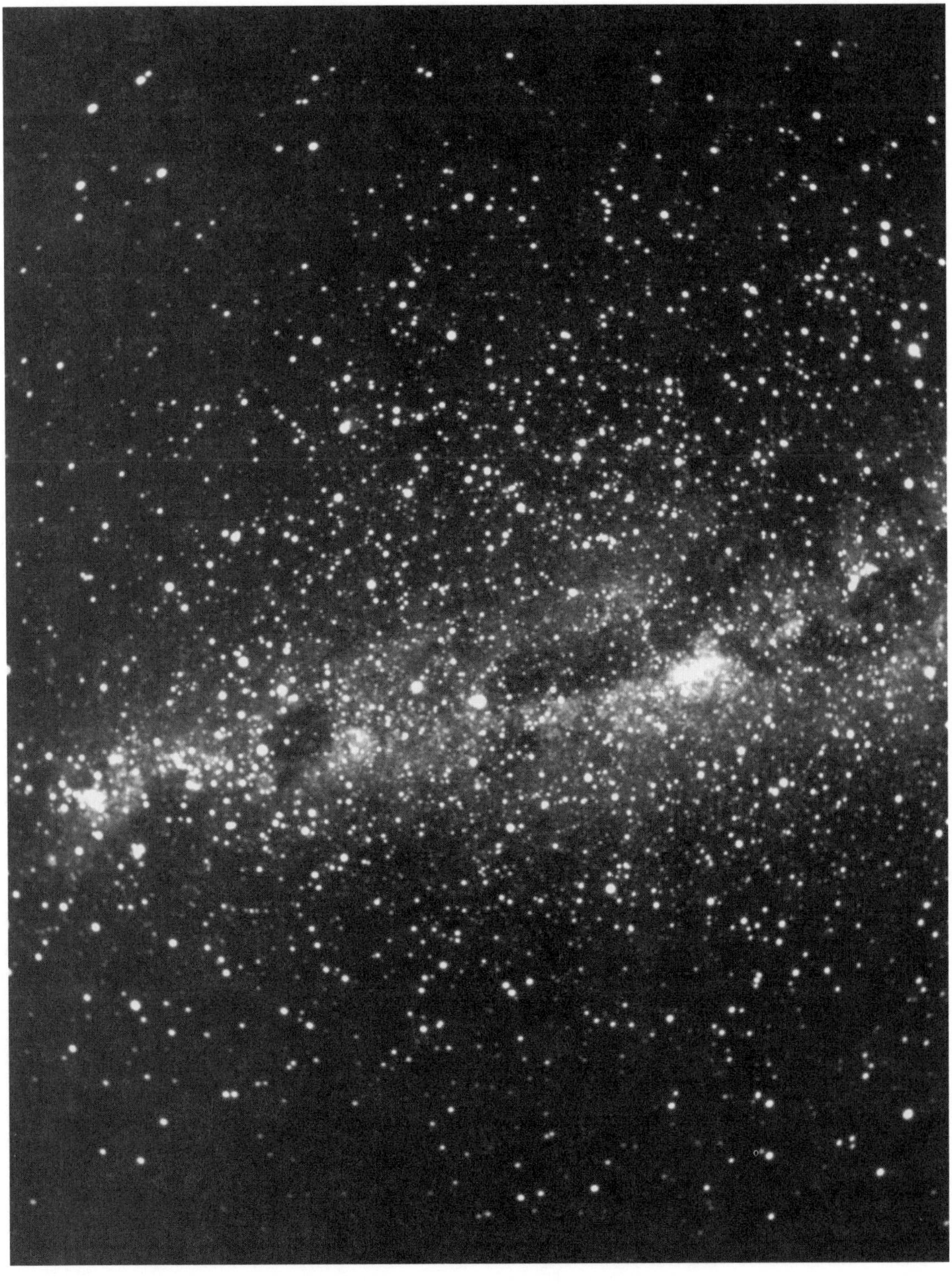

Empedocles: The maturing of the four-elements theory

Heracleitus and Parmenides thus approached the questions of "the one and the many," and of continuity and change, from opposing sides. Both views had their merits and their flaws, and together they revealed the weakness of attempts to explain the universe in terms of a single substance. This opened the way to multiple-substance theories, most notably that of Empedocles (em-PED-uh-kleez; c. 490–430 B.C.E.)

Drawing on the teachings of his predecessors, Empedocles taught in his poem *On the Nature of Things* that fire, air, water, and earth are the four elements or roots of the cosmic order. According to Empedocles, these four swirl around one another, with no space in between; thus Empedocles helped establish the tradition whereby Greek philosophers refused to believe in the existence of a void, or an area without matter or physical substance. All things, according to Greek philosophy, are composed of these four elements in varying proportions: bone, for instance, is two parts earth, two parts water, and two parts fire.

The combination and separation of the elements, Empedocles explained, is governed by two forces, which he called Love and Strife, that constantly vie with one another for supremacy. Initially all four elements were blended together by the love of the gods, but Strife eventually broke apart the elements. Ultimately, Empedocles taught, the four elements would completely separate from one another into four spheres, and only then would Love reenter the equation, bringing these four spheres back together.

Empedocles's teachings sound more religious than scientific, and indeed they influenced the unscientific belief in the Four Humors, the belief that human health is governed by a balance of four bodily fluids, which caused much misery before it was finally discarded at the beginning of the modern era. (See essay "Greek Physicians Transform the Life Sciences" in the Life Science chapter.) Yet it would be a mistake to dismiss him as a nonscientist. Empedocles was the first thinker to emphasize the use of experimentation in science, and his theory of the four elements, though crude by modern standards, represents a serious early attempt to explain the chemical makeup of the world.

Atomism: A surprisingly modern view

A contemporary of Empedocles was the Greek philosopher Leucippus (flourished in the fifth century B.C.E.), who, with his student Democritus (de-MAHK-ri-tus; c. 460–c. 370 B.C.E.), is known as the leading proponent of atomism. As its name suggests, atomism is based on the concept that the physical world is made up of atoms, which might sound like a very modern idea. In fact it is more than twenty-four hundred years old.

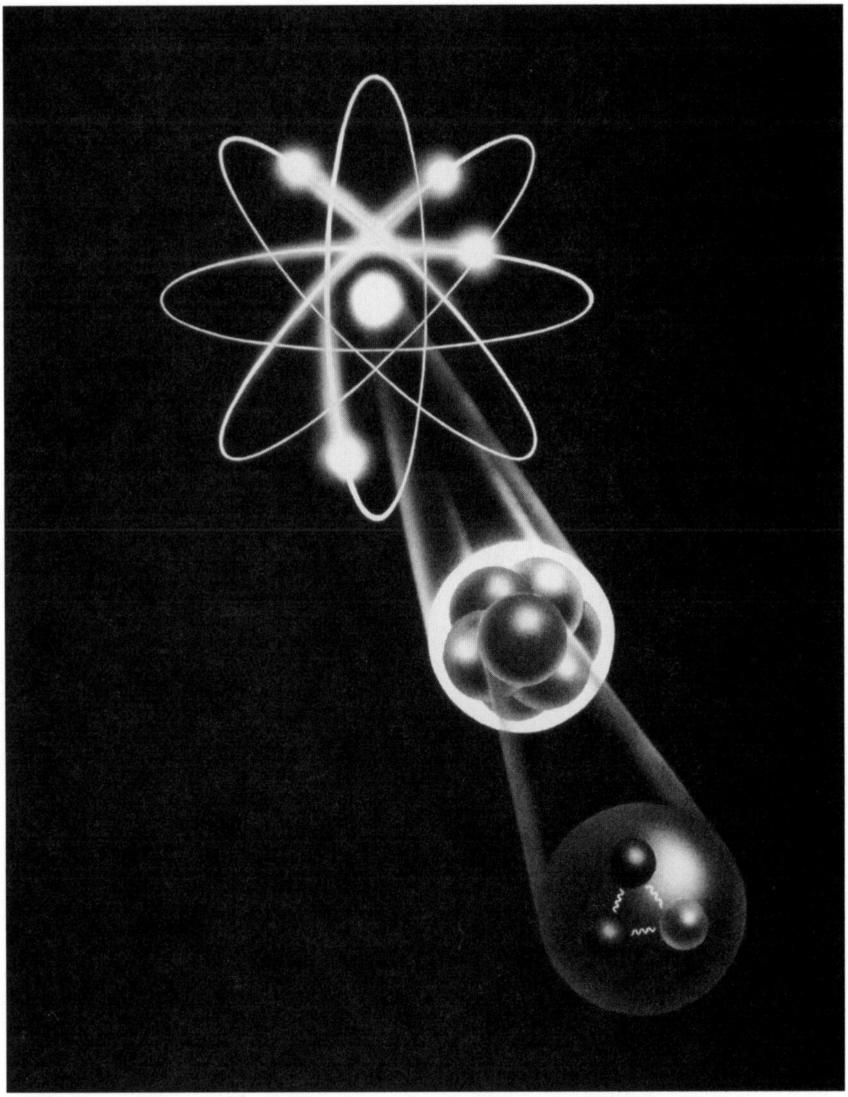

A diagram showing the structure of an atom. Greek philosophers Leucippus and Democritus proposed that everything on Earth was composed of atoms in the fifth century B.C.E. **(Photograph by Michael Gilbert. Reproduced by permission of Photo Researchers, Inc.)**

The atomic theory taught by Democritus (little is known about Leucippus or his specific teachings) depicted a world composed of tiny, indivisible units (*atomos* in Greek) that exist eternally and are in constant motion. Collisions among them are responsible for change of all kinds, while the shape, position, and arrangement of atoms accounts for the differences in appearance between larger physical objects.

According to Democritus, qualities such as color, taste, and texture are mere illusions resulting from the interactions between atoms. "By custom sweet and by custom bitter, by custom hot, by custom cold, by custom

The "Real" Elements

An element is a substance, made up of only one kind of atom that cannot be broken down chemically into another substance. Contrary to the teachings of Empedocles (c. 490–430 B.C.E.) and other ancient Greeks, there are not just four elements in the world; there are more than a hundred. Ninety-two of these elements occur naturally; the rest were created artificially, usually in laboratories.

The ancients actually knew of many elements, such as gold, silver, lead, and iron, but the first individual credited with discovering an element was German chemist Hennig Brand (died c. 1692), who discovered phosphorus in 1669. Around the same time, English physicist and chemist **Robert Boyle** (1627–1691; see biography in this chapter) defined an element as a substance that cannot be broken down chemically into another, and a century later, French chemist **Antoine-Laurent Lavoisier** (1743–1794; see biography in this chapter) distinguished elements from compounds, in which two or more elements are chemically bonded.

Most of the elements are solids at room temperature, while a handful are gases, and just two, mercury and bromine, are liquids. Some elements are extremely common and useful; others, such as praseodymium, are far from household words. Just eighteen elements make up 99.51 percent of Earth's crust, oceans, and atmosphere, while only ten compose almost the entire mass of the human body. Oxygen is by far the most abundant element in both Earth and the body, but not elsewhere. A staggering 99.99 percent of the entire mass of the universe is made up of just two elements, hydrogen and helium.

Incidentally, none of the Greeks' four elements is actually an element. Water comes the closest, being a compound, while air and earth are both mixtures, or combinations of various compounds. (Coffee, metal alloys, and wood are other examples of mixtures.) As for fire, it is simply the result of combustion, an example of an oxidation-reduction chemical reaction.

color; but in reality atoms and void," he explained. Democritus believed that all atoms are the same, but as they interact they produce differing impressions or images (*eidola* in Greek). According to Democritus the human soul itself is composed of atoms and disintegrates at death, returning the atoms to the universe. There is therefore no concept of immortality (living forever) in Democritus's philosophy, and the gods themselves are merely giant *eidola*.

Democritus's atoms and modern atoms

Democritus tried to explain what most people would call spiritual matters (the soul, the gods) in terms of physical ones, and thus he attempted to go far beyond the realm of science. He was speaking more as a philosopher than as a scientist when he asserted that the perceived differences between groups of atoms is an illusion; yet there is much of value in this, as well his other ideas.

Today chemists understand that the differences between different types of atoms (and hence of different elements) are very real: for instance, carbon atoms have six protons, gold atoms have seventy-nine. Still, Democritus was at least partially right in suggesting that the arrangements of atoms cause differences between substances. For instance, when two highly flammable gases, hydrogen and oxygen, chemically bond in just the right way, they produce water, which is similar to neither. And if these bond with carbon, a powdery black substance found, for instance, in coal, in just the right configuration, they can produce sugar, which is nothing like carbon, hydrogen, oxygen, or water.

Democritus was the first Greek philosopher to consider the possibility of a void, or empty space, what modern scientists would call a vacuum. According to Democritus, "Nothing exists but atoms and the void," and in fact this is true. Not only is the world composed of atoms, as he said, but those atoms are mostly empty space. The majority of matter in the atom lies in the nucleus, which compares in size to the rest of the atom the way a BB would to a sports arena; in between the nucleus and the edge of the atom is empty space through which electrons spin.

The rediscovery of the atomic idea

It would be a mistake to give Democritus too much credit for modern atomic theory, which has its roots in the work of English chemist John Dalton (1766–1844). Indeed, not even Dalton, or any other scientist of the nineteenth century, had any concept of electrons, protons, and neutrons, which were discovered in the period from 1897 to 1932. Still, Democritus was closer to the truth than any thinker for the next twenty-two hundred years.

The atomic idea survived in the work of the Greek philosopher Epicurus (341–270 B.C.E.), the Greek physician Asclepiades of Bithynia (c.

130–40 B.C.E.), and the Roman poet Lucretius (c. 100–c. 55 B.C.E.) Then it virtually died out until Dalton published his atomic theory in 1803. Meanwhile another view, one that drew from Empedocles's four-elements theory, prevailed. (See essay "Aristotle and Ptolemy: Wrong Ideas That Defined the World" in this chapter.)

ARISTOTLE AND PTOLEMY: WRONG IDEAS THAT DEFINED THE WORLD

The Greek philosopher Democritus (c. 460–c. 370 B.C.E.) developed an amazingly accurate explanation of the physical world. All matter, he taught, is composed of atoms, a model accepted by scientists today. Yet modern atomic theory only came into existence after 1800, some twenty-two hundred years after Democritus.

During most of the intervening time, Western thinkers generally accepted another theory of matter, one put forward by the Greek philosopher **Aristotle** (384–322 B.C.E.; see biography in Life Science chapter). Aristotle had more influence on the shaping of Western philosophy than any individual, and in the sciences, he made especially valuable contributions to biology. Yet he had a perhaps even greater—and certainly less positive—impact on the physical sciences.

Aristotle accepted the idea of four elements put forward by the philosopher Empedocles (c. 490–430 B.C.E.), and this led to misguided theories of both chemistry and physics, a scientific discipline whose name goes back to Aristotle's book by the same title. Only in the 1500s did Aristotle's physics begin to come under serious and sustained challenge, but his negative influence in chemistry would last until almost 1800.

One reason for this is that Empedocles's theory of matter, though it was much further from the truth than Democritus's, seemed more logical to the those living in ancient times because it involved things one could see and touch—earth, air, fire, and water—instead of invisible atoms. (See essay "Early Greek Theories of Matter: What *Is* Everything?" in this chapter.) Furthermore, Democritus's atomic theory made no allowance for the existence of God, whereas the Aristotelian model included the concept of a "Prime Mover," or God, which controlled the universe. This led to much greater acceptance of Aristotelian science with the rise of Christian influence in Europe during the period after about 300 C.E.

Similar factors influenced the acceptance of ideas put forward by the Greco-Roman astronomer **Ptolemy** (c. 100–c. 170; see biography in this chapter), who maintained that Earth was at the center of the universe. Ptole-

Words to Know

alchemy: A set of mystical beliefs based on the idea that ordinary matter can be perfected. In the Middle Ages, this became a semi-scientific discipline concerned, for instance, with attempts to turn various metals into gold.

celestial: Of the skies or heavens.

chemistry: An area of the physical sciences concerned with the composition, structure, properties, and changes of substances, including elements, compounds, and mixtures.

cosmology: A branch of astronomy concerned with the origin, structure, and evolution of the universe.

cosmos: The universe.

eclipse: An event in which one celestial body covers, or otherwise makes it impossible to see, another. In a solar eclipse, the Moon passes between Earth and the Sun, covering the Sun. In a lunar eclipse, Earth comes between the Sun and the full Moon, placing the Moon in its shadow.

geocentric: Earth-centered.

heliocentric: Sun-centered.

kinematics: The study of how objects move.

mechanics: A branch of physics concerned with the study of bodies in motion.

physics: An area of the physical sciences that is concerned with matter, energy, and the interactions between them.

retrograde motion: The apparent backward movement, or reversal of direction, by outer planets in the solar system. In fact retrograde motion is simply an optical illusion, created by the fact that Earth is orbiting the Sun much faster than the outer planets are.

terrestrial: Of the Earth.

vacuum: An area devoid of matter, even air.

my was not the first to take this position, but he constructed an elaborate model of the universe that seemed to make sense to premodern Europeans.

Before Aristotle

Empedocles, Democritus, and the other thinkers are called pre-Socratic philosophers, a term that emphasizes the importance of the Greek philosopher Socrates (c. 470-399 B.C.E.). Whereas the pre-Socratics had been chiefly concerned with explaining the nature of the physical world, Socrates steered philosophy toward more human concerns with questions such as "What is justice?" or "What is the good life?"

Socrates's pupil Plato (c. 428–348 B.C.E.), who was probably the most influential thinker in Western history, aside from his own student, Aristotle, approached a whole range of issues. Like Socrates, he was concerned with human society, yet in his book *Timaeus* he offered a theory of the universe in which he brought together the idea of the four elements with the concept of atomism.

Plato's universe

Governed by a divine craftsman he called the Demiurge (DEM-ee-urj), Plato's universe was made up of the four elements. These elements appeared as atoms shaped like four of the five "Platonic solids," while the fifth existed in outer space. Plato's atomism seems to have been influenced more by the mathematician **Pythagoras** (c. 580–c. 500 B.C.E.; see biography in Mathematics chapter) than by Democritus. Just as Pythagoras sought to explain the universe in terms of numbers, which he regarded as examples of spiritual perfection, Plato saw perfection in the shapes of the five solids.

Plato also accepted the lead of earlier philosophers who maintained that Earth is the center of the universe. In order to maintain this belief, however, it was necessary to develop a model of the cosmos that accounted for apparent irregularities in planetary motion. Today, scientists understand that those irregularities are a result of the fact that the planets are not moving around Earth at all, but around the Sun. However, it was possible, with a bit of hard thinking, to create a system in which the planets moved around Earth, and to make sense of such a system. During Plato's time, an astronomer attempted to do just that.

Eudoxus and the concentric spheres

In Plato's ideas it is easy to see a few concepts later adopted by Aristotle. Not only did Aristotle put forward his own Demiurge concept, which he called the Prime Mover, but like Plato he believed that the material composition of outer space was different from that of Earth.

Similarly, Plato's contemporary Eudoxus of Cnidus (c. 400–c. 350 B.C.E.) provided an early example for Ptolemy by envisioning a set of concentric spheres (that is, spheres within spheres) that marked the planetary orbits around Earth.

These concentric spheres were connected to other spheres, for a total of twenty-seven, which collectively seemed to account for the planets' movements and preserved the idea of a geocentric (Earth-centered) universe. Later, Callippus (flourished in the fourth century B.C.E.) improved on Eudoxus's system, and made it even more complicated.

Aristotelian cosmology

Aristotle himself added still further "improvements" (and complications) until there were a total of fifty-five spheres, all moving in relation to Earth. As Aristotle conceived them, these spheres were not just orbital paths, but actual material bodies rather like wheels spinning on axles, kept in motion by the action of the Prime Mover. Though it was almost entirely inaccurate, Aristotle's cosmology, or model of the universe, was powerful in presentation and thorough in scope, and thus was extraordinarily influential within Western society. The same is true of his ideas about chemistry and physics, which are closely related to his cosmology.

Thomas Aquinas interpreted Aristotle's Prime Mover as the Christian God, and thus made Aristotelian ideas acceptable to the Catholic Church.
(The National Gallery, London/Corbis. Reproduced by permission of the Corbis Corporation.)

In Aristotle's spherical, or round, cosmos, there were two principal regions: a celestial, or heavenly realm above the orbit of the Moon, and a terrestrial, or earthly one in what was known as the sublunary (below the Moon) region. Virtually everything about these two realms differed. The celestial region never changed, whereas change was possible on Earth. Earth itself consisted of the four elements, whereas the heavens were made up of a fifth substance, which he called "ether." (As with other Greek philosophers, except for Democritus, Aristotle denied the existence of a vacuum, or empty space).

Interactions of the four elements

Aristotle explained these four elements as combinations of four qualities, or two pairs of opposites: hot-cold and wet-dry. The combination of hot and dry produced fire; cold and wet made water; hot and wet produced air; and cold and dry yielded earth. In a departure from Empedocles, Aristotle believed that the elements were changeable, and that one element could be transformed into another, an idea that provided a basis for later experiments in alchemy (See essay "Alchemy, Astrology, and Education in Medieval Europe" in this chapter.)

Empedocles taught that Strife tends to pull the four elements apart, and that Love brings them back together, but Aristotle took just the opposite approach. He believed that if left undisturbed, the four elements would completely segregate into four concentric layers, with earth at the center, surrounded by water, then air, then fire, bounded at the outer perimeter by the ether. However, the motion of bodies above the Moon's sphere caused the elements to behave unnaturally, and thus they remained mixed and in a constant state of agitation.

Aristotelian physics

The distinction between natural and unnatural (or violent) motion was one of the central ideas in Aristotle's *Physics,* a book compiled by one of his students from his lectures. Despite its title, *Physics* actually addresses a wide variety of sciences, yet its focus is on motion and change. These are among the principal concerns of physics, particularly the area known as mechanics and its subdiscipline, kinematics.

In Aristotle's view, natural motion is that which moves a body to its natural position, which in turn is determined by the weight or lightness of the body. It is natural that earth, the element, would tend to fall toward the center of the universe, since it is the heaviest of all; similarly, fire, as the lightest of the four sublunary elements, has a tendency to rise to the outermost level of the realm below the Moon. The heavier an object, the faster it tends to fall toward its natural position. Whereas there is nothing to stop natural motion, violent motion, movement that takes an object away from its natural position, must overcome forces that would impede it. If a rock falls to the ground, this is natural motion, but if a person throws the rock up toward the sky, the motion is violent or unnatural.

Force and resistance

Aristotle claimed that everything that moves is moved by something, a concept that led him to his idea of an original source of motion—the Prime Mover, a "changeless source of change"—which Christian writers later equated with God. He also believed that the force responsible for motion had to be in constant physical contact with the body that moved.

Obviously the thrower's hand is not in constant contact with the stone, but Aristotle maintained that by setting the stone in motion, the thrower activates the surrounding medium, in this case, air. The air parts in front of the stone and circles back to maintain a continuous force pushing the stone upward or forward. This force gradually diminishes due to the resistance of the air or other medium. When it completely dissipates, the stone falls downward according to its natural motion.

In Aristotle's kinematics, two factors affected the speed of a body in motion: the force with which it is set in motion, and the resistance of the medium. If the resistance was zero, the speed of the moving object would be infinite, and for this reason he rejected the idea of a vacuum because infinite speed is impossible. Furthermore, he believed that bodies of different weights fall at different speeds; those speeds being directly proportional to their weight. However, he realized that without a material medium, lighter bodies would move just as swiftly as heavier bodies. (This part, at least, is true: in a vacuum, all objects fall at the same speed.)

Evaluating Aristotle as a physical scientist

Aristotle's writings dominated subsequent Greek philosophy and the studies of Byzantine (medieval Greek) and Arab scholars. (See essay "The Islamic World Takes the Lead" in this chapter.) Later, when western Europe discovered his work in translations from the Arabic, European philosophers, most notably Thomas Aquinas (1225–1274), blended ideas from Aristotle and other Greek philosophers with concepts from the Bible. Together, these principles formed the basis of Western thinking throughout the Middle Ages (c. 500–c. 1500 C.E.) and created a legacy whose effects are still felt today: indeed, it would be impossible to imagine Western civilization without the influence of Aristotle.

In addition, Aristotle's works became the foundational texts of science as taught in European universities from the 1200s to the 1500s. This was unfortunate, because virtually every aspect of his teaching was incorrect. Stones do not fall because they are seeking their natural position; they fall because of Earth's gravitational field. Heavier objects seem to fall faster than lighter ones, but as noted, they would fall at the same speed in a vacuum, and vacuums do exist, despite the fact that Aristotle refused to believe in them. As for the idea of the four elements and the belief that space is made of a different substance than Earth, both now seem a bit far-fetched.

Whereas Aristotle believed that curved motion is natural and eternal, and straight-line motion comes to a stop, the laws of motion (see essay "The Scientific Revolution" in this chapter) developed by **Isaac Newton** (1642–1727; see biography in this chapter) show quite the opposite. Though Newton is credited with overturning the faulty Aristotelian model, in fact his work built on that of **Nicolaus Copernicus** (1473–1543; see biography in this chapter) and **Galileo Galilei** (1564–1642; see biography in this chapter). These men in turn owed much to a handful of skeptics during the Middle Ages, men who dared challenge Aristotle when his word reigned supreme.

Andrea Bregno's sculpture of Nicholas of Cusa (left) with St. Peter (center) and an angel. Nicholas, who believed Earth revolves around the Sun, opposed Aristotle's ideas on astronomy. (Reproduced by permission Alinari-Art Reference/Art Resource, New York.)

In Aristotle's defense

Much can be said in Aristotle's defense, including the fact that, for all his flaws, he was still one of the greatest minds in history, who contributed enormously to human understanding of subjects ranging from drama to zoology. In addition, he lived at a time when the most basic concepts of science had yet to be discovered; nor could he have known that, from about 200 to 1200 C.E., the Western world would produce few thinkers of distinction who would develop or challenge his ideas.

Furthermore, as noted earlier, Aristotle's explanation of the physical world seemed to make sense. Unlike Democritus's atomic theory, it related to things that people could see and touch; allowed for the existence of a deity; and brought together cosmology, chemistry, and physics in a neat, consistent package. By contrast, an ancient person, if confronted with the concept of gravity, might well say that it sounded absurd.

A series of discoveries about the world

There is another reason not to dismiss Aristotle as a physical scientist: it was he who first proved that Earth is spherical. This was the first of three great discoveries concerning the planet and its relation to the rest of space. Next came the heliocentric (Sun-centered) model of the universe put forward by the astronomer Aristarchus of Samos (flourished c. 270 B.C.E.), and last was an astoundingly accurate measure of Earth's circumference made by **Eratosthenes** of Cyrene (c. 276–c. 194 B.C.E.; see biography in Mathematics chapter).

Plato had first suggested the idea of a spherical Earth, but he asserted this for the very nonscientific reason that a sphere is perfect, and Earth in its perfection must be spherical. Aristotle, who, for all his failings, is rightly considered the father of Western science, set out to prove (or disprove) this belief through experiment. During a lunar eclipse, he observed that the shadow cast on the Moon by Earth has a rounded edge, indicating that Earth is a sphere.

Aristarchus and Eratosthenes

Later, Aristarchus of Samos took a further step toward a sophisticated understanding of Earth and the solar system, which the Greeks thought was the entire universe. The movement of objects in the sky, he proposed, could best be explained if Earth rotated on its axis once every day and revolved with the other planets around the Sun. He also correctly suggested that the Sun is larger than Earth.

Less successful was Aristarchus's attempt, through the use of trigonometry, to measure the distance to the Sun. Though his reasoning was sound, his instruments were so primitive that they produced a far from accurate reading, leading him to the conclusion that the Sun is twenty times farther from Earth than the Moon is. (In fact it is more like three hundred ninety times as far away.)

Two centuries after Aristarchus, Eratosthenes used similar methods to make a measurement of Earth's circumference that produced a figure very close to the one accepted today (24,662 miles [39,459 kilometers], according to Eratosthenes, versus 24,901.55 miles [39,842.48 kilometers], the figure used today). (For more about Eratosthenes's measurement of Earth, see sidebar to "Angles, Curves, and Surfaces" in the Mathematics chapter. That chapter also contains a biography of Eratosthenes.)

Ptolemy sets the pattern for fifteen hundred years

Sadly, only one of these discoveries—Aristotle's proof of a spherical Earth—gained wide acceptance in the years that followed. Then again, virtually all of Aristotle's ideas (good or bad) received a hearing, simply because they came from the master himself. Aristarchus, by contrast, commanded no such attention, and his heliocentric model had few defenders.

Contrary to popular belief, Europeans in the time of Italian explorer Christopher Columbus (1451–1506) knew that the world is round, but due to the rejection of Eratosthenes's measurement, they had an extremely inaccurate estimate of its size. Perhaps if Columbus had known just how far it really was to Asia, he would never have set sail. But like most educated Europeans of the preceeding centuries, he believed that the distance around Earth was only about 18,000 miles (28,800 kilometers). This was much smaller than Eratosthenes's figure of 24,662 miles (39,459 kilometers) or the measurement accepted today, which is 24,901.55 miles (39,842.48 kilometers).

Columbus's ignorance in this matter owes much to the most influential figure in the physical sciences (other than Aristotle himself) prior to 1500: Ptolemy. Though he came from the same town as Eratosthenes—Alexandria, Egypt—and was aware of Eratosthenes's calculations, Ptolemy rejected these in favor of incorrect figures furnished by the philosopher Posidonius (c. 135–c. 51 B.C.E.). Nor was this the only misguided idea Ptolemy helped popularize.

Ptolemaic cosmology

Ptolemy's most influential work later became known to Europeans as the *Almagest,* not the title he gave it, but a version of the name bestowed to it by the Arabs, who called the book *al-majisti,* or "the greatest." And indeed, like the writings of Aristotle on physics, Ptolemy's system of astronomy and cosmology is impressive, though highly flawed.

Drawing on ideas that date back to Eudoxus, Ptolemy depicted the universe as a series of concentric spheres with circular orbits centered on Earth. In order to account for irregularities such as retrograde motion, he created an incredibly detailed system in which he essentially invented planetary paths and types of motion that made the geocentric system work.

Though Ptolemy exhibited brilliance in the way that he propped up the geocentric model, ensuring that it would remain dominant for many centuries to come, what he did was the exact opposite of science. He started with the conclusion that Earth is at the center of the universe, then adjusted the facts, and the interpretation of the facts, to fit this. True science, on the other hand, places its emphasis on facts, not theory, and when facts and theory do not line up, then it is the theory, not the facts, that must be adjusted or discarded.

Ptolemy's contribution to geography

In the area of geography, as opposed to astronomy, Ptolemy's ideas were much more valuable. As noted, even his use of Posidonius's incorrect measurement of Earth had its uses, since it indirectly influenced the beginning of European voyages to the Americas in 1492. Furthermore, in his eight-volume work *Hyphegesis geographike* (Guide to geography), Ptolemy helped popularize the use of latitude and longitude lines. First conceived by the Greek astronomer and mathematician Hipparchus (flourished 146–127 B.C.E.), these imaginary lines make it possible to pinpoint the location of a spot on Earth's surface.

In Ptolemy's time, people had no idea of the Earth's full size, so latitude and longitude measurements were made in relation to known places, such as Alexandria, Egypt. Furthermore, accurate measurements of longitude would not be possible until the 1700s, with the British development of precision timepieces, which provided exact information regarding the relationship between a particular spot and the Sun. Therefore many of Ptolemy's longitude figures were highly inaccurate, but at least he made an attempt to provide coordinates based on the knowledge available to him at the time.

Rejecting the widespread belief that a vast ocean, known to the ancients as "the Ocean Sea," surrounded the entire world, Ptolemy argued that in order to keep Earth in balance, there had to be a southern continent equal in weight to the area known by the Greeks and the Romans, Europe, north Africa, and western Asia. This southern continent he called *terra australis incognita,* or "unknown southern land." In fact much more of Earth's land is north of the Equator than south of it, but there were indeed not one but two southern continents, unknown to

Christopher Columbus departing on his first voyage. Scientists and explorers knew the world was round, but they seriously underestimated its size.
(© Bettmann/UPI-Bettmann. Reproduced by permission of the Corbis Corporation.)

A 1570 map of the Americas, drawn by Abraham Ortelius of Antwerp. Ptolemy popularized the use of longitude and latitude lines, as seen on this map, to pinpoint locations on Earth. **(© Bettmann. Reproduced by permission of the Corbis Corporation.)**

Europeans until centuries later: Australia and Antarctica. (At that time no one could imagine another entire hemisphere existed as well, the Western Hemisphere.)

Ptolemy had a major impact on cartographers, or mapmakers, for centuries after his death. For one thing, he presented a set of workable mathematical principles for representing the spherical surface of Earth on a flat page, always a problem for cartographers. He also established the practice of orienting maps with north at the top of the page. Today people take this for granted, but prior to Ptolemy, cartographers depicted the direction of the rising Sun, east, at the top of their maps. Ptolemy, however, chose to use a northward orientation, because the Mediterranean region that he knew extended twice as far east to west as it did north to south. In order to represent the area on a scroll, the form in which books appeared during his time, it was easier to make maps with north at the top.

The effect of Ptolemy's work

The greatest impact of Ptolemy's work came not from his geography, but from his astronomy and cosmology. In large part because he was among the last important scientific figures in the West for about a thousand years, the geocentric model of the universe became virtually set in stone. Whereas modern people must face the frightening awareness that Earth is just a tiny speck at the edge of the universe, people in the Middle Ages (c. 500–c. 1500 C.E.) lived with the comforting illusion that the cosmos was small and centered on Earth.

The Platonic Solids

The Greek philosopher Plato (c. 428–c. 348 B.C.E.) maintained that there are five shapes that illustrate perfection. This perfection lies in the fact that these are the only five three-dimensional objects that have vertices (edges) that are all alike, as well as faces that are a single kind of regular polygon (a closed shape with three or more sides, all straight.)

The simplest of these Platonic solids is the tetrahedron, a pyramid-like shape composed of four equilateral triangles, or triangles with sides of equal length. "Tetra-" means "four," signifying the four faces of that solid, while the octahedron, as its name suggests, has eight faces, and is composed of two four-sided pyramids, bottom-to-bottom. The icosahedron has five equilateral triangles around each of the vertices, making twenty faces, the maximum number of faces for a Platonic solid made of triangles.

The other two solids are composed, respectively, of squares and pentagons. The first of these is the cube, which needs no explanation, while the second is the dodecahedron (doh-dek-uh-HEED-rahn). The dodecahedron, which looks a little like a beach ball with squared sides, is what Plato suggested was the shape of atoms in outer space. Likewise he associated the other four solids with elements on Earth: fire (tetrahedron), earth (cube), air (octahedron), and water (icosahedron).

These ideas are useless to modern science, but the Platonic solids are still of interest—chiefly to mathematics—because they are the only closed shapes in which the faces and vertices are all the same. By contrast, a pyramid, for instance, has one four-sided face. Likewise the design of a soccer ball has interspersed hexagons and pentagons, because it would be impossible to fully cover a spherical object only with pentagons.

Actually, during much of the medieval period (or Middle Ages; c. 500–c. 1100 C.E.), Ptolemy himself was largely forgotten in Europe, along with most scholarship from the ancient world. Nonetheless, the geocentric model made as much sense to medieval people as it did to the ancients. By then, Aristotelian ideas about physics had won wide acceptance (though

Aristotle's writings themselves were largely unknown), and this reinforced geocentrism. Obviously Earth weighed a great deal, whereas the Moon, planets, and stars must be very light, since they floated in the sky—ideas that seemed to confirm Aristotle's assertions about the elements seeking their natural levels.

In medieval times, the Muslim world rediscovered Aristotle and Ptolemy, whose writings helped influence the burgeoning of Islamic science. Later, the writings of these Greek thinkers passed on to western Europe, where they became linked with Christian doctrine. Given that God had created man in his own image, as the Bible said, it seemed only appropriate that he would place his creation at the center of the universe, as Ptolemy's cosmology indicated.

But the heliocentric model of the universe proved to be much simpler to maintain than the geocentric one, because it did not involve the sorts of elaborate tricks required to make Ptolemy's cosmology workable. Thus the heliocentric model presented by Copernicus in 1530 was easier to understand than Ptolemy's, yet in the years to follow, it would face harsh opposition before gaining acceptance. (See essay "The Scientific Revolution" in this chapter.)

THE ISLAMIC WORLD TAKES THE LEAD

The Roman Empire began to decline in about 200 C.E., signaling the beginning of the end of the ancient world, which also meant an end to European progress in science. Within two centuries, the empire had divided into eastern and western halves, the western portion of which ceased to exist in 476. By that time, western Europe had been plunged into darkness that would last until about 1100, a period in which the focus was on mere survival rather than progress.

The Eastern Roman, or Byzantine, Empire, fared better. Based in Greece, it retained the teachings of the ancient world, but rather than moving forward, the Byzantines were content to rest on the successes of the past. The Mediterranean world was therefore ready for a fresh new force, an empire as dynamic as Greece and Rome had once been. By the mid-600s, it had emerged from Arabia, and within a century it had conquered most of western Asia, north Africa, and parts of Europe. This was the realm controlled by the Muslims, adherents of the Islamic faith.

Al-Ma'mun and the House of Wisdom

The first Islamic leader was the prophet Muhammad (c. 570–632), who upon his death designated a caliph, a spiritual and political leader, to suc-

Words to Know

astrolabe: A small instrument, used during ancient and medieval times, for calculating the positions of bodies in the heavens.

cosmology: A branch of astronomy concerned with the origin, structure, and evolution of the universe.

cosmos: The universe.

diffraction: That which occurs when a light ray passes close to an object and bends or separates as a result.

geocentric: Earth-centered.

heliocentric: Sun-centered.

optics: A realm of scientific study concerned with the formation and transmission of light.

reflection: That which occurs when light rays strike a smooth surface and bounce off at an angle equal to that of the incoming rays.

refraction: The bending of light as it passes at an angle from one transparent material into a second transparent material. Refraction accounts for the fact that objects under water appear to have a different size and location than they have in air.

ceed him. Early generations of caliphs concerned themselves with conquering new lands, but by the time of the caliph al-Ma'mun (ruled 813–833), they had turned their attention to other interests. Seeking to encourage scholarship in his empire, al-Ma'mun in 832 established the House of Wisdom in his capital city of Baghdad (in present-day Iraq.)

An early model for the scientific organizations and think tanks of today, the House of Wisdom served two purposes: translation and research. Initially its scholars focused on translating texts of Greek philosophy and science, ensuring that the wisdom of the ancients—which western Europe had largely forgotten—would be preserved. These translation

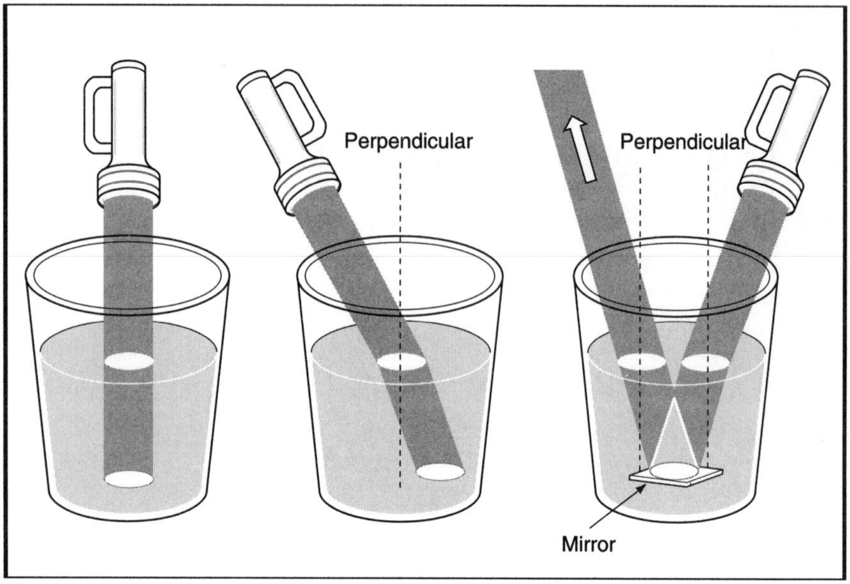

An illustration showing refraction, the perceived bending of light when viewed through a medium other than air. **(Reproduced by permission of the Gale Group.)**

efforts in turn encouraged new scholarship, and the next few centuries saw enormous scientific progress in the Muslim world.

Optics

Optics is the area of scientific study concerned with the production and transmission of light. It is a part of the physical sciences, though in premodern times it often involved an area more relevant to the life sciences: the mechanics of human vision. Another important aspect of early studies in optics was the interaction of light with physical objects, through reflection, refraction, or diffraction.

Reflection—what happens when one sees oneself in a mirror—occurs when light rays strike a smooth surface and bounce off at an angle equal to that of the incoming rays. Refraction is the bending of light as it passes at an angle from one transparent material into a second transparent material, and it accounts for the fact that objects under water appear to have a different size and location than they have in air. Finally, diffraction occurs when a light ray passes close to an object and bends or separates as a result.

Early studies

Arab and Persian studies in optics provide a clear example of the way in which Muslim scientists took inspiration from the Greeks, yet moved beyond Greek ideas. Concerned primarily with vision rather than light itself, Greek studies in optics had involved highly misguided ideas regarding how the eye sees. In a tradition dating perhaps to the great mathemati-

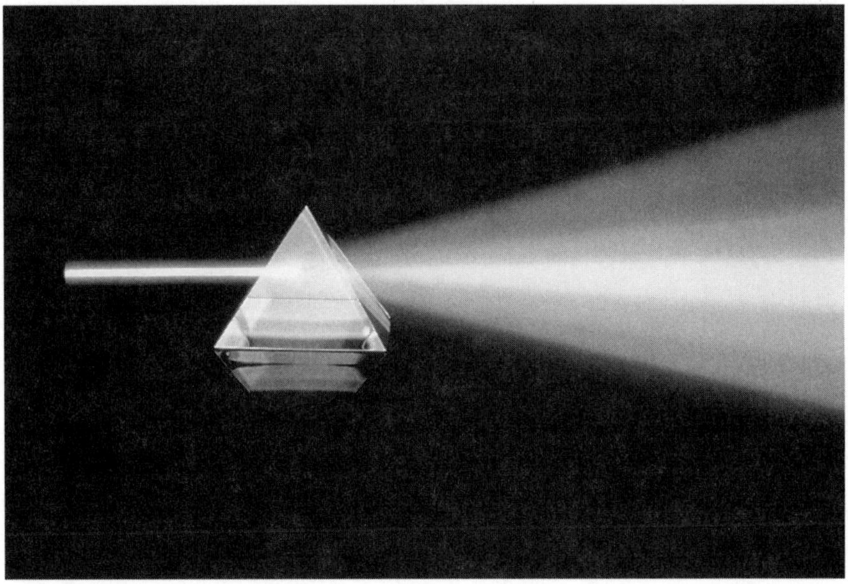

An illustration of a prism diffracting a beam of light into a spectrum of colors. (Photograph by Peter Angelo Simon. Reproduced by permission of the Stock Market.)

cian **Euclid** (c. 330–c. 260 B.C.E.; see biography in Mathematics chapter), the Greeks believed that light does not come from the Sun or some other external source; rather, they believed, it emanates from the eye, which sends out rays that make objects visible.

In addition to this theory, known as extromission, the Greeks had another, almost equally preposterous notion, known as intromission, the idea that vision is the result of objects emitting thin films or images of themselves, which the eye receives. The Arab philosopher al-Kindi (died c. 870) successfully critiqued intromission theory: if intromission were true, he suggested, then a circle would always look perfectly circular, whereas in fact a circle viewed on edge looks like a straight line.

Alhazen

The first scientist to challenge extromission was **Alhazen** (965–1039; see biography in this chapter), whose work emphasized experimentation and critical thinking. In his *Book of Optics* (about 1027), Alhazen discussed the subject of vision and light, explaining correctly that the eye receives light rays rather than sending them out. Furthermore, he extended optics beyond the subject of vision to the study of light propagation (transmission).

Alhazen conducted extensive experiments in reflection and refraction, outlining the basic laws of refraction and establishing the practice of using a laboratory for experimental optical research. He also attempted to develop a theory of rainbows more accurate than that offered by **Aristotle**

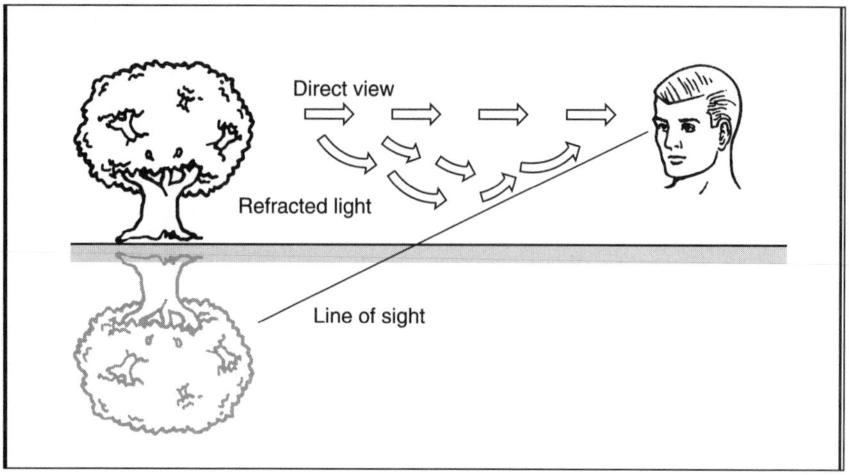

An illustration demonstrating how refracted light can create a mirage in a person's line of sight. **(Reproduced by permission of the Gale Group.)**

(384–322 B.C.E.; see biography in Life Science chapter). According to the great Greek philosopher, water droplets in clouds form a continuous surface, rather like a mirror. Alhazen agreed with this basic premise, but whereas Aristotle had envisioned a convex (curved like the outside of a sphere) mirror, Alhazen proposed a concave one, that is, curved like the inside of a sphere.

Though he never reached a real understanding of the rainbow phenomenon, Alhazen established a useful method for studying rainbows by transmitting sunlight through glass spheres filled with water. He was also the first thinker to observe the refraction of light in the atmosphere, which distorts the appearance of objects near the horizon. (This is the cause behind a mirage, for instance.)

Later Muslim optical studies

Alhazen's contemporary Avicenna (Ibn Sina; 980–1037; see biography in Life Science chapter) dismissed both Aristotle's and Alhazen's explanation of the rainbow. After carefully observing sunlight diffracted by water droplets formed while watering a garden, Avicenna concluded that the rainbow resulted from the reflection of light off of individual droplets rather than entire clouds.

Two centuries later, the Persian scientist Qutb al-Din al-Shirazi (1236–1311) inspired his student Kamal al-Din Farisi (c. 1260–c. 1320) to reexamine Alhazen's optical theories, particularly his ideas about the rainbow. As a result, Farisi correctly recognized that the spheres of water Alhazen had used should be compared to droplets of water, not a mass of cloud, and that the rainbow resulted from the refraction of sunlight on and in the droplet. At the same time, a European scholar, German monk

A Muslim at prayer. Muslims always face in the direction of Mecca when praying. **(Photograph by Charles Rex Arbogast. Reproduced by permission of AP/Wide World Photos.)**

Dietrich (or Theodoric) von Freiburg (c. 1266–c. 1308), was studying the same problems and reached similar conclusions—but he went even further than Farisi in understanding the causes of the rainbow.

Astronomy

Astronomy was important in the Muslim world for several reasons, not the least because the Koran, Islam's holy book, encourages Muslims to use the stars for guidance. Since the Islamic calendar is lunar, or based on the Moon's cycle's, the times of Ramadan (the holy month in which Muslims go without food during daylight hours) and various other religious festivals are regulated by the Moon. Likewise the hours of the five daily prayers, required of all Muslims, could be determined through the observation of celestial bodies.

Furthermore, the prayer wall in mosques (Muslim houses of worship) is always aligned along the *qibla*, the direction of Islam's most sacred site: a shrine called the Ka'aba in the holy city of Mecca (now in Saudi Arabia). Once again, astronomical readings were necessary in order to provide accurate data for the placement of the *qibla*.

The influence of Ptolemy

Ptolemy's *Almagest* (see essay "Aristotle and Ptolemy: Wrong Ideas That Defined the World" in this chapter) first appeared in Arabic during the early 800s. Despite its many flaws, the *Almagest* was far more advanced and comprehensive than any other astronomical work up to that time, and Islamic astronomers readily adopted Ptolemy's geocentric (Earth-centered) view of the universe.

Soon, however, scholars at the House of Wisdom began finding errors in Ptolemy's work. They initially responded to this by attempting to improve the mathematics involved, so that the equations would work out as Ptolemy had intended them. In time, however, Muslim scientists began to challenge the assumptions at the very heart of Ptolemy's cosmology, or model of the universe.

Once again, Alhazen was in the lead. Intent on establishing a harmony between the mathematical and the physical aspects of astronomy, he rejected the use of mathematical models that did not correspond to the actual movement of bodies in space. Rather than simply prop up Ptolemy's flawed calculations, he argued that Ptolemy's mathematics should be abandoned, along with some of his ideas concerning planetary motion. Alhazen stopped short of rejecting the Ptolemaic system altogether; yet the Persian astronomer Abu Ubayd al-Juzjani (died c. 1070) went so far as to construct a non-Ptolemaic model of the universe.

Spanish Arab astronomers

Though al-Juzjani's efforts were ultimately unsuccessful, Muslim astronomers, particularly in Spain, continued to challenge the Ptolemaic system. In most cases, they did this not because they disagreed with his geocentric model, but because the complicated forms of planetary motion Ptolemy had introduced, simply to make his cosmology workable, disagreed with Aristotle's physics. According to Aristotle, all the planets should be moving in fixed circles around Earth and only around Earth; however, Ptolemy's astronomy required that planets move in other ways as well.

This line of criticism reached its height in the work of the Spanish Arab philosopher and scientist **Averroës** (1126–1198; see biography in Life Sciences chapter). Averroës had probably been influenced by his teacher, the philosopher Ibn Tufayl (Muhammad ibn 'Abd al-Malik ibn Muhammad ibn Muhammad ibn Tufayl al-Qaysi; died c. 1185), whose students also included the astronomer al-Bitruji (died 1204). Al-Bitruji attempted to reform the Ptolemaic astronomy by returning to the less complex model presented earlier by Eudoxus (see essay "Aristotle and Ptolemy: Wrong Ideas That Defined the World" in this chapter), but this system proved even less accurate than Ptolemy's.

The observatory at Maragheh

The astronomers gathered at the famous observatory in Maragheh took a different approach. Located in what is now Azerbaijan, the observatory was established by Hülegü Khan (c. 1217–1265), grandson of the fierce Mongol conqueror Genghis Khan (c. 1162-1227). Hülegü, who established an empire that controlled much of southwestern Asia, placed the Persian astronomer al-Tusi (1201–1274) in charge. Al-Tusi created an observatory that drew some of the best Muslim, Christian, Jewish, and Chinese astronomers of the time.

The scholars at the Maragheh school, led by al-Tusi, sought to restore Ptolemy's system by simplifying it and removing some of its inconsistencies. To this end, they built physical models of the solar system, intending to show how a version of Ptolemy's system could be workable. Thus their approach was the opposite of Alhazen's: instead of reforming the mathematics, they intended to develop a better understanding of the actual movement of the planets. All such efforts were ultimately doomed to failure in light of subsequent discoveries about the universe. (See essay "The Scientific Revolution" in this chapter.) But in their willingness to discard Ptolemy's insistence that the planets moved in perfect circles, the Maragheh astronomers helped open the way for later progress.

Astronomical tools

It should be remembered that prior to the invention of the telescope in the early 1600s, astronomers had no tools for observation other than the naked eye. They did, however, possess other tools, most notably the astrolabe, a small instrument for calculating the positions of heavenly bodies. Used during the late ancient (up to about 500 C.E.) and medieval (or Middle Ages; c. 500–c. 1500 C.E.) periods, the astrolabe was essentially a flat model of the universe, consisting of a movable framework with markings representing various bright stars. The astrolabe could be used to find the time of day, or the times when a star would rise, set, or be at its highest point in the night sky.

Arab astronomers made a number of modifications and expanded the usefulness of the astrolabe, for example, by making special models for use at particular latitudes or locations. Later, Europeans were so slavish in their imitation of Muslim-built astrolabes that they produced models whose markings provided incorrect readings in Europe, which was farther to the north than the Arab world. Another common astronomical instrument was the quadrant, or quarter-circle, which calculated the angle of a star or the Sun. As with the astrolabe, Islamic astronomers improved upon the design of ancient quadrants, making them bigger and more versatile.

Tables, timekeeping, and trigonometry

Muslim scientists used the measurements they made with these instruments to calculate astronomical tables listing the positions of planets, the lunar phases, predictions of eclipses, and other astronomical phenomena.

Arabic calligraphy. Arabic requires an entirely different script than the Latin alphabet, the basis of many modern languages. **(Reproduced by permission of Cory Langley.)**

The most popular of these tables was also one of the earliest, created by the Arab astronomer and mathematician al-Battani (c. 858–929). His astronomical tables were adopted by Europeans and used until the middle of the fifteenth century.

Many of the problems Islamic astronomers were called upon to solve required the development and use of new mathematical methods. For instance, determining the *qibla* involved complex problems in spherical trigonometry, which led to new developments in mathematics by **al-Khwarizmi** (c. 780–c. 850; see biography in Mathematics chapter) and others. The determination of the exact time that prayer was to begin involved spherical geometry and influenced Ibn Yunus (950–1009) in the establishment of new methods. In addition, Ibn Yunus compiled useful timekeeping tables that were widely imitated. The timekeeping tables of the astronomer al-Khalili (c. 1320–c. 1380) in Syria proved so accurate that they remained in use well into the 1800s.

Europe learns from the Muslim world

While Islam flourished, western Europe stagnated; then, in about 1100, the West began to recover. Much of this recovery resulted from contact with the Muslim world, a fact that involved many ironies. First of all, at a time when western Europe had retreated to a primitive state, and the Byzantine Empire had virtually shut its doors to the West, it was the Arabs and the Persians who preserved European learning. Secondly, European-Muslim contact, ultimately so beneficial to the West, was almost entirely a result of wars based in bitter religious and cultural hatreds.

The Rainbow Connecting Muslim and European Scientists

Following the lead of **Alhazen** (965–1039; see biography in this chapter), the Persian scientist Kamal al-Din Farisi (c. 1260–c. 1320) used spheres filled with water as a means of studying the rainbow. He correctly recognized that the rainbow came from the reflection and refraction (bending) of sunlight on and in an individual water droplets, not an entire cloud.

By the time of Farisi, a number of European scholars were also studying optics. The first of these was the English theologian Robert Grosseteste (c. 1175–1253), whose student, **Roger Bacon** (c. 1220–1292; see biography in Technology and Invention chapter), was the first to suggest that lenses could correct poor eyesight. Great scholars such as Albertus Magnus (c. 1200–1280) also investigated the properties of lenses and the causes behind rainbows.

Around the same time that Farisi had his breakthrough in this area, the German monk Dietrich (or Theodoric) of Freiburg (c. 1250–c. 1310) reached similar conclusions, and went further. Dietrich also used glass spheres filled with water and recognized that the rainbow came from the interaction of sunlight with the individual cloud drops. Likewise he described and depicted the particular types of reflection and refraction that produce a rainbow. In addition, however, he correctly explained that the different colors of the rainbow were a result of the sunlight striking the water droplets at different angles.

Though they were almost exact contemporaries, working in the same area of study, it is unlikely, given the technology of communication and travel existing at the time, that Dietrich and Farisi knew of one another. Therefore Dietrich's discoveries were almost certainly independent of Farisi's; nonetheless, like most European scientists of the late Middle Ages (c. 1100–c. 1500 C.E.), Dietrich owed an enormous debt to Arab thinkers such as Alhazen, who had kept learning alive at a time when it had virtually died out in Europe.

In addition to the Crusades (1095–1291), religious wars fought primarily in what is now Israel, Lebanon, Syria, and Egypt, Europeans engaged Muslims in southern Italy and Sicily, parts of which were in Arab hands from the 800s to the early 1000s, and Spain. The Muslims conquered southern Italy and Sicily in 711, but over the centuries Christian forces gathered their power and finally drove out the last Arab rulers in 1492. Though these efforts at reconquest may have been justified (unlike the Crusades, which were clearly an unprovoked invasion of Arab lands), it is questionable whether the resumption of European and Christian rule improved the quality of life in Spain and Sicily.

At least some of the Muslim kingdoms that controlled these areas had been relatively enlightened, for instance treating Jews with great toleration, whereas the European kingdoms that took their place, particularly in Spain, were typically anti-Semitic. Furthermore, it is hard to imagine that scholarship would have flourished in these areas if they had remained under European rule during the Middle Ages (c. 500–c. 1500 C.E.). As it was, the new European conquerors of Spain, Sicily, southern Italy, and parts of the Holy Land (the area equivalent to modern-day Israel and Lebanon), which Europeans controlled for a few years, inherited vast intellectual riches, which they ultimately passed on to the European continent as a whole.

Translations of scientific texts

Just as the Muslims had once translated Greek texts into Arabic, now Europeans began translating Arab versions of Greek texts back into a European language, Latin. They also translated original Arabic works by Avicenna, Averroës, and others. The translators were virtually all monks and men of the church, as indeed were most learned men of the Middle Ages, and they came from a variety of countries. Among the most important medieval translators were the Englishmen Adelard of Bath (flourished in the twelfth century) and Robert of Chester (flourished 1140s); France's William of Moerbeke (c. 1215–c. 1286); and the Italians Gerard of Cremona (c. 1114–1187) and Campanus of Novara (died 1296).

Greatest among these was Gerard, who in about 1140 traveled from northern Italy to Spain in search of Ptolemy's *Almagest*. He found a copy in the city of Toledo, and learned Arabic in order to translate it into Latin. While there he became aware of numerous Arabic texts on many other subjects and devoted the next thirty or forty years to translating these. Most of his predecessors (the first text translated from Arabic appeared in Europe during the 900s) had prepared translations word-for-word from Arabic into Latin, which resulted in nonsensical sentences and mangled meanings. Gerard, however, had such a good command of the languages, and such a clear understanding of the subject matter, that he was able to produce highly accurate and readable translations.

ALCHEMY, ASTROLOGY, AND EDUCATION IN MEDIEVAL EUROPE

From about 800 to 1200 the Islamic world held the lead in the physical sciences, especially in the study of optics and astronomy. Then, beginning in about 1100, Europe began to recover from centuries of stagnation, and the pace of progress gradually increased from a standstill to a full-fledged scientific revolution by the 1500s. This recovery was largely a result of contact with the Muslim world, much of it, ironically, in the form of war, especially the religious conflicts known as the Crusades (1095–1291).

This was only one of several ironic facts about the European recovery of the late Middle Ages, a time in which many a force for progress proved also to be a barrier against it. Universities, which emerged in the 1100s as centers of study in the physical science, within a few centuries became bastions of outmoded ideas. Likewise, the texts used in those schools—ancient Greek or medieval Arab writings on science—contained at least as much misinformation as they did genuine knowledge. And toward the end of this period, the church, which had long supported learning, acted to protect itself against new wisdom that threatened its authority.

Two of the principal areas of study in the physical sciences during the Middle Ages, astrology and alchemy, were not scientific at all. The first of these—the study of the positions and the movements of the stars, planets, and other heavenly bodies in the belief that these have an effect on people's individual lives—had existed since ancient times. In the medieval (or Middle Ages; c. 500–c. 1500 C.E.) world it acquired such respect that it became a regular course of study in universities.

On the other hand, alchemy was an "outlaw" discipline, practiced primarily by magicians, mystics, and others on the fringes of society, including some true scientists. Founded on the idea that common things can be transformed into extraordinary ones, for instance, that ordinary metals can become gold, alchemy is rooted in misconceptions about the physical world. Yet by encouraging experimentation with various substances, it was actually a forerunner of chemistry and helped end the dominance of the four elements theory.

The rebirth of European education

The establishment and development of schools was critical to the European recovery that took place during the period from about 900 to 1200. Prior to that time, Europeans had few examples of education other than that provided by the Roman Marcus Terentius Varro (116–27 B.C.E.), who had outlined the model of the nine liberal arts taught throughout the Roman

Words to Know

alchemy: A set of mystical beliefs based on the idea that ordinary matter can be perfected. In the Middle Ages this became a semi-scientific discipline concerned, for instance, with attempts to turn various metals into gold.

astrology: The study of the positions and the movements of the stars, planets, and other heavenly bodies in the belief that these have an effect on people's individual lives.

astronomy: The scientific study of the stars and other heavenly bodies, in particular, their positions and movements.

cosmology: A branch of astronomy concerned with the origin, structure, and evolution of the universe.

geocentric: Earth-centered.

Scientific Revolution: A period of accelerated scientific discovery that completely reshaped the world. Usually dated from about 1550 to 1700, the Scientific Revolution saw the origination of the scientific method and the introduction of ideas such as the heliocentric universe and gravity. Its leading figures included Nicolaus Copernicus, Galileo Galilei, and Isaac Newton.

zodiac: An imaginary band in the heavens, divided into twelve constellations or astrological signs.

Empire. Later, medicine and architecture were dropped from the lineup, leaving just seven. Of these, three were known as the trivium—grammar, rhetoric (the art of speaking and writing), and logic—while four others constituted the quadrivium: arithmetic, geometry, astronomy, and music.

One of many popular misconceptions about the Middle Ages is the idea that the Catholic Church was the enemy of education. In fact, with the decline and fall of the Roman Empire and the subsequent rise of Christianity (about 200 to 600 C.E.), the church became the home and protector of educated men. Nonetheless, education suffered severely when recently nomadic tribes such as the Goths (a Germanic people who overran the Roman Empire in the early centuries following its decline)

A Benedictine monk studying in a monastery library. Contrary to popular belief, the church was a friend to learning throughout most of the Middle Ages.
(© Stephanie Maze/Corbis-Bettmann. Reproduced by permission of the Corbis Corporation.)

and the Huns (a nomadic people from central Asia who seized control of large portions of central and eastern Europe under its leader Attila around 450 C.E.) took the place of the sophisticated Romans as the rulers of western Europe.

The greatest western European ruler between about 350 and 1100 was Charlemagne (742–814), who controlled what is now France, Germany, and the countries in between. (This was the first version of the Holy Roman Empire, which in various incarnations would remain a potent force in European politics for almost a thousand years.) Disgusted by the poor state of education, Charlemagne commissioned the English scholar Alcuin (c. 732–804) to reform the schools in his empire. The same period also saw the establishment of the first European institution of higher learning, the medical school at Salerno in southern Italy. (For more about Salerno, as well as Bologna [discussed below], see "The Reawakening of the Life Sciences in Europe" in the Life Science chapter.)

Universities

The first true university was established in the Italian city of Bologna (buh-LOAN-yuh) during the late 1000s. Students came from far away to study at Bologna, and the residents of the city often discriminated against them, for instance, by charging them higher rates for food and lodging. Then in 1158 the Holy Roman emperor Frederick I Barbarossa (c. 1123–1190) granted privileges to the students at Bologna, rights that would eventually be extended to students all over Europe.

The mid- to late 1100s saw the establishment of famous universities in Paris, France, and Oxford, England. During the next few centuries, universities (the term itself was coined in 1221) sprang up all over Europe. Once again, the students often found themselves in conflict with the locals, a situation also true in many university towns today. Furthermore, the universities often faced internal conflicts that led to the formation of new schools. Thus for instance a group of disgruntled professors and students from Bologna established the University of Padua in 1222.

The style of teaching in these medieval universities was very different from that of modern schools. Classes consisted of a professor reading aloud, and commenting on, an established text, usually by one of the great thinkers of ancient Greece, while the students copied down the lecture word for word. This gave the students both the original text and a learned commentary from the professor. All lectures were in Latin, the language of educated men (no women attended universities in medieval times) throughout Europe.

Though universities attempted to cater to the needs of the public, especially since students paid lecturers directly and could boycott a teacher they did not like, they tended to stick to old models, including the seven liberal arts of Roman times. For a time, this arrangement worked well, but as Europeans' educational horizons began to expand in the 1300s (thanks, once again, to continued contact with the Islamic world), the universities began to seem stuck in the past. By the 1500s many critics regarded the universities as places of backward, unimportant studies. (This may be the origin of the association between the trivium and trivia, or facts of limited significance.)

Scholasticism

While medieval universities still flourished during the 1200s, they became home to such great medieval minds as the German scientist Albertus Magnus (c. 1200–1280) and his more famous pupil, the Italian philosopher Thomas Aquinas (1225–1274). Both were priests, as indeed were most learned Europeans up until about 1300, and Thomas is notable for his role as a leading figure in the scholastic movement.

As its name implies, scholasticism had its roots in the universities. Its focus lay in the joining of Christian theology with Greek science and philosophy, particularly the ideas of **Aristotle** (384–322 B.C.E.; see biography and essay "Aristotle and Ptolemy: Wrong Ideas That Defined the World" in Life Science chapter). Earlier, **Averroës** (1126–1198; see biography in Life Science chapter) and Moses ben Maimon (Maimonides; 1135–1204) had attempted the same synthesis between Aristotelian ideas and the Muslim and Jewish faiths respectively. Then, the French philosopher Peter

A statue of Charlemagne from the Aachen Cathedral in Germany. The Holy Roman Emperor, with the help of the English scholar Alcuin, attempted to reform education. **(© Archivo Iconografico, S.A./Corbis. Reproduced by permission of the Corbis Corporation.)**

Abelard (1079–c. 1144) had begun the movement to apply the same concept within the realm of Christianity.

Originally scholasticism met with hostility from church leaders, who rejected it because Aristotle was not a Christian. Yet Thomas Aquinas and others succeeded in showing that there was no necessary conflict between Aristotelian thought and Christianity, and indeed that certain ideas of Aristotle's—for instance, the concept of a Prime Mover in the universe—actually fit well with Christian beliefs. Within a short time, Aristotelian ideas became so firmly entrenched that thinkers who challenged them risked being perceived as opponents of Christianity.

The science of astrology

Astrology has a long history that dates back to ancient Babylonia (see essay "Gazing at the Stars: How Science Began," in this chapter). Eventually astrological ideas made their way west, but in the heyday of Greek civilization, scholars were at least as interested in genuine astronomy as they were in the false science of astrology. (They knew of no distinction between the two, since they believed that astrology was real.)

OPPOSITE PAGE Exeter College Chapel's spire rises above the sixteenth-century buildings of Brasenose College of Oxford University in England. **(© Eye Ubiquitous/Corbis. Reproduced by permission of the Corbis Corporation.)**

As Greece began to decline and Roman influence increased during the period from about 300 to 100 B.C.E., astrology took on a different character. Instead of focusing on grand predictions regarding the fate of whole societies, astrologers began to concern themselves with everyday matters. Among the areas of interest to astrologers in late Roman times was the application of their art in the area of medicine.

Most astrological literature of Roman times was written in Greek, a language largely unknown in the West during the early Middle Ages, so even the non-science of astrology was lost to Europeans of that time. Then, during the 1100s and 1200s, the discovery of Arabic texts, and the rediscovery of Greek texts in translation from the Arabic, finally exposed European scholars to astrological studies.

Horoscopes

The late medieval period (or late Middle Ages; c. 1100–c. 1500 C.E.) also saw the use of astrology to cast individual astrological charts, or horoscopes. Based on the position of the stars at the moment of a person's birth, astrologers believed, it was possible to predict his or her future. In addition, astrologers cast horoscopes for specific events; for instance, in preparing for war, a king might consult an astrologer to ensure that the time was right. Medical astrologers, on the other hand, could cast retroactive or back-dated horoscopes to determine the configurations of planets that had caused particular diseases.

If events happened to occur as predicted, or, in the case of medical astrology, if the patient happened to get better, then both the astrologer and the science of astrology received credit. If, on the other hand, things did not go as planned, the practitioner might be condemned, but the reputation of astrology itself did not suffer.

Powerful endorsements

For all its absurdity, astrology seemed to enjoy approval from some of the Western world's greatest minds, not to mention God himself. In his influential work *Timaeus*, Plato (c. 428–c. 348 B.C.E.) had discussed the divine nature of certain heavenly bodies and their direct relationship to life on Earth, ideas that seemed like an endorsement of astrology. More impor-

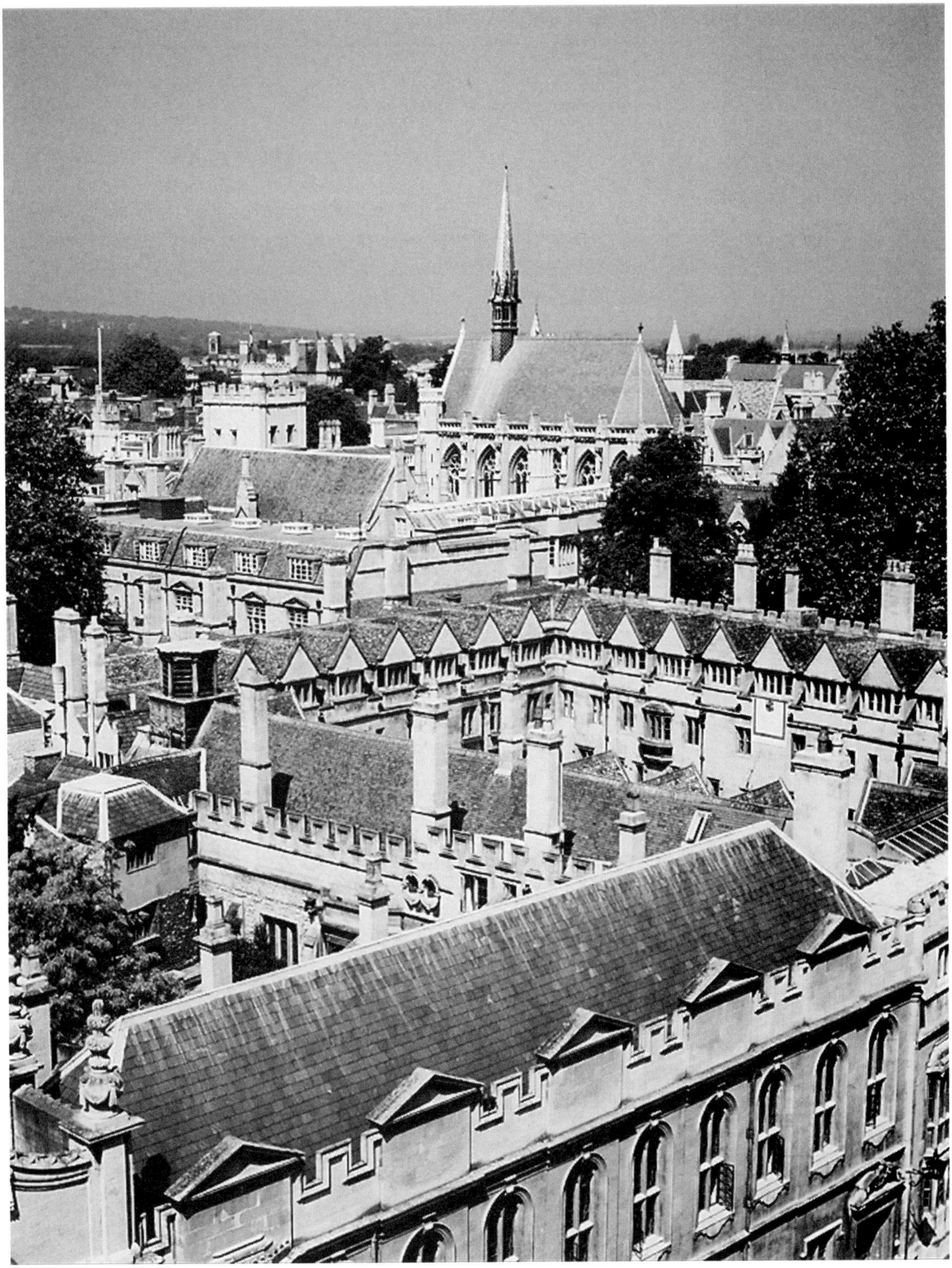

tantly, Plato's student Aristotle, generally not a friend of mystics, had suggested that events in the sublunary sphere (see essay "Aristotle and Ptolemy: Wrong Ideas That Defined the World" in this chapter) were determined by the movement of heavenly bodies, guided by divine influence.

Proponents of astrology even pointed to the Christian church, which has typically condemned all forms of fortune-telling and soothsaying, including astrology. Yet since God had sent a star to announce Jesus Christ's birth, this seemed like an endorsement from on high, and medieval zodiac charts sometimes showed an image of Christ. Indeed, Christian theologians of the Middle Ages typically opposed only those forms of astrology that were based on the idea that neither God nor humans could change the fate decreed by the stars. As long as an astrologer's interpretation allowed for human free will and divine intervention, two cornerstones of Christian faith, church leaders were willing to accept it.

A respectable field of study

European interest in astrology coincided with an age of increasing intellectual activity. During the Middle Ages (c. 500–c. 1500 C.E.), also called the Dark Ages to reflect the lack of intellectual pursuits, people were actually so unenlightened that they had no concept even of pseudo- or false sciences such as astrology, let alone real science.

The curious relationship between astrology and the reemerging European intellectual community is illustrated by the adoption of astrological studies as a part of the curriculum (the course of studies offered) in many universities. As strange as it may seem, there was actually a time when the most prestigious schools in Europe offered degrees in astrology, something with no more scientific basis than palm-reading.

The end of astrology

In fact, astrology reached its peak as a respectable field of study in the 1400s and 1500s, when Europe was fully out of the Middle Ages and embarking on the period of rapid change, and intellectual and artistic rebirth, known as the Renaissance. Far from being seen as superstition, astrology in medicine, for instance, seemed to link the medical practice to the world of science and mathematics. Furthermore, demonstrating competence in astrological computations was one of the ways a learned physician could separate himself from a quack.

Yet whenever something reaches its peak, that also means it is beginning to decline, and so it was with astrology. The 1500s saw the birth of the three men who would bring an end to astrology as a serious field of study: **Nicolaus Copernicus** (1473–1543; see biography in this chapter), **Galileo Galilei** (1564–1642; see biography in this chapter), and **Johannes Kepler**

(1571–1630; see biography in this chapter). Astrology really only makes sense if Earth is the center of the universe, and by destroying the old geocentric model, these men dealt it a blow from which it would never recover. They also helped usher in the Scientific Revolution (about 1550–1700), a period that saw the emergence of new ways to study the physical world, a scientific approach that made pursuits such as astrology seem downright silly.

Alchemy

Alchemy, which is based on the idea that physical substances can be perfected, had its origins in ancient Egypt and China. In the West, the Egyptian city of Alexandria, a center of the Greek-speaking world, likewise became a center of alchemical study. Among the alchemists who resided there was Mary the Jewess (flourished in the first century C.E.), one of the few notable female physical scientists prior to 1800, whose inventions was the double boiler, still known in French-speaking countries as the *bain-marie* or "Mary's bath."

An astrological chart showing Christian imagery (top), zodiacal signs (middle), and Earth below. **(Reproduced by permission of the Corbis Corporation.)**

When the Arabs conquered Egypt in 642, alchemy spread within Islamic culture. Among its leading proponents was Geber (Jabir ibn Hayyan; c. 721–c. 815), who synthesized several new compounds. Arab alchemists worked with mercury and sulfur, believing that these could be combined in various proportions to produce different metals. Alchemy made its way to Europe through Arab-controlled Spain but did not become widely known until the 1100s, when Spanish scholars translated Arabic works into Latin. Many common chemical terms, such as "alcohol" and "alkali," as well as the word "alchemy" itself, derive from the Arabic.

Beliefs of alchemists

Alchemists believed that if they could only manipulate conditions properly, they could change the balance of elements in a substance, thus causing a change. They therefore sought what they called the philosopher's stone, a magical substance that would make such a change, or transmutation, easier.

Gold was key to the philosophy of alchemy, not only because of the metal's rarity and corresponding value, but also because it did not decay, rust, or tarnish. Thus the idea of changing ordinary metals into gold became associated with the concepts of incorruptibility and regeneration, or renewal. Just as the Chinese believed that eating from golden dishes led to long life, medieval Europeans came to associate gold and alchemy with immortality (everlasting life) and resurrection. The transmutation of lead or other "base metals" into gold became a symbol of God's grace in the religious conversion of a sinner.

Astrology was an important part of the alchemist's studies because the positions of the planets and the stars were believed to influence the outcome of their work. Each celestial body supposedly corresponded to a particular metal. For instance, the Sun was associated with gold, the Moon with silver, Mars with iron, Venus with copper, Jupiter with tin, Saturn with lead, and Mercury with the metal mercury, or quicksilver.

Alchemy's contributions to science

Alchemists invented the process of distillation, which became one of their most important techniques. Distillation is the use of heat to separate the components of a liquid and/or gas; for instance, distilling water separates the water from salt and other impurities. To the alchemists, however, distillation of a substance meant that they were separating its essence or spirit from its lower elements. This idea is still reflected in the use of the word "spirits" to describe certain substances.

Using distillation, False Geber (a later Spanish mystic who modeled his work on that of Geber in the 1300s) produced *aqua regia,* a mixture of hydrochloric and nitric acids, the first known liquid in which gold would dissolve. Aqua regia came to be known as the alkahest, or universal sol-

Medical Astrology

In the late Middle Ages, astrology not only seemed like a genuine science, but one that could provide an aid to doctors in diagnosing and treating patients. Medical astrologers believed that the twelve signs of the zodiac governed specific parts of the body, and astrological charts of the era often included lists of herbs said to be particularly effective at specific times.

Astrological medicine required knowing the exact time at which the patient became ill. Combining this with knowledge of the astrological correspondences among the "seven planets" (see essay "Gazing at the Stars: How Science Began" in this chapter) and the seven metals known in the Middle Ages (gold, copper, silver, lead, tin, iron, and mercury), the physician could supposedly predict the course that the illness would take.

Combining astrology with another theory that had even less merit, physicians used the zodiac charts to help determine the imbalance of the Four Humors (see essay "Greek Physicians Transform the Life Sciences" in Life Science chapter) in an ill patient. For example, the Moon supposedly influenced the flow of blood in the veins just as it did the tides, so before a surgeon bled a patient (bloodletting was then a common practice), he checked the position of that planet.

Doctors might also recommend that a patient wear a specific talisman, or magic charm, containing an appropriate astrological image engraved on a precious stone. However, the relationships that supposedly existed between the heavenly bodies and the human body were so complex, numerous, and contradictory that in practice it was impossible to carry out any operation without breaking some astrological rule.

vent, the next best thing to the philosopher's stone. In addition, alchemists discovered a number of other acids, most notably sulfuric acid. These acids ultimately had a number of practical applications, and their uses in industry later helped fuel the Industrial Revolution that began in about 1750. More importantly, alchemists' ceaseless experimentation with, and study of, chemicals formed the basis for what became chemistry.

Alchemy spreads and changes

European alchemists of the Middle Ages included some of Europe's greatest scientists, such as **Roger Bacon** (c. 1220–1292; see biography in Technology and Invention chapter) of England, as well as Ramon Llull (c. 1235–1316) and Arnau de Villanova (c. 1235–1312) of Spain. Bacon exemplified the ways in which alchemy gradually moved in the direction of genuine science: though he experimented with a number of mystic ideas, he had a generally good scientific grounding (at least, for the time in which he lived), and helped steer European thinkers in progressive directions.

By the 1500s scientists were beginning to turn away from the more mystical elements of alchemy and instead began to apply the practical knowledge it had given them to the study of medicines and disease. A leading figure in this movement was **Paracelsus** (1493–1541; see biography in Life Science chapter), who greatly influenced Renaissance medicine.

The true turning point between alchemy and chemistry came with the publication of *The Sceptical Chymist* (1661) by British scientist **Robert Boyle** (1627–1691l see biography in this chapter), who, though trained in alchemy, moved beyond it. Boyle, often regarded as the father of chemistry, introduced the idea of elements as substances that cannot be broken down to form other substances, and he rejected the alchemists' claim that one element can become another.

Thereafter, while alchemy continued to exist, it became associated primarily with magic and the occult (involving supernatural or supernormal powers). Mainstream chemists were often embarrassed by it while continuing to make use of the substances and techniques developed by their alchemist predecessors. In fact, they had no need for such shame. Though alchemy is based on impossibilities, it is much closer to true science than astrology. And whereas astrology ceased to be useful to science in ancient times, alchemy greatly advanced human learning, paving the way for the many great developments in chemistry that followed during later centuries.

THE SCIENTIFIC REVOLUTION

With the exception of early studies in astronomy and a few contributions by thinkers of the Middle Ages (c. 500–c. 1500 C.E.), the physical sciences experienced very little progress prior to about 1500. This stagnation resulted primarily from continued acceptance of the mistaken ideas put forward by **Aristotle** (384–322 B.C.E.; see biography in Life Science chapter) and **Ptolemy** (c. 100–c. 170; see biography in this chapter).

For centuries, developments in the physical sciences lagged far behind those in mathematics and technology or, to a lesser extent, the life sci-

Words to Know

acceleration: A change in velocity over time. The acceleration due to gravity, for instance, is 32 feet (9.8 meters) per second per second, meaning that for every second an object falls, its velocity is increasing as well.

celestial: Of the skies or heavens.

cosmology: A branch of astronomy concerned with the origin, structure, and evolution of the universe.

cosmos: The universe.

geocentric: Earth-centered.

heliocentric: Sun-centered.

inertia: The tendency of objects in motion to remain in motion, and objects at rest to remain at rest, unless acted upon by some outside force.

kinematics: The study of how objects move.

mechanics: A branch of physics concerned with the study of bodies in motion.

retrograde motion: The apparent backward movement, or reversal of direction, by outer planets in the solar system. In fact retrograde motion is simply an optical illusion, created by the fact that Earth is orbiting the Sun much faster than the outer planets are.

scientific method: A set of principles and procedures for systematic study, introduced primarily by Galileo Galilei, and still used in the sciences. The scientific method consists of four essential parts: the statement of a problem to be studied; the gathering of scientific data through observation and experimentation; the formulation of hypotheses or theories; and the testing of those hypotheses. The results of testing may lead to a restatement of the problem, or an entirely new problem to be analyzed, which starts the process over again.

Scientific Revolution: A period of accelerated scientific discovery that completely reshaped the world. Usually dated from about 1550 to 1700, the Scientific Revolution saw the origination of the scientific method and the introduction of ideas such as the heliocentric universe and gravity. Its leading figures included Nicolaus Copernicus, Galileo Galilei, and Isaac Newton.

vacuum: An area devoid of matter, even air.

velocity: Speed in a certain direction.

ences. Yet none of those areas experienced anything like the turning point that confronted the physical sciences in the period from 1550 to 1700.

So profound were the changes produced in these one hundred fifty years that they have been given a name—the Scientific Revolution. The Scientific Revolution was a period of accelerated progress and new reliance on what became known as the scientific method, a means of systematically developing and testing theories based on observation.

Those who made the Scientific Revolution

The central figure of the Scientific Revolution was **Isaac Newton** (1642–1727; see biography in this chapter), who may in fact have been the most influential scientist of any kind prior to the twentieth century. Newton's explanation of gravitation and the laws of motion not only explained the workings of the physical universe, but also opened up the Western world to the idea that the application of scientific reasoning could solve a variety of problems.

Newton was far from the only significant figure in the Scientific Revolution, however. **Nicolaus Copernicus** (1473–1543; see biography in this chapter) launched it with his discovery that Earth is not the center of the universe. **Galileo Galilei** (1564–1642; see biography in this chapter) greatly advanced that revolution by popularizing Copernicus's ideas, pioneering the scientific method, and conducting experiments on falling bodies that influenced Newton.

Beyond the big three

Newton, Copernicus, and Galileo are not the only notable figures of this time. **René Descartes** (1596–1650; see biography in Mathematics chapter) led mathematicians and philosophers in the effort to relate numbers and scientific data. He suggested that the world was a machine whose workings could be understood, a model reinforced by the discoveries of Newton and others.

Tycho Brahe (1546–1601) made astronomical observations that provided the data that formed the basis for the three laws of planetary motion put forward by **Johannes Kepler** (1571–1630; see biography in this chapter), laws essential to Newton's later work. Also prominent were **Robert Boyle** (1627–1691; see biography in this chapter), father of modern chemistry; **Christiaan Huygens** (1629–1695; see biography in this chapter), whose wave theory of light rivaled Newton's corpuscular (particle) theory; and Robert Hooke (1635–1703), who is important for work in areas ranging from physics to biology. (See essay "An Explosion of Knowledge" in this chapter.)

Isaac Newton was a central figure of the Scientific Revolution and one of the most influential scientists of all time. **(Reproduced by permission of Archive Photos, Inc.)**

Before Copernicus

Johann Müller (known as Regiomontanus; 1436–1476), whose criticism of Ptolemy's cosmology influenced Copernicus, was an important forerunner of the Scientific Revolution. He was also the last in a long line of men who, over the years, gradually chipped away at the Aristotelian and Ptolemaic models. Others included the Byzantine philosopher John Philoponus (flourished in the sixth century), who questioned Aristotle's ideas on motion; the French physicist Jean Buridan (1300–1358), who took that criticism further; and Nicholas of Cusa (1401–1464), who suggested that Earth revolves around the Sun.

Philoponus anticipated Newton's first law of motion by nearly twelve hundred years in his critique of Aristotelian physics. When a person throws a stone, for instance, Aristotle maintained that the stone is moved by the medium through which it travels, that is, the air. In his view, it was as though the thrower handed off the stone to the air, which propelled it. Philoponus argued convincingly that the medium is not the agent or cause of continued violent motion; otherwise, it would be possible to move an object by simply agitating the air behind it.

Instead, Philoponus held that the thrower transfers to the projectile (for example, a stone) something he called "impetus," or what modern physicists would call kinetic energy, the energy associated with movement. Muslim scholars, among them Avicenna (Ibn Sina; 980–1037) and Ibn Bajja (c. 1095–1138), adopted and developed impetus theory. Eventually impetus theory made its way to Europe, and by 1320 it was being taught at the University of Paris, in France.

One of its leading proponents was Buridan, who went much further than Philoponus in his critique of Aristotle. With amazing accuracy, Buridan hypothesized that an object imparts to another a certain amount of energy, in proportion to its velocity (speed in a certain direction) and mass, that causes the second object to move a certain distance. He was also correct in stating that air resistance slows an object in motion.

New mathematical techniques

One of the difficulties facing Europeans studying kinematics, or the science of how objects move, was a tradition that dated back to the Greek mathematician **Euclid** (c. 330–c. 260 B.C.E.; see biography in Mathematics chapter). Euclid had claimed that it was logically impossible to express a ratio between two different sorts of quantities, such as distance and time. In his mind these were, to use a modern expression, like apples and oranges, and this meant that people of medieval times (or of the Middle Ages; c. 500–c. 1500 C.E.) had no notion of ideas such as miles per hour.

Thomas Bradwardine (c. 1290–1349) and other mathematicians at Merton College, a part of England's Oxford University, brought about a critical change in the understanding of such ratios. In order to understand the Aristotelian/Ptolemaic model of the cosmos, the Merton College mathematicians realized, it was necessary to understand the meaning of concepts such as speed and acceleration. To do that required a mathematical formula expressing the relationship between the distance an object moved, and the amount of time it took it to move that distance; therefore they reluctantly discarded Euclid's incorrect notion.

Also important was the work of Nicole Oresme (c. 1325–1382), a French mathematician who came up with the idea of representing motion by a picture, diagrams that were a forerunner of the graphs later developed by his countryman, Descartes. Nicole realized that different laws of motion governed different motions in the physical world. Like Bradwardine and other medieval thinkers, he was hampered by the old Aristotelian view, but each forward step helped prepare the way for the Scientific Revolution.

Copernicus

In the fifteenth century, the Austrian astronomer and mathematician Georg von Peuerbach (1423–1461) pointed out to his student, Regiomontanus, the inaccuracies of existing astronomical tables and the need for better translations of Greek texts. Peuerbach attempted to produce a revised and corrected version of Ptolemy's *Almagest,* but he died before finishing it. Therefore the job fell to his distinguished pupil.

The *Epitome of Astronomy,* begun by Peuerbach and completed by Regiomontanus, would prove to be a turning point in astronomy. Like their medieval predecessors, the two men set out to pay tribute to Ptolemy, but by showing the errors in his work, they were actually criticizing him. This fact was not lost on a young Polish astronomer named Nicolaus Copernicus (Mikolaj Kopernik).

Copernicus's break with tradition

Like many great thinkers before and after his time, Copernicus did not set out to change the world but only to solve a problem. Indeed, he remained convinced of uniform circular motion, the idea that the planets form perfect circles as they revolve around the center of the solar system. Uniform circular motion dated back to Aristotle and would only be refuted by Kepler long after Copernicus's time.

But Copernicus recognized the unworkable nature of the geocentric model maintained by Aristotle and Ptolemy and instead put forward a heliocentric one. (It would still be some time before astronomers realized that even the Sun is nowhere near the center of the entire universe.) Equally shocking and unorthodox was his claim that Earth rotates on its axis.

Relative motion and frame of reference

Copernicus provided a logical explanation for two questions likely to be raised by a heliocentric view of the universe. First, how is it that Earth can be moving around the Sun, when the Sun appears to be moving around Earth? And second, how can Earth be rotating on its axis, when it does not seem to move at all? To answer both, he applied the ideas of relative motion and frame of reference.

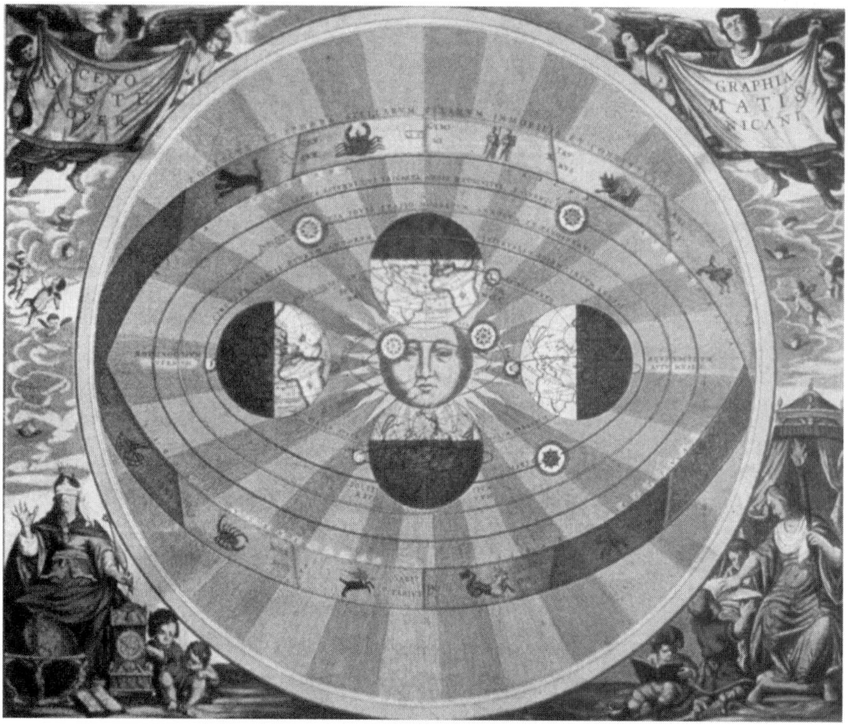

A 1660 illustration of Nicolaus Copernicus's view of the universe. The idea of the Sun—not Earth—being at the center of the universe was considered radical in Copernicus's time. **(© Corbis-Bettmann. Reproduced by permission of the Corbis Corporation.)**

From the viewpoint of Earth, the Sun seems to rise in the sky and set over the horizon, but this is only because people's perspective is too limited to make them aware of Earth's movement around the Sun. Likewise, Earth does not seem to be rotating, because it is not moving relative to the people on it. To use an analogy unavailable to Copernicus, this is a bit like being on a moving bus and watching buildings go by outside: the buildings are moving relative to the observer, but the floor of the bus itself is not.

The immediate impact of Copernicus's ideas

Not only did Copernicus's heliocentric model make more sense than Ptolemy's, it also explained a number of problems with the geocentric model, such as retrograde motion. In the Ptolemaic system, a distant planet such as Jupiter seemed sometimes to be moving strangely in relation to Earth and the Sun. Thanks to Copernicus, it became apparent why: Jupiter was indeed farther away than the Sun, as Ptolemy had observed, but it lay in the opposite direction and was moving around the Sun just as Earth was, only with a much larger orbit.

Though Copernicus's system marked a radical change from Ptolemy's because it maintained uniform circular motion, it did not represent a full break with the past. Nonetheless, Copernicus recognized that his ideas would be shocking and controversial, because the Catholic Church—still among the most powerful forces in Europe during his time—had given its full approval to the Ptolemaic system. The Ptolemaic system seemed to agree with the Bible by placing humanity, created in God's image, at the center of the universe; therefore any challenge to Ptolemy and Aristotle would seem like a challenge to Jesus and God.

Copernicus first described his heliocentric system in the brief essay "Commentariolus," which he circulated privately. Then, in 1530, he completed his full work, *De revolutionibus,* but delayed publication until 1543, the year of his death. At the time of publication, a Lutheran minister named Andreas Osiander (1498–1552) wrote a preface in which he maintained that the heliocentric idea was just a mathematical model and not intended as a true description of the universe.

Osiander's idea was to ward off attacks against Copernicus, by saying in effect that he should not be taken too seriously. Yet church officials soon responded to the challenge posed by Copernicus. In 1600 the Italian philosopher Giordano Bruno (1548–1600) was burned at the stake for his support of Copernicus's ideas, and one thinker who took the obvious message from this was Galileo.

Despite Earth's revolving around the Sun, the setting Sun gives the appearance that the Sun revolves around Earth. **(Photograph by Robert J. Huffman. Reproduced by permission of Field Mark Publications.)**

Galileo

In 1609 Galileo built and used one of the very first telescopes. As a result he made a number of discoveries that corroborated Copernicus's findings and pointed out a number of flaws in the ideas of Aristotle and Ptolemy. As he showed in *Sidereus nuncius* (1610), Jupiter had its own moons, and this meant that not everything in the universe revolved around Earth. In addition, contrary to Aristotle's claim that the lunar surface is perfectly smooth, he showed that the Moon's surface has mountains and depressions.

Church leaders responded to Galileo's outspoken defense of Copernican ideas by attempting to silence him. However, the cardinal who became Pope Urban VIII in 1623 was a friend and permitted Galileo to present a two-sided comparison of the Copernican and Ptolemaic systems. Yet the resulting work, *Dialogue Concerning Two Chief World Systems* (1632), weighed in heavily on the side of Copernicus.

The church tried and convicted Galileo for heresy, or opposition to official doctrine, and placed him under house arrest for the remainder of his life. During those years he produced *Two New Sciences* (1638), in which he laid the groundwork for modern physics by emphasizing new ideas that included experimentation, demonstration, and quantifiable results. In other words, he introduced the scientific method.

The foundations of gravitational study

In part, the book presented the results of Galileo's attempts to test Aristotle's ideas on gravity, for instance, the Greek thinker's claim that objects fall to their natural position, and that heavier or larger objects fall faster than lighter or smaller ones. Galileo, on the other hand, predicted that two metal balls of differing sizes would fall with the same rate of acceleration.

To test this, he could not simply drop two balls from a rooftop, or have someone else do so while he stood on the ground, because they would fall too fast to be studied. Instead, he rolled them down an incline, and through a series of mathematical steps, he showed that the rate of acceleration in free fall within a vacuum is not dependent on weight.

Obviously something was causing those balls to fall, and clearly it had nothing to do with Aristotle's notion of natural positions. In fact that force was gravity, an idea later explored in much greater depth by Newton. Newton also made considerable use of a concept initially formulated by Galileo: inertia, which Newton later defined as the tendency of objects in motion to remain in motion, and of objects at rest to remain at rest, unless acted upon by some outside force.

Kepler

In 1572 Brahe observed a nova, a star that suddenly becomes very bright before fading again to its former state. This contradicted Aristotle's claim that the heavens were perfect and unchanging. Then, five years later, in 1577, he witnessed a comet that had clearly passed through several of the planetary spheres that supposedly existed, something that would have been impossible if those spheres were solid, as Aristotle claimed they were.

Reluctant to accept Copernicus's heliocentrism because he genuinely believed it conflicted with the Bible, Brahe adopted a compromise position. He instead advanced the theory that all planets but Earth orbit the Sun, while the Sun and the rest of the planets revolve around a stationary Earth. Though Brahe's theory gained acceptance during the next half-century, the tide had already turned against the old views, and one of those leading the new movement was Brahe's assistant, Kepler.

Philosophy, Politics, Religion, and Newton

The outgrowth of the optimistic spirit fostered by **Isaac Newton**'s (1642–1727; see biography in this chapter) work on gravity and motion was the Enlightenment, an age whose philosophy and politics reflected the attitude that human reason reigned supreme. That attitude is embodied in the work of Newton's countryman John Locke (1632–1704), a philosopher whose ideas inspired the American Revolution. Similarly, Newton influenced French thinkers such as Voltaire (1694–1778) and Jean-Jacques Rousseau (1712–1778), whose principles exerted an enormous impact on the French Revolution of 1789.

Though the American and French revolutions are often compared to one another, because both were made in the name of liberty, there were some significant differences. Not least among these was the fact that the French Revolution generated the Reign of Terror (1793–94) that took the life of French chemist **Antoine-Laurent Lavoisier** (1743–1794; see biography in this chapter) and many others, and ultimately led to the dictatorship of Napoleon Bonaparte (1769–1821). In addition, the French Revolution was violently antireligious, whereas the American Revolution helped establish the freedom of religious groups to worship as they pleased.

Indeed, both the friends and the foes of religious belief found something to value in Newtonian physics, whose principles were also extended to religion as well. Christians, Newton among them, saw in his work a proof that the universe was orderly, governed by regular laws that provided glimpses of a God who oversees it all. Others, however, took Newton's ideas to mean that a mechanical, mathematically explainable universe had no need for a God.

Kepler's laws of planetary motion

Brahe was a meticulous observer and recorder of astronomical events, and when Kepler secured control of Brahe's data after his death, this proved to be a treasure of incomparable value. From it, Kepler discovered that not only do the planets orbit the Sun, but that orbit is not, as Copernicus had believed, a perfect circle. Instead, it is an ellipse, or an oval.

The elliptical orbit of the planets is embodied in Kepler's first law of planetary motion, which destroyed the last remnants of the Ptolemaic/Aristotelian universe. In his second law, Kepler showed that planets move faster when closer to the Sun, while his third law established a mathematical relationship between the distance from the Sun and the planet's speed. Later, Newton would show that the reason for this speeding up is that the Sun exerts a gravitational pull on the planets.

Newton

Newton's *Philosophiae naturalis principia mathematica* (1687) is widely regarded as one of the most important books ever written. In it he established his law of universal gravitation, as well as his three laws of motion. These ideas not only confirmed the concepts put forward in the realm of astronomy by Copernicus, Galileo, and Kepler, but they completely reformed physics and ultimately the sciences as a whole. And their influence went far beyond the sciences, into areas that included religion, politics, and philosophy.

Building on Galileo's research of falling bodies and Kepler's observation of planetary velocity, Newton asserted that gravity is a universal property of all matter, one that works at a distance, without direct contact. All things exert a gravitational force on one another, but only if at least one of those objects possesses enormous mass is the gravitational pull significant.

Mass, force, and gravity

What is mass? According to Newton's second law of motion, it is the ratio of force to acceleration; or, to put it another way, force is equal to mass multiplied by acceleration. Mass is a measure of inertia, which Newton defined in the first law. Mass is not the same as weight, which is simply gravitational force. As a matter of fact, the metric unit known as the kilogram is a unit of mass, whereas the pound, which is part of the English system of measures, is a unit of force. On Earth they are essentially equivalent (1 pound = 2.2 kilograms), but in space their values would not be so easily translated.

A person's weight on Earth is equal to his or her mass multiplied by the downward acceleration due to gravity: 32 feet (9.8 meters) per second per second (meaning that for every second an object falls, its velocity is increasing as well). On the Moon, one's weight would differ from the weight on Earth, but one's mass would be the same. This means that it would be easier to lift a person, but just as hard to push that person from side to side. Why, then, is the gravitational pull of the Moon smaller than that of Earth? Because its mass is less than Earth's, and as Newton showed, gravitational attraction is directly related to mass.

Astronauts Neil Armstrong and Edwin "Buzz" Aldrin plant an American flag on the lunar surface, July 20, 1969. Because gravity is directly related to mass, one's weight would change on the Moon, but not one's mass.
(© NASA/Roger Ressmeyer/Corbis. Reproduced by permission of the Corbis Corporation.)

Newton's third law of motion states that when one object exerts a force on another, the second object exerts on the first a force equal in magnitude but opposite in direction. This is sometimes rendered as "For every action, there is an equal and opposite reaction." A chair holds a person up because the chair pushes upward with a force equal to that with which the person's body pushes downward. If the body pushes down with too great a force, that is, if the person weighs too much for the chair, the chair will give way, and the person will fall through to the next object capable of holding his or her weight (probably the floor).

Newton's law of gravitation provides a formula for the gravitational force exerted between two bodies. The gravitational force exerted between two bodies is equal to the product of the two bodies' mass divided by the square of the distance between them, and multiplied by a quantity known as the gravitational constant, *G*. In other words, the larger the two bodies are, and the smaller the distance between them, the greater the gravitational attraction.

The impact of Newton's work

The value of *G* was unknown to Newton and only calculated much later by English physicist and chemist Henry Cavendish (1731–1810). This made it possible to calculate the mass of Earth, as well as that of the Sun and the planets.

Newton's law of gravitation proved to be a precise and effective tool wherever applied. A truly universal law, it could be verified by the simplest fall of an apple, or measured against the most detailed observations of celestial movements. In the twentieth century Newtonian mechanics, based in part on Newton's laws of universal gravitation, still proved accurate enough to guide the navigation of spacecraft.

Although Newton's law of gravitation offered no explanation of why gravity existed, it yielded rich insight into the workings of the natural world. Scientists tried to use Newton's law to explain other phenomena that took place at a distance, for instance, magnetism. Of even greater importance to science, however, was the idea that the world behaved in a rational way, that things could be explained and understood.

For the first time, it became possible to picture the universe as a machine, with predictable behaviors that could be quantified, or mathematical values could be assigned to them. It is no accident that the Industrial Revolution, a period of rapid acceleration in technology, began just a quarter-century after Newton's death: thanks to Newton's revolution in thinking, it seemed for the first time in history that humans could apply scientific ideas to solve all possible problems.

AN EXPLOSION OF KNOWLEDGE

During and after the period of great changes described in the essay "The Scientific Revolution," the physical sciences underwent changes far beyond the areas of astronomy and physics known respectively as cosmology and mechanics. These changes accelerated enormously during the 1700s, a period known as the Enlightenment. The term "enlightenment" refers to an awakening of the mind, and such was the case in the eighteenth century, old ways were rejected and a new emphasis on the ability of the human mind to solve problems was adopted.

In the field of astronomy Edmond Halley (1656–1742) identified the comet that today bears his name, along with the discovery of Uranus, the first planet discovered since prehistoric times, by William Herschel (1738–1822). At the same time, studies in physics entered new territories with research into the nature of light, heat, and sound, as well as electricity and magnetism.

Words to Know

cosmology: A branch of astronomy concerned with the origin, structure, and evolution of the universe.

geology: The scientific study of Earth, particularly as revealed through its rocks.

matter: Physical substance that occupies space, possesses mass, and is ultimately convertible to energy. Matter can be a gas, liquid, or solid.

mechanics: A branch of physics concerned with the study of bodies in motion.

optics: A realm of scientific study concerned with the formation and transmission of light.

refraction: The bending of light as it passes at an angle from one transparent material into a second transparent material. Refraction accounts for the fact that objects under water appear to have a different size and location than they have in air.

Scientific Revolution: A period of accelerated scientific discovery that completely reshaped the world. Usually dated from about 1550 to 1700, the Scientific Revolution saw the origination of the scientific method and the introduction of ideas such as the heliocentric universe and gravity. Its leading figures included Nicolaus Copernicus, Galileo Galilei, and Isaac Newton.

thermodynamics: The study of the relationships between heat, energy, and work. (Work, closely related to the concept of power, is a term in physics that has a definition different from its everyday meaning.)

velocity: Speed in a certain direction.

The eighteenth century also saw the maturation of the earth sciences, along with the first theories that Earth and the universe are very, very old.

The Enlightenment produced few scientific figures on a stature with those of the Scientific Revolution. As with the life sciences, the physical sciences in the eighteenth century were more noted for their achievements than for the people who made them. Yet a few names do stand out, among them Swiss physicist and mathematician **Daniel Bernoulli** (1700–1782; see Technology and Invention chapter for a biography), who developed the field of hydrodynamics, the study of the motion of fluids. Particularly notable were the chemists: **Antoine-Laurent Lavoisier** (1743–1794; see biography in this chapter), who took his discipline into the modern age; as well as Joseph Black (1728–1799), Joseph Priestley (1733–1804), and others.

Light: Wave or particle?

During the Enlightenment, particularly during the period known as the Scientific Revolution (approximately 1550–1700), great advances were made in the field of optics, or the study of light. Whereas medieval (or of the Middle Ages; c. 500–c. 1500 C.E.) studies in optics had focused primarily on the mechanism of vision, optical research during the Scientific Revolution was concerned primarily with the nature of light itself.

Thus began a heated debate fought by two influential figures. On the one side was Dutch physicist **Christiaan Huygens** (1629–1695; see biography in this chapter), who maintained that light travels in the form of waves. On the other was **Isaac Newton** (1642–1727; see biography in this chapter), who upheld the corpuscular theory of light, or the idea that light travels in the form of particles.

Particle theories of matter

As physicists today know, light is a form of energy, not matter; but scientists of the 1600s and 1700s had no such knowledge. In fact, Newton's corpuscular theory was actually part of a rising trend toward particle theories of matter. This would lead to a full-scale revival of atomic theory at the beginning of the nineteenth century by British chemist John Dalton (1766–1844).

The atomic idea, however, dates back to the Greek philosopher Democritus (c. 460–c. 370 B.C.E.) but was long rejected in favor of the erroneous four elements theory. (See essay "Early Greek Theories of Matter: What *Is* Everything?" in this chapter.) One reason for this rejection had to do with the belief that Greek atomism left no place for God; therefore, in order to resurrect atomic theory, this objection had to be overcome. The turning point came with the work of French priest and philosopher Pierre Gassendi (1592–1655), who explained atoms as having been created and set into motion by God.

The great minds of Gassendi's time and thereafter accepted the atomic idea, which evolved through the work of **Galileo Galilei** (1564–1642; see biography in this chapter); French mathematician **René Descartes**

(1596–1650; see biography in Mathematics chapter); and British chemist **Robert Boyle** (1627–1691; see biography in this chapter). As with so much else, however, it was Newton who gave shape to the emerging idea, which he applied in his theory of optics.

Optics through the mid-1600s

During the late Middle Ages (c. 1100–1500 C.E.), information of Greek and Muslim studies in optics—most notably those of **Alhazen** (965–1040; see biography in this chapter)—reached Europe from the Middle East. Late medieval scientists such as Albertus Magnus (c. 1200–1280) and **Roger Bacon** (c. 1220–1292; see biography in Technology and Invention chapter) conducted fruitful research in optics, but their ideas still harkened back to those of **Aristotle** (384–322 B.C.E.; see biography in Life Science chapter) and Alhazen.

The modern concept of vision had its beginnings with the work of **Johannes Kepler** (1571–1630; see biography in this chapter). Inspired by a growing interest in realistic painting and the use of perspective in art, Kepler argued that light rays are refracted through the eye to form an inverted, or reversed, image. Shortly thereafter, Dutch astronomer and mathematician Willebrord Snel (1580–1626) discovered the law of refraction, a mathematical formula for determining the angles of refracted rays.

Descartes extended the application of mathematics to optics with his own wave theory, which Huygens adopted and developed. Meanwhile, Descartes's contemporary, **Pierre de Fermat** (1601–1665; see biography in Mathematics chapter), analyzed Snel's law of refraction and found evidence in it that light must travel more slowly in a denser medium. (A medium is anything, such as air or water, through which something else travels.) Fermat's conclusion was in fact correct, but most thinkers of the day, Descartes included, believed that light travels instantaneously, that it takes literally no time to travel from Point A to Point B.

Newton and Huygens

Using a prism, a three-dimensional glass shape for dispersing light rays, Newton in 1666 revealed that white light is composed of different colors refracted through characteristic angles. He interpreted this to mean that white light is composed of streams of particles, which are sorted and diverted to produce the spectrum or range of colors.

Newton's particle theory showed the influence of Descartes, while Huygens's wave theory reflected the ideas of Fermat, including the concept that light has a finite velocity. In 1676 Danish physicist Ole Rømer (1644–1710) conducted observations which led him to conclude that Jupiter and Earth are far enough apart that light takes a noticeable amount of time to travel between the two. Based on Rømer's findings, Huygens calculated the velocity of light as 140,000 miles (225,000 kilometers) per second, which, while it was much smaller than the actual figure of 186,000 miles (297,600 kilometers), was still an impressive achievement.

The years that followed saw a bitter dispute between Newton's and Huygens's followers, a battle that continued long after the death of both men, and pitted British adherents of corpuscular theory against continental European advocates of wave theory. Newton's ideas dominated for most of the 1700s; then Huygens's came to the fore in the 1800s.

Dutch physicist Christiaan Huygens. Huygens argued in the seventeenth century that light travels in the form of waves. (Reproduced courtesy of the Library of Congress.)

Resolving the problem

More than two centuries after Newton, when Albert Einstein (1879–1955) analyzed the work of his distinguished predecessor, something seemed wrong to him. Newton had treated gravity, like light, as an instantaneous phenomenon, which Einstein perceived as a flaw. By then the speed of light had long since been established, and in the course of his research Einstein discovered that nothing can travel faster than light.

Though the name of German physicist Max Planck (1858–1947) is not as famous as that of Einstein, in fact Planck's quantum theory, which he put forward a few years before Einstein introduced his theory of relativity, actually did more to transform the world of physics. Quantum theory, which relates to energy at the atomic and subatomic levels, would ultimately transform science, bringing about a new understanding of the universe, much as Newton's gravitational theory and laws of motion had in late 1600s. Among the many fruits quantum theory bore was a resolution to the old dispute between Newton and Huygens: light behaves as both particles and waves.

The nature of heat

Eighteenth-century chemists, along with physicists working in the area of thermodynamics (the study of the relationships between heat, energy, and work), made enormous strides in their understanding of heat and temperature. Along the way, however, they had to overcome a highly inaccurate idea, almost a throwback to the Middle Ages, that hampered progress for some time. This was the phlogiston (floh-JIS-tun) theory of fire, which had its origins with German chemists Johann Becher (1635–1682) and George Ernst Stahl (1660–1734).

Becher, who dabbled in alchemy, seemed to have a fondness for tall tales. He sold the Dutch government rights to a process for turning silver and sand into gold, and told stories of handling a stone that made him invisible. Perhaps, then, he was just spinning another yarn when, borrowing on both alchemy and the medieval idea of the four elements, he proposed the existence of an "oily spirit."

Becher remained rather vague about this idea, and therefore it fell to his pupil, Stahl, to develop it. According to Stahl, a much more serious individual, this oily spirit was phlogiston, a material that escaped from objects when they burned. In the act of escaping, the phlogiston caused violent motion: the flames, sparks and explosions of combustion. After an object burned, the ash that remained had little or no phlogiston left.

Johann Becher's notion that an "oily spirit" is given off when an object burns fueled the eighteenth-century debate about the phlogistan theory of fire. **(Reproduced courtesy of the Library of Congress.)**

The rise and fall of phlogiston theory

A few thinkers, among them Robert Hooke (1635–1703), opposed what they thought was nonsense and proposed (correctly) that air supports combustion. Unfortunately, phlogiston theory would prevail throughout much of the eighteenth century. During that time, applications of phlogiston theory expanded, until it became the center of a whole system, the first unifying theory of chemistry. Breathing, as well as the rusting of metals, came to be seen as examples of phlogiston being expelled.

The first cracks in phlogiston theory began to show at mid-century, as supporters became divided over the subject of the substance's weight. By then, Becher and Stahl's claim that it had no weight had begun to seem ridiculous, since all matter must weigh something. Yet there was a problem with the idea of phlogiston having weight: a metal that rusted actually weighed more than one that did not, something that should not be the case if it had lost phlogiston. This led some scientists to the bizarre claim that phlogiston actually had a negative weight.

All this debate about phlogiston only illustrates the fact that it was not really a scientific idea at all: instead of seeking the truth, adherents of phlogiston were determined to save the theory itself. The beginning of the end of phlogiston came with the discovery of oxygen by Swedish chemist Carl Scheele (1742–1786), which was credited to Priestley because he published his findings earlier. As Lavoisier later showed, it was oxygen, not the fictional phlogiston, that enabled combustion and rusting.

Priestley and Lavoisier

Priestley himself remained an advocate of phlogiston theory and insisted on calling oxygen "dephlogisticated air." This is particularly ironic in light of the fact that Priestley did much more than Lavoisier, whose contributions were mainly in the area of theory, to expand chemists' understanding of specific gases. It was Priestley, for instance, who discovered the use of carbonation to make soda water, and he was one of the first to recognize the role of oxygen and carbon dioxide in a plant's respiratory cycle.

In fact Priestley and Lavoisier often found themselves at odds, even politically. Both supported the French Revolution, which began in 1789, but Priestley, a political radical, continued to do so when the revolution took an extremist turn in 1793, spawning the Reign of Terror that claimed Lavoisier among its victims. (Eventually, Priestley's views became too much for his British neighbors, and he fled to America where he was received warmly.)

Yet it would be wrong, as some historians have done, to simply characterize Priestley as a foolish defender of an outmoded theory. Today it seems clear that phlogiston theory was finished, but it was not so obvious at the time. Even Lavoisier, in debunking phlogiston, actually introduced a similar concept, which he called "caloric," because no one really understood the nature of heat.

Thermometers

Before discussing the discoveries about heat that took place at the end of the eighteenth century, it is necessary to mention a development at the beginning of it: the creation of thermometers and temperature scales. The idea of measuring temperature had first been suggested by the Greco-Roman physician **Galen** (129–c. 199; see biography in Life Science chapter), but little progress occurred until about fifteen hundred years later, when Galileo built an early type of thermometer called a thermoscope.

The first true thermometers appeared about the time of Galileo's death in 1642, and in 1664 Hooke conceived the idea of applying a scale for measuring temperature. For the zero point, Hooke chose the temperature at which water freezes, thus establishing a standard still used today in the Fahrenheit and Celsius scales. In 1702 Danish astronomer Rømer initiated the use of water's boiling temperature as a second reference point.

Up until this time, thermometers used alcohol, but German–Dutch physicist Daniel Fahrenheit (1686–1736) introduced the first mercury thermometer in 1714. Thermometers measure the amount of temperature-dependent expansion and contraction in a substance, and mercury has a much more uniform rate of expansion and contraction. Fahrenheit also debuted the temperature scale that bears his name and was the first to use degrees as a measurement of temperature.

The Fahrenheit and Celsius scales

Whereas a circle has 360 degrees, Fahrenheit imagined half that many, 180, separating the freezing and boiling points of water on his scale. He had discovered that water can be super-cooled, or kept in a liquid state at temperatures below freezing, by the use of salt, a method still applied to deice roads today. He therefore equated 0 degrees on his thermometer with the lowest possible temperature for water, while 32 degrees was the normal freezing temperature, and 212 degrees (exactly 180 degrees above freezing) became the boiling point.

In 1742 Swedish astronomer Anders Celsius (1701–1744) created a rival scale. Instead of using the cumbersome numbers associated with the Fahrenheit scale, he determined to set the freezing and boiling points of water exactly 100 degrees apart. The first Celsius thermometer actually had the freezing point at 100 degrees, and the boiling point at 0 degrees; only later was it changed to its present configuration. When France adopted the metric system in 1799, it chose to use the Celsius, or centigrade, scale.

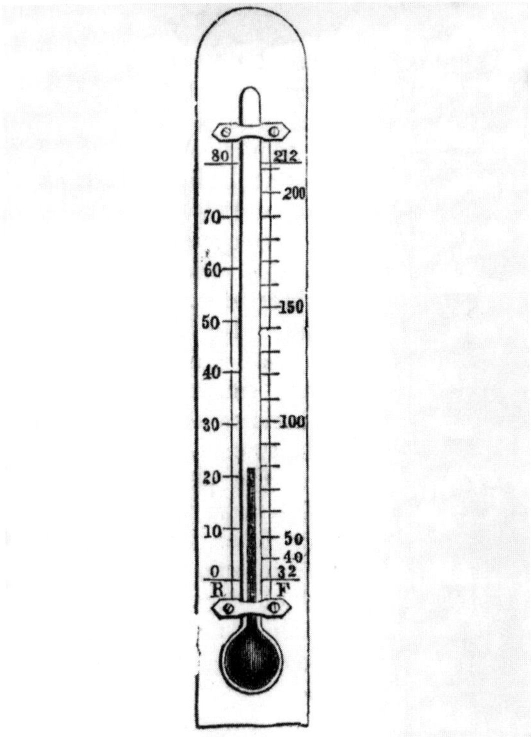

Fahrenheit's thermometer. Daniel Fahrenheit was the first scientist to measure temperature in degrees. **(© UPI/Corbis-Bettmann. Reproduced by permission of the Corbis Corporation.)**

Black's heat capacity and latent heat

Building on experimental results derived by Fahrenheit, British chemist Joseph Black (1728–1799) concluded in 1760 that the heat in an object does not depend on its volume or mass, as had been formerly believed. Instead, he argued, different substances have differing responses to heat. Establishing an important principle of physics and chemistry, he defined the amount of heat required to raise the temperature of a unit mass of a given substance by one degree as its heat capacity.

In his attempt to refute phlogiston theory, Lavoisier had introduced the idea of caloric, a concept that, like phlogiston, reflected a prevailing view of heat as a fluid substance. Black's work, which showed heat to be a measurable physical quantity distinct from temperature (though related to it), ultimately helped disprove the fluid theory of heat.

With the use of Fahrenheit's mercury thermometers, Black showed that when substances go through a change of phase (for example, when ice melts to form water), they absorb heat without changing temperature. He called this "latent heat." Heat is a form of energy, not a substance, and Black's latent heat results from the fact that when melting, the ice expends a certain amount of energy simply changing from solid to liquid, energy that cannot therefore be directed toward increasing the temperature.

Prévost and heat transfer

In 1791 Swiss physicist Pierre Prévost (1751–1839) introduced his theory of heat exchanges. Still accepted today, this theory describes how heat is transferred from one object to another. For example, an ice cube in a hot cup of coffee does not cool the coffee down, even though that is the way people normally describe it. Rather, the coffee warms up the ice cube, transferring heat to it and in the process losing heat of its own. Certainly the coffee does become cooler, but what has been transferred is heat, not cold. In terms of physics, there is no such thing as cold, only heat and the absence of heat.

Prévost's ideas had enormous impact and helped form the basis for the three laws of thermodynamics, formulated over a period of about sixty years beginning in the 1840s. Together these laws led to vast improvements in machinery during the Industrial Age, an era reliant on steam power. They also proved the impossibility of creating a perfectly efficient machine, or one that directs all the energy put into it to the purpose of output. (An automobile, for instance, uses up more than half the energy put into it simply to keep running; only a relatively small portion is directed toward moving it forward.)

Thompson and Davy point the way

As valuable as his contributions were, Prévost continued to uphold the idea of heat as a liquid. In 1798, however, British physicist Benjamin Thompson (also known as Count Rumford; 1753–1814) proposed that heat is not a fluid, but a type of motion. He based this conclusion—which is not correct but closer to the truth than the idea of heat as a fluid—on his observations of cannonmaking in Munich, Germany. Workers used tools to bore the insides of brass cannons, and Thompson noted that this process gave off an enormous amount of heat.

According to caloric theory, this heat resulted from the release of caloric as the brass was broken down into shavings. Thompson, however, believed differently, and experimentation revealed that it was the motion of the boring tool, not caloric, that generated heat. Around the same time, English chemist Humphrey Davy (1778–1829) discovered that a block of ice submerged in supercooled water would melt when rubbed. He concluded that the rubbing motion was converted to heat and that this heat was sufficient to melt the ice. These observations helped pave the way for nineteenth-century research that unveiled much of the mystery surrounding the nature of heat.

Electricity and magnetism

Another area of eighteenth-century study that would yield dramatic results during the nineteenth century was that of electricity and magnetism. In 1865 Scottish physicist James Clerk Maxwell (1831–1879) published a paper in which he showed the relationship between electricity and magnetism. Electromagnetic force, as Maxwell explained it, is a fundamental interaction of the universe, akin to Newton's gravitation.

Electricity and magnetism are, almost literally, two sides of the same coin, a fact that can be demonstrated by analogy to the human hand. Hold out your right hand, palm perpendicular to the floor and thumb upright. Your thumb points in the direction of the electrical field, as does the heel of your hand, while your palm and the back of your hand indicate the direction of the magnetic field.

These two fields are mutually perpendicular, and are likewise perpendicular to the direction that an electromagnetic wave moves, a direction comparable to that of your four fingers. The Sun, for instance, emits electromagnetic waves, which at various frequencies carry radio and TV signals; infrared, visible, and ultraviolet light; X rays; and other forms of electromagnetic energy. Electromagnetism is a complex, involved subject, and and scientists' understanding of it first began to mature during the Enlightenment.

Early understanding of electricity and magnetism

The ancient Greeks and Romans were aware of electricity in a form that many people have experienced in daily life: static electricity, which can be generated (for instance) by running a comb through one's hair on a cold, dry day. They were also aware of magnets, as were the Chinese, who in the 1100s developed the first magnetic compasses (a topic discussed in the Technology and Invention chapter.)

The first experimental study of magnetism was the work of the French physicist Petrus Peregrinus de Maricourt, or Pèlerin de Maricourt (flourished in the thirteenth century), who described a magnet as having two poles. Then, in 1600, English scientist William Gilbert (1544–1603) presented an amazingly advanced theory of electricity and magnetism. He discussed Earth's magnetic field, as well as what modern scientists would call conducting and nonconducting materials.

A long line of scientists during the 1600s and early 1700s experimented with electricity and magnetism, adding new concepts to the emerging picture of this dual form of energy. One of the principal tools of experimentation developed during this time was the Leyden jar, a glass flask filled with water that served as a means of drawing electric sparks. During those years, a number of scientists conducted experiments in which they exposed themselves to pain and even the danger of death.

Notable Enlightenment studies

The most famous such example was the kite experiment of **Benjamin Franklin** (1706–1790; see biography in Technology and Invention chapter.) Franklin is also notable for replacing the prevailing dual-fluid explanation of electricity, put forward by French chemist Charles-François Dufay (1698–1739), with a theory that introduced the now-familiar concepts of positive and negative charges. Franklin, too, is credited with the first useful technology associated with electricity: the lightning rod, used to slowly draw electricity from the sky before it could strike a house or other building.

The description of electricity as a fluid, still current at mid-century, reveals that, as with heat, scientists did not yet understand that electricity was a form of energy, not a substance. The work of French physicist Charles-Augustin Coulomb (1736–1806), however, helped to identify electromagnetism as a force. Using a delicate instrument called a torsion balance, Coulomb was able to show that electrical and magnetic fluids act in a manner similar to gravitation as explained by Newton.

Besides Franklin's lightning rod, few applications for electricity were devised in the eighteenth century. Only at the end of the 1700s did Italian physicist Alessandro Volta (1745–1827), who also discovered the concept of electric current, invent the battery. Later, units of electric measure were named after Coulomb and Volta (the coulomb and volt, respectively), who, along with Franklin, were just some of the eighteenth-century scientists who contributed to the understanding of electricity and magnetism.

Understanding Earth

In studying Earth's magnetic field, which makes the use of a compass possible, English astronomer Henry Gellibrand (1597–1636) showed that the field has changed over time. This was one of the first indications that the planet's history can be studied scientifically, even though humans have no direct information regarding the origins of Earth. Ironically, Gellibrand, a minister, helped open the way to geological theories that called into question the account of creation in the biblical Book of Genesis.

The ancient Chinese had studied seismology, or the branch of the earth sciences concerned with earthquakes and other disturbances, but in the West understanding of the Earth had been limited until the later Renaissance, a period of intellectual and artistic rebirth from about 1350 to 1600 C.E. Part of this limitation was due to reliance on the biblical account of a six-day creation; but to a larger extent, Western ignorance resulted simply from a lack of proper tools or methods.

Nonetheless, eventually Europeans began to notice fossils, which indicated the existence of long-gone animals unlike any known on Earth in historic times, one of the first indications that Earth is actually very old. Likewise the discovery of the Americas by Christopher Columbus (1451–1506) further damaged the authority of ancient texts, including writings by Aristotle and **Ptolemy** (c. 100–c. 170; see biography in this chapter). If these writers, and the author of Genesis, did not know about the existence of other continents, what else did they not know?

Renaissance geology

During the period leading up to the Enlightenment, a number of figures contributed to the understanding of geology, the study of Earth, among them German mineralogist Georgius Agricola (Georg Bauer; 1494–1555); **Leonardo da Vinci** (1452–1519; see biography in Technology and Invention chapter); Danish geologist Niels Stensen (1638–1686); Robert Hooke, and others. Geology could not yet be considered a full-fledged science, but by the end of the 1600s it was nearly to that point.

Leonardo was among the first Western thinkers to speculate that fossils might have been made by the remains of long-dead animals, and Stensen supported this idea with research. Stensen also studied the age of rock beds, and he, along with Hooke and others, began to confront the fact that the Earth had to be much older than the six thousand years suggested by a strict interpretation of Genesis.

Geological theories of the 1700s

During the 1700s, German geologist Johann Gottlob Lehmann (1719–1767), building on ideas introduced by Stensen concerning the formation of rock beds, put forward the theory that certain groups of rocks tend to be associated with each other. Each layer of rock, he proposed, is a sort of chapter in the history of Earth.

Aspects of his theory were incorrect, but the general principle marked an advancement over previous ideas in geology and helped point the way toward a new view of the earth sciences. Previously geology had been qualitative and descriptive, meaning that earth scientists used very generalized terminology and failed to possess a grasp of larger issues. Thanks to

Lehmann and others who followed, the earth sciences would become more truly quantitative and predictive, offering explanations of what had happened in the past, along with justifiable theories concerning what might happen in the future.

German geologist Abraham Gottlob Werner (1749–1817) suggested a theory that was largely incorrect, yet one that nonetheless advanced the earth sciences. His neptunist theory was based on the idea that water had been the main force in shaping Earth's surface. Though this was not accurate, his idea was nonetheless significant, because it constituted the first well-ordered geological theory of Earth's origins and early history.

The question of Earth's age

That history was turning out to be very long indeed. In 1774 Georges Louis Leclerc, comte de Buffon (1707–1788) applied Newtonian ideas to the study of Earth and estimated its age at seventy-five thousand years. Privately he admitted that he actually thought Earth was billions of years old, but he did not think such a figure would be understood. At the time, after all, the concept of a billion was hardly a familiar one, as it is today. More importantly, the idea of Earth being that old was shocking and downright frightening to people who accepted a strict interpretation of the biblical account.

Unlike in the time of Galileo, Europeans had little fear of actual arrest or execution for endorsing ideas that seemed to go against the Bible (with the possible exception of the Spanish, whose land was home to the dreaded Spanish Inquisition, a period of several hundred years in which the Roman Catholic Church in Spain tortured and executed large numbers of people deemed to be heretics). However, a scientist could still lose his job for supporting the wrong principles, and thus Buffon was forced to renounce his position on threat of losing his post at the University of Paris, in France.

At the same time, the case for a very old Earth continued to accumulate. In England, James Hutton (1726–1797) printed his *Theory of the Earth* (1795), which suggested that the weathering effects of water produced the sedimentary layers of Earth. However, based on observation of river flow and mud content, Hutton realized that this process would require much longer than six thousand years.

The debate continued well into the next century. Today, however, there is really no debate at all: studies of the radioactive decay of uranium have revealed that Earth is about 4.7 billion years old, and if that figure changes in the future, it is likely to increase, not decrease. This does not, however, prove that the Bible is wrong, or that it should be ignored completely as a book of spiritual (though not scientific) truths.

A new look at the heavens

Even as geologists gained a new understanding of the ground beneath their feet, astronomers discovered whole new worlds, quite literally, in the skies. Astronomy, the first of the physical sciences, developed in Babylonia thousands of years before, would continue to yield new riches in the late 1600s and 1700s. Much of this activity took place in England, a nation poised to build a vast empire in the eighteenth and nineteenth centuries.

British interest in space began even before Newton published his groundbreaking *Principia,* with its laws of universal gravitation, in 1687. Twelve years earlier, in 1675, the Royal Observatory was founded at Greenwich, England, and it would remain one of the preeminent sites for astronomical observation during the next two centuries.

The Greenwich observatory also became a world center for timekeeping, and as a result, in 1767 it was established as the site for the primary line of longitude on the world map. Today, time is still computed in terms of Greenwich, hence the expression Greenwich mean time, (GMT) as a means of providing data that can be converted to local time anywhere in the world.

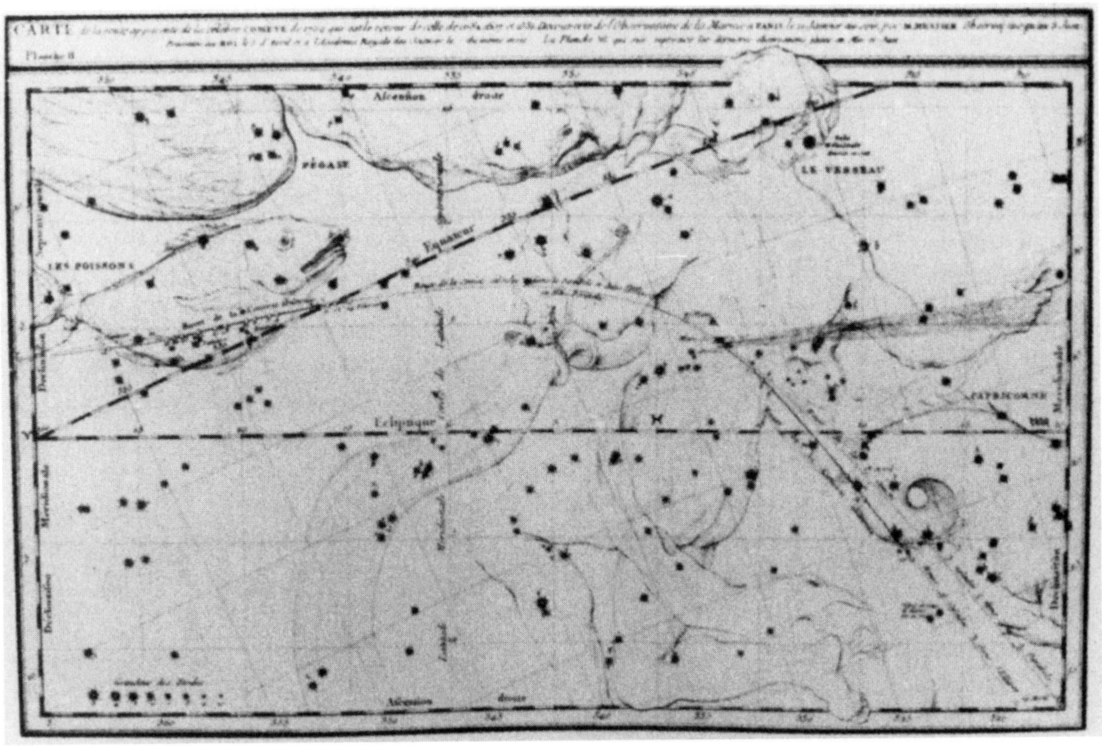

A celestial chart from 1759 showing the path of Halley's comet among the constellations. **(Reproduced courtesy of the Library of Congress.)**

Halley's comet and Uranus

Among the two most striking achievements of British astronomers were the identification of Halley's comet and the discovery of Uranus. Halley did not, as is popularly believed, discover the comet; Chinese astronomers had first observed it in 240 B.C.E. However, he was the first to recognize that the comets that had reappeared at intervals of seventy-five to seventy-six years over the centuries were all the same one.

In 1705 Halley collected the observational records of twenty-four comets between 1337 and 1698, and applying Newtonian methods, he predicted that the comet would be visible again in 1758. Unfortunately, he did not live to see it, but his prediction proved correct, thus serving as additional proof of Newton's ideas concerning gravitational attraction. As Halley showed, the comet actually orbits the solar system, pulled by its gravitational field. Halley's comet last appeared in 1986.

Then there was the discovery of Uranus by the German-born Herschel, who had settled in England. A musician and an amateur astronomer, he began observing the night sky in 1767 and started building his own telescopes. Eventually he involved his brother Alexander and sister Caroline in his research, and later Caroline became an astronomer recognized in her own right, an unusual feat for a woman in the 1700s.

All the planets as far away as Saturn had been known from prehistoric times; then, in 1781 Herschel discovered what the director of the Royal Observatory confirmed was a "new" planet. Initially it was to be named "George's Star," for King George III (1738–1820), but astronomers ultimately chose to continue the tradition of naming planets after Roman deities. Therefore the name of Uranus, Saturn's father and Jupiter's grandfather, was chosen.

Where does God, or humanity, fit in it all?

Herschel's discoveries extended beyond the solar system and began to reveal what scientists could scarcely have suspected. More than two centuries earlier, the work of **Nicolaus Copernicus** (1473–1543; see biography in this chapter) had revealed that Earth was not the center of the universe; still, astronomers had continued to believe that the universe consisted primarily of the solar system and the stars visible from Earth. Thanks to Herschel, however, it slowly became apparent that the universe is extremely large, so large that no astronomer, even today, knows exactly how big it is.

During the last quarter of the eighteenth century, French mathematician Pierre-Simon de Laplace (1749–1827) put forth the theory that the origins of the universe, as well as an explanation of its workings, could be

In the Beginning Was...What?

Studies in geology during the 1700s first revealed that Earth is very old. Today, in fact, data based on the radioactive decay of uranium shows that it is very, very old, about 4.7 billion years. If that span of time were likened to a single year, then the entire scope of history since civilization began in about 3500 B.C.E. would occupy the space of a few seconds just before midnight on December 31.

On the other hand, a very strict reading of the biblical Book of Genesis suggests that the Earth was created in 144 hours, just six days. During the 1600s the Irish bishop James Ussher (1581–1656) took this idea to an extreme, and calculated that God finished making the Earth at 9:00 A.M. on Sunday, October 23, 4004 B.C.E. Today few people take Ussher's estimate seriously, but some Christians nonetheless find it difficult to accept the idea that Earth was not created in six, twenty-four hour days.

However, the fact that Earth is 4.7 billion years old does nothing to disprove the core message of the Bible. The Bible is not a book of science; instead, it is the unfolding story of sin, redemption, and salvation, of God's relationship with humankind.

explained fully without any reference to God. His theory that the solar system originated from a cloud of gas has continued to find adherents, even in the twenty-first century.

BIOGRAPHIES

ALHAZEN (IBN AL-HAYTHAM; 965–1040)

Arab physicist, astronomer, and mathematician

The greatest Arab physical scientist of the Middle Ages (c. 500–c. 1500 C.E.), Ibn al-Haytham, known to the West as Alhazen, contributed to the understanding of astronomy, mathematics, and medicine. His greatest achievement, however, was in the field of optics, or the study of the production and transmission of light. Alhazen's *Kitab al-manazir* (Book of optics; about 1027) proved the most important and influential work on the subject between the time of **Ptolemy** (c. 100–c. 170; see biography in this chapter) and **Johannes Kepler** (1571–1630; see biography in this chapter).

Born in the city of Basra, in what is now Iraq, Alhazen was attracted to science because it seemed like a way to resolve the conflicts between various competing religious sects. As he came to see it, truth could only be discovered through thoughtful inquiry and observation.

OPPOSITE PAGE The Aswan High Dam was created to control the annual flooding of the Nile River. Water that would otherwise flood the region is captured in Lake Nasser, formed when the dam was built in the 1960s. **(© Corbis-Bettmann. Reproduced by permission of the Corbis Corporation.)**

Taking the wrong job

Early in his career, Alhazen achieved fame as a scholar and soon received a special invitation from al-Hakim (996–1021), the caliph, or ruler, of Egypt. Al-Hakim needed someone to develop a means of controlling the flow of the Nile River, whose periodic flooding had been a problem for the Egyptians since the beginning of time. Alhazen insisted that he was equal to the task.

After he sailed down the river and observed the magnificent structures built by the ancient Egyptians, however, he realized that if the river's flooding could be controlled at all, it would have been done thousands of years before. (In fact, it was only in the 1960s that the Egyptian government was able to construct a dam—the Aswan High Dam—to successfully overcome the problem.) Fearful of al-Hakim's reaction, he pretended to be insane and remained confined to his house until after the caliph's death.

By the time Alhazen was free to travel again, he was over fifty years old. Yet during the period of his virtual house arrest, he must have had time to do a great deal of thinking and experimentation, which he later poured into writings in the last years of his life. In addition to his work as a scientist, he earned a living copying scientific and mathematical manuscripts.

Critique of intromission theory

Greek thinkers, from the most advanced society of the Mediterranean world prior to Alhazen's time, had put forward two conflicting theories on optics. One of these was intromission, or the idea that vision is the result of objects emitting thin films or images of themselves, which the eye receives. The other was extromission, the belief that the eye emits an invisible fire, which touches objects to reveal their colors and shapes.

Long before Alhazen, the Arab philosopher al-Kindi (died c. 870) had debunked intromission theory by noting that if it were true, a circle would always look perfectly circular, whereas a circle viewed from the edge actually looks like a straight line. In the *Kitab,* Alhazen argued against the extro-

mission view on the grounds that a material flowing from the eye could not possibly fill the area around it fast enough to make vision possible.

Though he did not arrive at the theory of vision known to virtually everyone today—that objects reflect light from the Sun and other sources, which the eye receives—Alhazen made far more progress in that area than anyone before his time. More importantly, he established a standard of thoughtful observation and experimentation that he put to use in other optical studies, and which served as a standard to later scientists.

The rainbow and other concerns

Other optical studies conducted by Alhazen involved mirrors and the angles of reflection and refraction (the bending of light) between them. He also conducted some of the first experiments on the dispersion of light into its constituent colors, something **Isaac Newton** (1642–1727; see biography in this chapter) would later achieve by separating the spectrum through the use of a prism.

Like many medieval scientists involved in optics, Alhazen was fascinated with the question of what made a rainbow. He pioneered the use of water-filled glass spheres, which provided the model for later theorists seeking to understand how rainbows were created.

ROBERT BOYLE (1627–1691)

British chemist and physicist

Though he never earned a college degree, Robert Boyle distinguished himself as one of the most influential figures of the Scientific Revolution (c. 1550–1700; see essay "The Scientific Revolution" in this chapter). As a physicist, he performed some of the earliest experiments with gases. Yet his role as a chemist eclipsed his many contributions in physics—because he helped to separate chemistry from alchemy, Boyle is sometimes known as the father of chemistry.

Born in Ireland, Boyle was the fourteenth child of a wealthy and aristocratic British family. A child prodigy, at the age of eight he was already studying Latin and Greek, and within three years he was traveling throughout Europe while being taught by a tutor. As a young man, he lived partly in England and partly on his estates in Ireland, and the death of his father provided him with inherited wealth that made possible the pursuit of scientific experimentation.

Work with gases

While residing at the University of Oxford from 1656 to 1668, Boyle, who was neither a student nor a professor, participated in meetings of scientists who favored experimentation over the use of pure reasoning or logic. Today this is hardly a controversial idea, but at the time it was, and the group called itself the Invisible College. Yet in 1663 they gained official recognition from King Charles II and became the Royal Society, destined to become one of the most influential scientific groups in all of Europe. Years later, in 1680, Boyle was elected president of the Royal Society, but he turned down the position.

At Oxford, with **Robert Hooke** (1635–1703; see biography in this chapter) as his assistant, Boyle conducted some of his first work on gases. He and Hooke constructed an air pump, which he used to remove air from a sealed container, thus producing a vacuum. Experimenting with the vacuum chamber, he produced a number of interesting findings: that air is necessary for combustion, the respiration of living things, and the transmission of sound. Again, these facts are hardly surprising to a person today, but Boyle, who published the results of his experimentation in *New Experiments Physio-Mechanicall, Touching the Spring of the Air and its Effects* (1660), was the first to discover them.

Robert Boyle.
(Reproduced courtesy of the Library of Congress.)

Boyle also found that air can be compressed, and in 1661 he reported what is now known as Boyle's law. Boyle's law states that when temperature is kept constant, the pressure and volume of a gas are inversely proportional; that is, as the volume increases, pressure decreases, and vice versa. His observations regarding the compressibility of air also led him to an early version of modern atomic theory: if air is compressible, he reasoned, it must consist of individual particles separated by empty space.

The birth of chemistry

Also in 1661 Boyle produced his most significant work, *The Sceptical Chymist*. Up to that time, chemistry was dominated by alchemy, a doctrine based on the idea that matter can be perfected, for instance, that ordinary metal can be turned into gold by chemical means. Today scientists know that this is impossible, because gold is an element, or a substance that cannot be chemically broken down into a simpler substance. The only means by which one element can be turned into another is through radioactive decay or nuclear reactions, which were not discovered for more than three hundred years.

Scientists in Boyle's day lacked a proper understanding of elements. Some still subscribed to the old theory of the four elements (earth, air, fire, and water) inherited from ancient Greece. Most alchemists believed that salt, sulfur, and mercury constituted the three basic substances, an idea that was much closer to the truth, since sulfur and mercury are at least true elements. Boyle, on the other hand, maintained that only experimentation could identify elements, which he was the first to define as substances that cannot be broken down into simpler substances.

In his *Experimental History of Colors* (1664), Boyle suggested a method of distinguishing between acids and bases. (Bases, called alkaline substances at the time, tend to be bitter. An example is sodium bicarbonate, often used as an acid neutralizer for cases of indigestion.) He described how blue solutions obtained from plants, such as syrup of violets, turn red in the presence of acids, and green when exposed to bases. This led to the use of acid–base indicators, still applied today to test the relative acidity, or alkalinity, of many substances.

NICOLAUS COPERNICUS (1473–1543)

Polish astronomer and mathematician

Nicolaus Copernicus inaugurated the Scientific Revolution, a period of accelerated progress in the sciences that lasted from about 1550 to 1700, with his discovery that Earth is not at the center of the universe. In so doing he broke with established scientific and religious tradition, and thus initiated the modern era in astronomy. His work constituted a true watershed for science, and therefore historians often speak of the "Copernican revolution."

Born and raised in Poland, Copernicus began his education at the University of Krakow. He then went on to the universities of Bologna, Rome, and Padua, in Italy, where he studied a range of subjects that included mathematics, astrology, astronomy, law, and medicine. He received a doctorate in canon law, or church law, an important subject at a time when the Catholic Church dominated many aspects of public and private life, from the University of Ferrara in Italy. Returning to Poland, he devoted his life to church administration as canon of Frombork Cathedral.

Develops his heliocentric theory

While studying in Italy, Copernicus learned that eighteen hundred years before, the Greek astronomer Aristarchus of Samos (flourished c.

270 B.C.E.) had proposed the idea of a heliocentric, or Sun-centered universe. This contrasted sharply with the received wisdom of Copernicus's time, which maintained that the Greco–Roman astronomer **Ptolemy** (c. 100–c. 170; see biography in this chapter) was correct in his geocentric (Earth-centered) model. Over time, a number of thinkers had challenged Ptolemy's cosmology, or theory on the structure of the universe, most recently the German philosopher Nicholas of Cusa (1401–1464), who suggested that Earth rotated on its axis and revolved around the Sun.

Fascinated by these ideas, Copernicus began to explore them in his spare time and soon became convinced that the heliocentric model correctly described the relative motion of Earth, the other planets, and the Sun. He worked without the aid of the telescope, which had yet to be invented; instead, he used the simple astronomical tools available then, as well as the sheer power of logic. Logic told him, for instance, that there must be something wrong with a system that, like Ptolemy's, required increasingly complex and convoluted mathematical and physical models to make it workable.

Nicolaus Copernicus. (Reproduced courtesy of the Library of Congress.)

Challenging religious authority

For all its merits, Copernicus was aware that his heliocentric model went against accepted church teachings. Church leaders claimed that Ptolemy's cosmology agreed with the Bible—a funny thing, since Ptolemy was not a Christian—and maintained that since God had created humanity in his own image, he had obviously placed Earth at the center of the universe. Given the immense power that the church possessed at the time, therefore, Copernicus had to be careful in presenting his ideas.

This was somewhat ironic because, in earlier centuries, the church had supported learning. However, in Copernicus's time, the church was under attack in the form of the Reformation, a breakaway religious movement that produced many of the Protestant denominations that exist today. In this atmosphere, church leaders had become paranoid and used the forces of the Inquisition, a religious court, to try and punish anyone who dared to defy established teachings.

De revolutionibus

Copernicus introduced his findings first in a short version, entitled *Commentariolus*, which he published in 1513 and distributed to friends and colleagues for comment. The full work, entitled *De revolutionibus orbium coelestium* (The revolutions of the heavenly spheres), was completed in 1530 but not published until 1543, the year of Copernicus's death.

When it finally did appear, it came with a preface, written by a church leader, explaining that Copernicus's theory was not being proposed as an actual explanation of Earth's motion and position. Rather, it was merely a mathematical model to make calculations with the Ptolemaic system easier. However, scientists were not fooled. Eventually **Galileo Galilei** (1564–1642; see biography in this chapter) adopted Copernicus's ideas, carrying them forward and helping to launch an unstoppable revolution in the sciences.

GALILEO GALILEI (1564–1642)

Italian astronomer, mathematician, and physicist

Three men are widely credited with creating the Scientific Revolution, which completely changed people's perspective on the universe. The first of these was **Nicolaus Copernicus**, (1473–1543; see biography in this chapter) who discovered that Earth is not the center of the universe, and the third was **Isaac Newton**, (1642–1727; see biography in this chapter) who explained gravity and the laws of motion, thus establishing the framework for physics into the early twentieth century. In between them was Galileo Galilei, usually known simply as Galileo.

Galileo seldom receives as much attention as Copernicus and Newton, but his work was far more wide-ranging than that of Copernicus, and it is hard to imagine Newton's discoveries without the foundation provided for him by Galileo. In addition to his famous support of Copernicus's heliocentric cosmology (a Sun-centered model of the universe) and his experiments with falling bodies, Galileo was the first scientist to use the thermometer and the telescope. Most significant of all was his development of the scientific method, a process of careful observation, experimentation, and testing still applied by scientists today.

Early career

Born on February 15, 1564, in Pisa, Italy, Galileo enrolled at that city's university to study medicine when he was seventeen, but his interests soon turned to mathematics. He made his first scientific discovery in 1582, when he realized that the period of motion for a pendulum remains approximately the same regardless of the amplitude of oscillation; that is, the amount of time it takes a pendulum to complete one full swing is not affected by the distance it has to travel: the greater the distance, the greater the speed with which it moves.

He left Pisa in 1585 without finishing his degree and continued his studies in Florence, Italy, where he completed his first scientific treatise, *La bilancetta* (1586). As professor of mathematics at Pisa from 1589 to 1592, Galileo conducted his first experiments on falling bodies, which he published in *De motu* (1590). From this work, and later experiments in the same area, would come a host of ideas that influenced Newton.

Galileo Galilei.
(© Corbis-Bettmann. Reproduced by permission of the Corbis Corporation.)

Using the telescope

In 1592 Galileo assumed the chair of mathematics at the University of Padua, in Italy, where he spent the next eighteen years. In early 1609 he heard reports of a device, invented in Holland the year before, consisting of two glass lenses that made objects at a distance appear closer. Based on this information, Galileo constructed his own telescope, and in early January 1610 he used it to observe the heavens.

His findings, which he published in *Sidereus nuncius* (1610), conflicted with the accepted geocentric, or Earth-centered, idea of the universe inherited from **Ptolemy** (c. 100–c. 170; see biography in this chapter) and recently challenged by Copernicus. As Galileo showed, Jupiter had its own moons, which meant that not everything in the universe (as people in his time called the solar system) revolved around Earth. He also challenged the other highly respected ancient authority on the physical sciences, **Aristotle** (384–322 B.C.E.; see biography in Life Science chapter), when he showed that the Moon's surface has mountains and depressions. (Aristotle had claimed it was perfectly smooth.)

To an even greater extent than Ptolemy, Aristotle was responsible for the misguided ideas that dominated the physical sciences. This is ironic, because it was Aristotle who introduced the idea that a scientist should draw his concepts from observation. Galileo, however, developed a much more thorough approach to science, which became known as the scientific method. Thanks to Galileo, scientists from then on would carefully study data to develop hypotheses that could be tested. Yet by challenging Aristotle's and Ptolemy's ideas about the world—ideas that had been accepted by the church because they seemed to agree with the Bible—Galileo had opened himself up to a great deal of trouble.

Trouble with the church

Rejecting a lifetime appointment at Padua, Galileo returned to Florence in 1610 as mathematician and philosopher to the Grand Duke of Tuscany. Shortly afterward, disputes with church leaders over his support of Copernican ideas brought him into conflict with the church. Copernicus himself was long dead, but scholars had come to accept his findings that Earth was not the center of the universe, which seemed to go against biblical principles.

Galileo received orders not to defend Copernican ideas in public, but when Urban VIII became pope in 1623, he obtained permission to present an impartial discussion of the Copernican and Ptolemaic systems. The discussion, which appeared in *Dialogue Concerning Two Chief World Systems* (1632), was anything but impartial; rather, it weighed in overwhelmingly on the side of heliocentrism. The church tried and convicted Galileo for heresy, or opposition to official doctrine, and placed him under house arrest for the remainder of his life.

During those years he produced *Two New Sciences* (1638), which deals in part with the principles of motion. Ironically, it was this work that ultimately ended the dominance of Aristotelian and Ptolemaic ideas. In it, he correctly stated that in a vacuum (an area devoid of matter, including air), bodies fall at the same rate, regardless of their weight, a direct contradiction of Aristotle. He also introduced the concept of inertia, or the tendency of a body in motion to remain in motion, and a body at rest to remain at rest. This helped provide a basis for Newton's laws of motion and gravitation, which fully established the truth of Copernicus's ideas.

CHRISTIAAN HUYGENS (1629–1695)

Dutch physicist

A scientist of wide-ranging interests and accomplishments, Christiaan Huygens is famous for his contributions in numerous areas of the physical sciences. He established the wave theory of light; helped explain the conservation of momentum and elastic collisions; produced the first theorems of centripetal force; and advanced mathematical studies in probability theory. He also made improvements to the telescope, discovered Saturn's moon Titan, and invented the pendulum clock.

Huygens was born on April 14, 1629, in The Hague, Netherlands, the son of Constantijn Huygens (1596–1687), a diplomat and well-known poet. The household received frequent visits from distinguished figures, including **René Descartes** (1596–1650; see biography in Mathematics chapter), who greatly influenced young Christiaan. Huygens was educated at home before entering the University of Leiden, in the Netherlands, to study law and mathematics in 1645. From 1647 to 1649 he studied law at the Collegium Arausiacum in Breda; then, rejecting the idea of a diplomatic career, he returned home in 1650 to devote himself to science.

Studies of colliding bodies

In 1652 Huygens began his study of colliding bodies, and by 1656 he arrived at an explanation of elastic collisions. An elastic collision is one in which kinetic energy, or the energy associated with motion, is conserved, or none of it is lost. When a cue ball strikes another pool ball, this is an almost perfectly elastic collision; only a little bit of the kinetic energy is lost, primarily in the form of sound.

On the other hand, if two lumps of clay hit each other, the collision is relatively inelastic. In this instance, a great deal of the kinetic energy is transferred in the form of heat and sound. Nonetheless, the total energy of the system remains the same, as does its total momentum, since both kinetic energy and momentum are proportional to the product of total mass and velocity. The physical law known as the conservation of momentum is attributed to Huygens and British scientists John Wallis (1616–1703) and Sir Christopher Wren (1632–1723), all of whom formulated it independently.

Christiaan Huygens. (Reproduced courtesy of the Library of Congress.)

The pendulum and other contributions to mechanics

In 1657 Huygens introduced the pendulum clock, which made possible accurate time measurements. This would ultimately enhance the accuracy of longitudinal measurements, always a problem for sailors at sea. When the Académie des Sciences was established as the principal French scientific society in 1666, Huygens became its most prominent member and continued his research on oscillatory systems (of which a pendulum is an example) in Paris. These culminated in the publication of *Horologium oscillatorium* (1673), which includes a mathematical analysis of the pendulum and discuses the relationship between the length of the pendulum and its period of oscillation, or the amount of time it takes to go through an entire cycle.

Huygens also studied centripetal force, or the inward pull that an object experiences in rotational motion. (Centripetal force, for instance, causes the cars on a circular amusement-park ride to tilt inward when the ride is moving at relatively high speeds.) His work on this subject provided a model for **Isaac Newton**'s (1642–1727; see biography in this chapter) laws of motion.

The wave theory of light

Newton and Huygens, and their followers, became embroiled in a debate over the nature of light. Newton had put forward a corpuscular theory of light, which depicted it as a set of particles, whereas in his *Traitá de la lumière* (1678), Huygens introduced the theory that light travels in waves. In the years that followed, British scientists primarily supported Newton, whose corpuscular theory held dominance until the early 1800s. Then continental European theorists, who tended to defend Huygens, got the upper hand, and the wave theory gained influence. The rise of quantum theory in physics during the early twentieth century, however, led to the realization that light behaves both as particles and as waves.

As an astronomer, Huygens and his brother Constantijn developed lens-grinding techniques that greatly improved the telescope. These they applied in observations, which led to Huygens's discovery of Titan, a moon of Saturn, in 1655. In the following year, he correctly described Saturn's ring (1656), and in 1659 he first observed surface markings on Mars. Huygens also invented a two-lens eyepiece—the Huygens ocular—and an improved micrometer.

Huygens lived in Paris for fifteen years, during which he returned to The Hague for two extended periods when he was ill. Illness brought him home a third time in 1681, and this time he decided to stay, because popular sentiment in France had turned against adherents of the Protestant faith. Huygens died in The Hague on July 8, 1695.

JOHANNES KEPLER (1571–1630)

German astronomer and mathematician

In the list of men who made the Scientific Revolution, three names stand supreme, but if any name deserves to be placed fourth, after **Nicolaus Copernicus** (1473–1543; see biography in this chapter), **Galileo Galilei** (1564–1642; see biography in this chapter), and **Isaac Newton** (1642–1727; see biography in this chapter), it is that of Johannes Kepler. A contemporary and acquaintance of Galileo, Kepler likewise influenced the acceptance of Copernicus's discovery that Earth is not the center of the universe.

He also applied the scientific method, pioneered by Galileo, in a discovery that went far beyond the findings of Copernicus. Copernicus still adhered to the old belief, which dated back to **Aristotle** (384–322 B.C.E.; see biography in Life Science chapter) and **Ptolemy** (c. 100–c. 170; see biography in this chapter), that the planets move around the center of the universe (that is, the solar system) in perfect circles. Kepler showed that this motion is instead an oval or ellipse, a fact that proved critical to Newton's law of universal gravitation.

Between two eras of science

The man noted for his extraordinary gifts of observation actually had problems with his vision from the time of his birth in Weil, Germany. Not only was he sickly, but he suffered from myopia (nearsightedness) and occasional bouts of double vision. After seeing the comet of 1577 when he was six years old, and an eclipse of the Moon when he was nine, Kepler became intrigued with astronomy. Though he attended seminary, intending to enter the church, his abilities as a mathematician led him instead to teach math in Graz, Austria.

His career placed Kepler in an interesting juncture between old-fashioned non-science and the scientific discoveries of the modern age. Many of his ideas were downright medieval or even ancient: for instance, he subscribed to the notion, introduced by the Greek mathematician **Pythagoras** (c. 580–c. 500 B.C.E.; see biography in Mathematics chapter), that the planets actually emit music as they move about in the heavens. Needless to say, the music of the spheres has absolutely no basis in fact.

Another aspect of Kepler's life that illustrates the mixture of science and non-science in his time is his service as an official astrologer while in Graz. Not only did he cast horoscopes for the local ruler, but he also supplemented his income by providing horoscopes for individual citizens. Yet even as he involved himself in the quasi-science of astrology, Kepler became convinced of a fact that would change the future of the sciences and society: that Earth revolves around the Sun, not vice versa.

In 1596 Kepler published the first of several works in which he furnished data that agreed with Copernicus's findings. Four years later, he moved to Prague (now in the Czech Republic), where he became assistant to the noted Danish astronomer Tycho Brahe (1546–1601). This proved important because Brahe was a tireless recorder of observations on the movements of heavenly bodies. When Brahe died, Kepler gained possession of his records, which he used in formulating his three laws of planetary motion.

Laws of planetary motion

Whereas physical scientists of ancient times tended to form ideas about the way that nature worked, then look for facts and formulas that confirmed those conclusions, Kepler took an exactly opposite approach. Like Copernicus and the new generation of scientists who transformed the world of knowledge in the period from 1550 to 1700, he recorded what he observed and then formed his laws to fit those observations.

Thus he did not set out to discard the idea of perfectly circular orbits, but by 1602 he had done so, simply because perfect circles did not fit with what he observed of planetary motion. He therefore postulated that a planet's distance from the Sun determined its speed, and calculated the exact relationship with precise accuracy. This became his second law. In 1605 he came to the conclusion that planets move in elliptical orbits, forming his first law.

Though discovered second, the 1605 law was first in the sense that elliptical orbits were necessary to understanding the variable speeds identified in the second law. His third law, formulated in 1618, extended these concepts by stating that the square of the time a planet takes to revolve around the Sun is proportional to the cube of its distance from the Sun. Together, these laws showed a clear relation between distance and speed, and though Kepler did not attempt to identify the reason that a planet sped up when closer to the Sun, Newton did: it was due to the Sun's gravitational pull.

Kepler and his family moved to Linz, Austria, where he published several books on astronomy, not only his scientific observations, but his speculations on the music of the spheres. Complex and hard to understand, these books found few readers; nor did it help Kepler's reputation that his mother was tried and briefly imprisoned for witchcraft in 1605. Yet Kepler, who died in November 1630 in Regensburg, Germany, had forever changed the way that scientists looked at the heavens.

ANTOINE-LAURENT LAVOISIER (1743–1794)

French chemist

With the exception of **Robert Boyle** (1627–1691; see biography in this chapter), no man so clearly deserves the title father of chemistry as Antoine-Laurent Lavoisier (luh-VWAH-zhay). Lavoisier discovered few new substances or processes; rather, his greatest contributions lay in the area of chemical theory. By showing the role that oxygen plays in combustion (burning), for instance, he successfully debunked the misguided phlogiston theory, which maintained that fire is an actual substance as opposed to a chemical reaction.

Among Lavoisier's other discoveries was the conservation of matter in chemical reactions. This meant that the product or products of a chemical reaction contain exactly the same chemicals (though now in different arrangements) that reacted in the first place. The chemical conservation of matter helped lead to the establishment of modern atomic theory; so too did Lavoisier's clarification of the difference between elements and compounds. He also played a part in the development of modern chemical names, as well as the metric system.

A child of privilege

Lavoisier was the son of a successful lawyer and studied law himself before turning to scientific studies at the College Mazarin in Paris, France. He won election to the prestigious Royal Academy of Sciences in 1768, when he was twenty-five, and four years later his father purchased a title of nobility for him. In an earlier era, one could only be born into a noble title such as that of a duke; but by Lavoisier's time it was possible for a person to receive such honors merely on the basis of wealth.

Antoine-Laurent Lavoisier. (Reproduced courtesy of the Library of Congress.)

With his newly elevated social position, Lavoisier became a member of the Farmers-General, a private company that collected taxes for the royal government. As a member of the Gunpowder Commission, he lived in the Paris Arsenal, where he set up a private laboratory to test the results of chemical experiments performed by others, and to carry out his own. There is a certain irony in the image of Lavoisier working in the middle of the explosives and ammunition at the arsenal, because in more ways than one, he was sitting on a powder keg.

France in the late 1700s was seething with discontent at the power of its king and nobility, and this would explode in the French Revolution of 1789. The original leaders of the revolution were liberals, and Lavoisier was among those who supported their aim of bringing democracy and reform to France. In time, however, extremists would gain control of the revolution, and Lavoisier would be among their most notable victims.

Contributions to chemical theory

During his all-too-brief career, Lavoisier contributed enormously to chemical theory. Though his English contemporaries Joseph Black (1728–

1799), Henry Cavendish (1731–1810), and Joseph Priestley (1733–1804) made far more discoveries, it was Lavoisier who confirmed, consolidated, extended, and explained those many discoveries. The result was a new understanding of chemical processes that provided the framework for the development of chemistry as a modern science.

Not only did Lavoisier discover the part that oxygen plays in combustion, thus debunking the notion of phlogiston, he also developed a larger theory that explained combustion as well as oxidation (for example, the rusting of metals) and respiration. Thus it is largely because of Lavoisier that scientists came to understand the critical role that oxygen plays in daily life.

Another significant aspect of Lavoisier's work was his emphasis on careful quantitative methods in chemistry. Quantitative, or number-based, analysis, is much more exact than the use of qualitative methods, or terminology such as hot or cold. Lavoisier and Pierre-Simon Laplace (1749–1827) pioneered the use of the calorimeter, a device for measuring the thermal (temperature-related) properties of various substances, thus paving the way for the subdiscipline known as thermochemistry. In addition, Lavoisier was the first to realize that all substances can exist in three states: gas, liquid, and solid.

He also played a role in developing a system of chemical nomenclature, or names. In the past, it had been sufficient for chemists to develop mere descriptive names for substances, but with the tens of millions of compounds that exist, it would be impossible for anyone to memorize all such names. Therefore chemists today use a system, which had its beginnings with Lavoisier, that employs specific rules for identifying substances in such a way that the name indicates the elements of which it is made. (For example, nitrous oxide, the anesthetic known by the common name of laughing gas, clearly contains nitrogen and oxygen.)

Death in the Reign of Terror

Lavoisier helped to establish the metric system, a valuable legacy of the French Revolution. Yet that revolution also left in its wake a great deal of misery, particularly after the takeover by the radical Jacobin faction in 1793. Lavoisier, appointed secretary of the treasury in 1791, fell afoul of the new leaders, who had him imprisoned in 1793. Within a year he had been tried and executed by guillotine, one of many thousands who met such a fate in what became known as the Reign of Terror.

For all his brilliance and his many contributions, Lavoisier was a difficult man. He often became embroiled in disputes with other scientists, sometimes claiming their discoveries as his own, and at other times using the results produced by others without acknowledging their work. Yet he was without a doubt one of the greatest thinkers of his generation, and his execution was one of the most tragic outcomes of the French Revolution. After his execution, mathematician Joseph-Louis Lagrange (1736–1813) commented, "It took them only an instant to cut off that head, and a hundred years may not produce another like it."

ISAAC NEWTON (1642–1727)

English physicist and mathematician

If any one person can be called the greatest scientist of all time, it would probably be Sir Isaac Newton. His work on gravitation and the laws of motion, published in his *Philosophiae naturalis principia mathematica* (1687), sometimes called just *Principia,* constituted the high point of the Scientific Revolution and one of the great turning points of world history. Building on the ideas of **Nicolaus Copernicus** (1473–1543; see biography in this chapter), **Galileo Galilei** (1564–1642; see biography in this chapter), **Johannes Kepler** (1571–1630; see biography in this chapter), and **René Descartes** (1596–1650; see biography in Mathematics chapter), Newton offered a new system for understanding the physical world, and his ideas set the tone for an entire age of scientific exploration.

Isaac Newton.
(© Corbis-Bettmann. Reproduced by permission of the Corbis Corporation.)

But the laws of gravitation and motion, important as they were, are far from the only contributions made by Newton. As a mathematician, he developed a form of calculus independent of, and different from, that established by Gottfried Wilhelm Leibniz (1646–1716; see biography in Mathematics chapter). He also revolutionized the area of physics known as optics, concerned with the production and transmission of light, by establishing the fact that white light breaks down to form the colors of the spectrum.

A troubled personal life

Newton was the son of an illiterate farmer who died before he was born, on Christmas Day 1642, the same year Galileo died, and later his mother married a man Newton hated. Therefore he went to live instead with his grandmother. Perhaps because of the troubles in his early life, Newton suffered mental and emotional breakdowns in 1678 and 1693 and has been described as suspicious, neurotic, tortured, and overbearing.

Some of these problems may be traced to his incredible intellect. It has been estimated that Newton had an IQ (intelligence quotient) of 210, about twice that of the average human being, yet as a boy he was not a good student. He took little interest in school and instead spent his time building mechanical contraptions such as water clocks and a mouse-powered mill. A turning point came when he got into a fight with a school bully; by fighting back he seemed to gain confidence, and his schoolwork improved as a result.

A fruitful break

In 1661 Newton entered Trinity College at Cambridge, in England, and while there he made the first of his important discoveries, developing the binomial theorem in mathematics. In 1665, the year he earned his bachelor's degree, the university closed for eighteen months due to an outbreak of the bubonic plague, and Newton retired to his family's home in the town of Woolsthorpe.

The break led to one of the most productive phases in Newton's career. By the time he returned to Trinity in 1667, he had discovered calculus; conducted experiments with prisms that led to his theory of colors; and developed the foundations of his gravitational theory. He was just twenty-five years old.

Newton received his master's degree in 1668 and became a professor of mathematics, a position he would hold for thirty-two years. He published his first paper, on the theory of color, in 1672, and was elected to the Royal Society, England's leading scientific institution, as a result of his invention of a reflecting telescope.

Work in optics

His subsequent studies in optics resulted in the foundation of that discipline in its modern version. Not only did Newton show that white light is composed of a spectrum of colors, but he developed new theories of light and color based on the mathematical treatment of observations and experiments.

To explain the way that light travels, Newton developed the corpuscular theory, based on the idea that light is made up of particles. Opposed to this was **Christiaan Huygens**'s (1629–1695; see biography in this chapter) wave theory of light, and in the years that followed Newton and his supporters would fight a bitter battle against Huygens and his.

Much the same took place in the field of mathematics, with British thinkers generally supporting Newton against Gottfried Wilhelm Leibniz

(1646–1716; see biography in Mathematics chapter) as the father of calculus. Nor was this the only quarrel involving Newton, who also had a long-running dispute with Robert Hooke (1635–1703) regarding authorship of gravitational theory.

The *Principia*

Despite his many achievements up to that point, Newton had yet to present his greatest work, the *Principia.* Though the book would prove to be one of the most influential works ever written, Newton had been in no hurry to publish it, and he only did so at the urging of astronomer Edmond Halley (1656–1742), who agreed to pay the printing costs.

The *Principia* quite literally explained the universe; that is, it provided a set of principles that identified the physical principles behind the movement and interactions of matter. In the book Newton established that gravitational force between two bodies is equal to the product of the two bodies' mass divided by the square of the distance between them, and multiplied by a quantity known as the gravitational constant. What this means is that the larger two bodies are, and the smaller the distance between them, the greater the gravitational attraction.

The law of universal gravitation explains how the universe holds together, while the laws of motion establish how and why objects interact with one another. The first law identifies inertia, or the tendency of an object in motion to remain in motion, and an object at rest to remain at rest, unless acted upon by some outside force. Inertia is measured in terms of mass, defined by the second law as the ratio of force to acceleration; in other words, force is equal to mass multiplied by acceleration. Finally, the third law shows that for every action, there is an equal and opposite reaction. Together, these laws explain all manner of physical events, from the behavior of heavenly bodies to the most mundane occurrences in everyday life.

Newton's legacy

Widely recognized and honored for his groundbreaking work, Newton was elected to Parliament in 1689 and 1701 and named master of the Royal Mint in 1696. In 1703 he was elected president of the Royal Society and was reelected each year until his death. In 1705 he was knighted.

In addition to his other work, Newton also studied and wrote in the fields of alchemy, history, music theory, chemistry, astronomy, and theology. A devoted Christian, he was always concerned with the effect his ideas might have on religious faith, an interesting parallel with one of the only men who warrants comparison with Newton: Albert Einstein (1879–1955). Einstein, whose relativity theory changed scientists' understanding of the universe as much as Newton's work had two centuries earlier, was also a man of deep religious faith who feared that his ideas would lead to a loss of belief in God.

With regard to Newton's principles, the conclusions people drew had a great deal to do with what they already believed. People who believed in God saw in his explanation of physical events a deep sense of order in the universe, which implied a loving Supreme Being. On the other hand, those who opposed religious faith believed that Newton had removed the need for God and made it possible to explain the universe in purely mechanical terms. These reactions show the powerful effect of Newton's work, which brought into being a new era that placed greater trust in science and the human ability to work out problems. Among the products of this climate were the principles embodied in the American Declaration of Independence and the U.S. Constitution.

PTOLEMY (c. 100–c. 170)

Greco–Roman astronomer and geographer

In his *Almagest,* Ptolemy described a view of the universe that prevailed for almost fifteen hundred years. Influenced by **Aristotle** (384–322 B.C.E.; see biography in this chapter), he identified Earth as the center of the cosmos, with the Sun and all other bodies moving around it. Over the centuries that followed, thinkers began to challenge these ideas, but criticism was muted until **Nicolaus Copernicus** (1473–1543; see biography in this chapter) showed that Earth revolves around the Sun, not vice versa.

Despite the flaws in his ideas, Ptolemy succeeded in offering a convincing version of cosmology, or an explanation of the arrangement and origins of the universe. His contributions were more clearly positive in the area of geography, a realm in which he established a number of now-accepted notions.

Ptolemy's time and place

Virtually nothing is known about the life of this thinker who so greatly influenced the future of world events. Though he is typically known simply as Ptolemy (TAHL-uh-mee), his full name was Claudius Ptolemaeus, and some scholars have taken the fact that he had a Latin name as a sign his family were citizens of the Roman Empire.

In any case, Ptolemy certainly lived in the Roman Empire, though whether as a citizen, a special status that involved much greater rights than those accorded to most members of the population, is not clear. Ethnically he was Greek, and he lived in Alexandria, Egypt, a center of Greek culture that had been founded more than four centuries before his time.

Ptolemy, who lived to be about seventy years old, was alive at the end of the great Greco–Roman civilization that had originated hundreds of years earlier in Greece. His was the final period of peace, prosperity, and progress in ancient times. Because of this, it would be more than a thousand years before the Western world produced scientists of his stature, and therefore his ideas would exert an enormous effect on Europeans' beliefs about Earth and space.

The *Almagest* and other works

Written about 150 C.E., the *Almagest* located more than a thousand stars and forty-eight constellations; explained how to calculate latitude and longitude; and predicted solar and lunar eclipses. It also presented complicated mathematical models that, when applied to the movement of objects in the heavens, made it possible to sustain the belief that Earth was at the center of the universe.

Ptolemy (seated). (Reproduced by permission of Archive Photos, Inc.)

Ptolemy was also interested in astrology and the impact of planetary position on human society. His four-volume *Apotelesmatica* became a primary reference for horoscope readers. Of more value to science was his *Geography,* in which he listed the latitude and longitude for many major cities; established the practice of showing north at the top of a map; and presented mathematical models describing how to depict the spherical Earth on a flat surface. He also wrote on music theory and optics.

Ptolemy might be described as a flawed genius: after all, one would have to be brilliant to devise a method, as he did, for making the geocentric or Earth-centered model of the universe workable. Yet he helped to influence centuries of ignorance, not only with his cosmology, but also with his geography. Rejecting the accurate measurement of Earth's circumference made by another Alexandrian, **Eratosthenes** of Cyrene (c. 276–c. 194 B.C.E.; see biography in Mathematics chapter), he instead accepted a much smaller figure calculated by the philosopher Posidonius (c. 135–c. 51 B.C.E.) Thanks to Ptolemy, Europeans remained convinced that Asia lay just a couple of thousand miles to the west, and in 1492 Christopher Columbus (1451–1506) set out to find it, only to discover an entirely new hemisphere.

BRIEF BIOGRAPHIES

GEORGIUS AGRICOLA (1494–1555)

Agricola, born Georg Bauer, was a German mineralogist and metallurgist (one who studies the science and technology of metals) often referred to as the father of mineralogy. He wrote a series of treatises on the principles of geology and mineralogy that proved highly influential to the early development of those fields. His most significant work was *De re metallica*, which presents a detailed and accurate account of sixteenth-century mining practices. The book, which discusses the extraction of metals, smelting, assaying techniques, and chemical technologies, remained the standard text on mining and metallurgy for over four centuries.

ALBERT OF SAXONY (c. 1316–1390)

Albert was a German philosopher and mathematician who wrote on mechanics (the area of physics dedicated to objects in motion) and geology. Around 1350 Albert presented a theory of impetus (an early version of the idea now known as kinetic energy) that distinguished between uniform and irregular motion, thus helping to call into question misguided ideas about physics that dated back to **Aristotle** (384–322 B.C.E.; see biography in Life Science chapter) In the field of geology, he introduced an influential but incorrect theory by maintaining that a process of uplift on land compensates for the force of erosion exerted on it by the oceans.

ARISTARCHUS OF SAMOS (FLOURISHED c. 270 B.C.E.)

Aristarchus was a Greek astronomer and mathematician famous for developing the first heliocentric (Sun-centered) planetary theory. For this, he has come to be known as the Copernicus of antiquity, or an ancient forerunner of **Nicolaus Copernicus** (1473–1543; see biography in this chapter). He also made an impressive, if ultimately unsuccessful, attempt to estimate the ratio of the distances between Earth, the Moon, and the Sun. His methods—he used trigonometry, and based his calculation on the measurement of angles—were correct, but the instruments available at that time were too primitive to yield reliable results. Therefore Aristarchus judged the distance to the Sun as twenty times that to the Moon, when in fact it is about three hundred ninety times as great.

AVICENNA (ABU 'ALI AL-HUSAYN IBN 'ABD ALLAH IBN SINA; 980–1037)

Avicenna (also known as Ibn Sina), was a Persian philosopher, physician, mathematician, and astronomer. Along with **Averroës** (1126–1198; see

Life Science chapter for full biographies of both men), he is often regarded as one of the two most important philosopher-scientists of medieval Islam. In his *Kitab al-shifa* (Book of healing; 1021–23), Avicenna criticized **Aristotle**'s flawed ideas on physics. He also anticipated a breakthrough discovery by Thomas Bradwardine by suggesting that time and motion must be interrelated since the one can have no meaning without the other. Avicenna also contributed to geological studies, maintaining that mountains are formed through sedimentation, and valleys through erosion. His division of minerals into salts, sulfurs, metals, and stones prevailed until the late 1700s. Influenced by Geber (Jabir ibn Hayyan; c. 721–c. 815; see sidebar), he embraced alchemy but sought to separate alchemical medicine from its more far-fetched aspects: unlike most alchemists, he did not believe it was possible to change one substance into another.

AL-BATTANI (c. 858–929)

Al-Battani, known in the West as Albategnius, is considered the greatest astronomer of the medieval Islamic world. He is best known for his astronomical handbook *Kitab al-zij,* which introduced new trigonometric methods for performing astronomical computations. He devised improved instruments and made accurate observations that allowed him to give corrected values for several astronomical constants in accordance with the system established by **Ptolemy.** However, al-Battani's observations also revealed errors in Ptolemy's *Almagest.*

THOMAS BRADWARDINE (c. 1290–1349)

Bradwardine was an English mathematician who developed the idea of applying mathematical formulas to physical laws. In order to do so, he had to overcome a problem that dated back to the great Greek mathematician **Euclid** (see biography in Mathematics chapter). Euclid had maintained that it is not possible to form a ratio between different types of quantities, such as distance and time. It is thanks to Bradwardine, then, that the modern world has concepts such as miles per hour.

TYCHO BRAHE (1546–1601)

Brahe was a Danish astronomer known as the greatest observer of activity in the sky prior to the invention of the telescope. His most notable observations included the 1572 nova (an extremely bright star) and the 1577 comet, both of which helped to undermine the belief, handed down from **Aristotle** (see biography in Life Science chapter), that the universe is perfect and unchanging. After Brahe's death, his assistant, **Johannes Kepler,** (see biography in this chapter) inherited his extensive astronomical data and used this information in establishing his famous laws of planetary motion.

GEORGES LOUIS LECLERC, COMTE DE BUFFON (1707–1788)

Leclerc, comte de Buffon (the count of Buffon, the name by which he is known) was a French naturalist famous for his multivolume encyclopedia of natural history. In *Histoire naturelle* (Natural history), published in forty-four volumes from 1749 to 1804, Buffon became one of the first scientists to suggest that the Earth is much, much older than a strict interpretation of the Bible's Book of Genesis would allow. He also contributed to probability theory (see essay "Patterns and Possibilities" in the Mathematics chapter) with what came to be known as Buffon's needle problem, involving the probability that a needle of a given length will fall on a line when dropped on a piece of lined paper. In his writings on natural history, Buffon commented on a wide variety of subjects, including geology, the origins of the solar system, biological classification, human evolution, extinct species, and the scientific method.

JEAN BURIDAN (1300–1358)

Buridan was a French physicist and philosopher who, more than three centuries before **Isaac Newton** (see biography in this chapter), anticipated Newton's first law of motion by stating than an object in motion will remain moving unless acted upon by outside forces. This put him at odds with the prevailing idea, passed down from **Aristotle** (see biography in Life Science chapter), who had maintained that a moving object requires continual application of force to keep it in motion. In a commentary on Aristotle's *Physics*, Buridan challenged the Greek philosopher's assertion that the air around an object in motion is what keeps it moving. Going much further than Johannes Philoponus had done eight centuries before, Buridan produced an amazingly accurate hypothesis: that one object imparts to another a certain amount of energy, in proportion to its velocity and mass, that causes the second object to move a certain distance. He was also correct in stating that the weight of an object may increase or decrease its speed, depending on other circumstances; and that air resistance slows an object in motion.

ANDERS CELSIUS (1701–1744)

Celsius was a Swedish astronomer and mathematician who in 1741 established the temperature scale, used throughout most of the world today, that bears his name. While taking meteorological, or weather, measurements, Celsius became frustrated with the lack of accurate thermometers, so he set about creating a more reliable instrument using a fixed scale based on two invariable, naturally occurring points. His lower fixed point was determined by immersing the instrument in melting ice, the upper point by placing it in boiling water. He set the upper point at 0 degrees and the lower at 100 degrees; later, his countryman, **Carolus Linnaeus** (see biography in Life Science chapter), inverted the scale.

Aristotle

Aristotle (384–322 B.C.E.) was a Greek philosopher who had more influence on the sciences than any ancient thinker. His impact on the life sciences was generally positive (see Life Science chapter for a biography and a discussion of Aristotle's contributions to biology), but his work in the physical sciences had a less beneficial effect.

Aristotle subscribed to the idea of four elements (earth, air, fire, and water), which supposedly make up all objects in differing proportions, and this had a significant impact on the ideas of physics and astronomy he put forward. According to Aristotle, Earth is the center of the universe, and all objects revolve around it in perfectly circular orbits; the heavens are unchanging and made of substances different from those found on Earth; heavier objects fall faster than light ones; and objects fall when dropped because the elements in them are seeking their natural position.

Every one of these propositions is wrong, even the one about heavier objects falling faster. (They only do so on Earth because of air resistance, which slows light objects. In a vacuum, or an area devoid of air, a stone and a feather would fall at the same speed.) Yet Aristotle's views on astronomy had a huge influence on **Ptolemy,** (see biography in this chapter) and the Aristotelian system would not be overturned for some two thousand years, until the time of **Nicolaus Copernicus, Galileo Galilei,** and **Isaac Newton** (see biographies in this chapter).

Despite his flaws, Aristotle was the first scientist to prove that the world is round. He was also an unmistakably brilliant thinker who wrote foundational texts on biology, rhetoric (the art of speaking and writing), politics, psychology, ethics (the philosophy of right and wrong), and drama.

ERNST CHLADNI (1756–1827)

Chladni (KLAHD-nee) was a German physicist who pioneered in the fields of acoustics and meteoritics. Because the study of sound waves and meteorites were in their infancy when Chladni first studied them, he is sometimes known as the father of both subdisciplines. A French scientist, Pierre Gassendi (1592–1655), had measured the speed of sound in air, but Chladni extended Gassendi's work by developing a method of measuring the speed of sound in other gases. He was also the first to propose that meteorites have an extraterrestrial origin.

CHU HSI (FLOURISHED c. 1175)

Chu Hsi was a Chinese scholar who became the first to observe, in his *Chu tsi shu chieh yao,* that fossils were once living organisms. In the book, Chu Hsi maintained that the universe had been created by violent friction, which in turn caused Earth, the Sun, and other bodies to remain in motion, an idea not unlike the Big Bang theory accepted by scientists today. He also accurately stated that "Should Heaven stop only for one instant, Earth must fall down."

CHARLES-AUGUSTIN COULOMB (1736–1806)

Coulomb was a French physicist and engineer best known for his contributions to the study of electricity and magnetism. In his early career, Coulomb focused on subjects such as structural supports and friction, producing a theory on friction that remained the standard until replaced by early twentieth-century studies involving molecular activity. He went on to develop the torsion balance, an instrument for measuring extremely small forces, which he applied in studying electric and magnetic phenomena. This led to the formulation of Coulomb's Law (1785), which states that the repulsion and attraction of two electrically charged objects is related to the product of their charges, and inversely related to the square of the distance between them. In his honor, the unit of electric charge is today called the coulomb.

DEMOCRITUS (c. 460–c. 370 B.C.E.)

Democritus was a Greek philosopher who, along with his teacher, Leucippus (flourished in the fifth century B.C.E.), introduced the idea that the world is made up of tiny objects called atoms. To resolve the many contradictions involved in theories of matter up to that point, Leucippus introduced the idea of an infinite number of indivisible units (*atomos* is Greek for "indivisible") that float in empty space. Democritus, who greatly developed Leucippus's ideas, maintained that these atoms were of different sizes, though not so big as to be visible, and collided in such a way that they either joined or reacted to one another. He also taught that all bodies emit thin films of atoms that interact with the sensory organs, which is indeed partially the case, since smell, for instance, is the result of objects emitting atoms and molecules absorbed by the nose. Today scientists recognize the atoms are divisible, but much else about Democritus's theory is correct; unfortunately, ancient thinkers rejected atomic theory in favor of the misguided theory of four elements.

DANIEL FAHRENHEIT (1686–1736)

Fahrenheit was a German–Dutch physicist and instrument maker who developed the first mercury thermometer, as well as the temperature scale that bears his name. He also established the fact that the boiling point of a substance varies with changes in pressure, and discovered that water can be supercooled, or brought to a temperature lower than its freezing point without freezing, by the use of certain kinds of salt. (This is the method often used today to melt ice on roads.) Influenced by Danish physicist Ole Rømer (1644–1710), Fahrenheit became convinced that alcohol was not the best thermometric substance, or the substance whose expansion and contraction a thermometer measures. He realized that mercury expands and contracts much more uniformly and built the first mercury thermometer in 1713. He introduced his temperature scale in 1724.

ROBERT GROSSETESTE (c. 1175–1253)

Grosseteste was an English physicist and philosopher noted for his studies of light and sound. The first important European scholar of optics (the area of physics concerned with the production and transmission of light), Grosseteste also wrote on astronomy, discussing comets and advancing a theory of tides. He correctly suggested that sound is the result of vibrations passing through air. Grosseteste is also remembered as the teacher of the distinguished scientist **Roger Bacon** (see biography in Technology and Invention chapter).

EDMOND HALLEY (1656–1742)

Halley was an English astronomer and physicist best known for predicting the return of the comet that today bears his name, and for the instrumental role he played in the publication of **Isaac Newton**'s (see biography in this chapter) highly influential *Principia* (1687). He also produced a fairly accurate measurement of the distance from Earth to the Sun, 95 million miles (152 million kilometers), which compares well with the presently accepted value of 92.9 million miles (148.64 million kilometers). Halley encouraged Newton to publish his work on gravitation and motion through the Royal Society, of which both were members. However, due to financial difficulties on the part of the organization, Halley chose to assume full financial responsibility for the publication of the book, which introduced Newton's laws of gravitation and motion. In 1695 Halley undertook his now-famous study of comets, which led him to believe that the comets of 1531, 1607, and 1682 were the same object. In 1705 he predicted that the object would reappear in December 1758, which it did, sixteen years after his death, thus helping to confirm Newton's gravitational theory.

WILLIAM HERSCHEL (1738–1822)

Herschel was a German–English astronomer and musician who in 1781 identified Uranus, the first planet discovered since ancient times. He also conducted the first thorough and systematic study of objects beyond the solar system and discovered infrared radiation emitted by the Sun and by other objects that send out electromagnetic radiation. Herschel's brother Alexander and sister Caroline (1750–1848) assisted him in his work, and Caroline became a recognized astronomer herself. She discovered eight comets and three nebulae (clouds of gas or dust in space) and received the gold medal from the Royal Astronomical Society in 1828.

ROBERT HOOKE (1635–1703)

Hooke was an English physicist best known for his research on elastic materials, as well as for his work as a microscopist (one who works with microscopes). Elastic materials are solids that will return to their original condition when the external force that has stretched them is removed. Hooke's experiments led to the discovery of what became known as Hooke's law, which states that the amount an elastic material will stretch under an external stress is proportional to the stress itself. This idea has a number of applications in areas from engineering to watchmaking. Hooke also gained wide recognition for his *Micrographia* (1665), an illustrated discussion of observations he made with a reflecting microscope he built himself. He coined the word "cell" to explain the microscopic biological structures he observed. Hooke also conducted important early research regarding gravitational attraction and planetary motion, and shared these ideas with **Isaac Newton**, (see biography in this chapter) who became much more famous for his work in those areas. As a result, the two were involved in a prolonged controversy regarding who should receive credit.

JAMES HUTTON (1726–1797)

Hutton was a Scottish geologist and chemist recognized as the father of modern geology. With no supporting data or earlier research to support his conclusions, his personal observations generated the concept of the rock cycle, which shows that the matter that makes up rocks is never created or destroyed. It is simply redistributed and transformed from one

Joseph Black

Joseph Black (1728–1799) was a Scottish chemist, physicist, and physician, best known for his work involving heat, carbon dioxide, and the study of chemical reactions. Black was the first to notice that when ice melts or water evaporates, heat is absorbed but the temperature does not change immediately. He called this "latent heat." He also observed that when the temperature for identical quantities of different substances is raised by the same number of degrees, different amounts of heat, which he defined as specific heat, are required.

These discoveries greatly influenced the development of calorimetry, which is concerned with the measurement of heat given off or absorbed in chemical and physical processes. Black's friend **James Watt** (1736–1819; see biography in Technology and Invention chapter) put these ideas to use in the development of the steam engine.

Carbon dioxide, known as fixed air, had been discovered previously by Stephen Hales (1677–1761) but was ignored until rediscovered by Black. His clear demonstration that fixed air differs chemically from ordinary air resulted in a clarification of the concept of gases as a state of matter separate from liquids and solids, and led to the discovery of various other gases.

Finally, Black's careful experimental studies played a major role in the development of chemistry as a modern quantitative science, or a science based on exact measurement, instead of vague descriptions and qualitative statements. (Terms such as hot and cold are qualitative, whereas 212 degrees Fahrenheit or zero degrees Celsius are quantitative.) Applying Isaac Newton's third law of motion to chemistry, Black reasoned that if one substance acts upon another, the second will exhibit a response to this action. Using this terminology, he explained the chemical change that occurs in such substances as a "reaction," a term still used today.

type to another in three stages. This principle, called uniformitarianism, is one of the foundations of modern geology.

JOHANNES PHILOPONUS (FLOURISHED IN THE SIXTH CENTURY C.E.)

Johannes, a Byzantine (medieval Greek) scholar, was the first thinker to challenge **Aristotle**'s (384–322 B.C.E.; see biography in this chapter) influential but incorrect ideas regarding motion. Known variously as John Philoponus (fuh-LAHP-uh-nus) and John the Grammarian, Johannes criticized Aristotle's claim that a body in motion requires a continued application of force to remain in motion. By contrast, Johannes maintained that a body will keep moving in the absence of friction or opposition, an idea that anticipated the first law of motion established by **Isaac Newton** (1642–1727; see biography in this chapter). Between Newton and Johannes lay a long line of thinkers who chipped away at Aristotelian physics, among them the Arab philosopher Avicenna (Ibn Sina; 980–1037), the French scholar Peter John Olivi (1248–1298), and French mathematician Jean Buridan (1300–1358); but it was Johannes who struck the first blow against Aristotle's system.

AL-KINDI (DIED c. 870)

Al-Kindi was an Arab philosopher, astronomer, mathematician, and physician whose greatest contribution to the physical sciences lay in his optical work. Al-Kindi, a member of the famous House of Wisdom in Baghdad (now in Iraq), successfully refuted intromission, the ancient theory that the eye sees objects because they emit thin films or images of themselves. If this were so, he maintained, a circle glimpsed from its edge would still look like a full circle. (Later, **Alhazen** (see biography in this chapter) overturned extromission, another, equally incorrect, theory of vision, which stated that light emanates from the eye, which sends out rays that make objects visible.) Al-Kindi also wrote on mineralogy and acoustics, the area of physics concerned with sound.

JOHANN GOTTLOB LEHMANN (1719–1767)

Lehmann was a German geologist who established the foundations of stratigraphy, or the scientific study of sedimentary rocks with regard to their order and sequence. His *Versuche einer Geschichte von Flotz-Gebrugen* (1756), in which he classified mountains and established a theory of their origins, was the world's first geologic profile. In it, he observed that the placement of rocks on the Earth's surface or below it is not random; rather, it reflects a history (*Geschichte*) in geological terms. Obvious as this idea might seem now, it was far from apparent in Lehmann's time, and not only did his book establish a framework for stratigraphy, it also spurred on local geology, or the investigation of specific sites.

MARY THE JEWESS (FLOURISHED IN THE FIRST CENTURY C.E.)

Mary, sometimes known as Miriam or Maria Prophetissa, was an alchemist in Alexandria, Egypt, and one of the few notable women in the physical sciences prior to 1800. It appears that in the "outlaw" world of alchemy, which never gained a great deal of acceptance among the recognized sciences, it was not unusual for women to become practitioners. Mary is noted for a number of inventions, in particular a water bath or double boiler still known in France as the *bain-marie* ("Mary's bath"). Mary wrote on the uses of alchemy for medicine and assigned to various metals the qualities of the male or female genders.

NICHOLAS OF CUSA (1401–1464)

Nicholas, sometimes known as Nicholas Krebs or Cryfts, was a German philosopher, mathematician, and astronomer who anticipated **Nicolaus Copernicus** (1473–1543; see biography in this chapter) in maintaining that Earth revolves around the Sun. He also held that the stars were other suns (though his definition of Earth as a star indicates that he misunderstood the meaning of the term), and that other habitable worlds like Earth orbited them. In a 1436 treatise, he made the case for calendar reform, which came to pass with the Gregorian reform of 1582. (See "Marking Time" in Technology and Invention chapter.)

PETRUS PEREGRINUS DE MARICOURT (FLOURISHED 1200S)

Peregrinus was a French crusader (religious warrior) and physicist who conducted the first systematic experiments on magnetism and invented improved nautical compasses. He was one of the few medieval scientists who conducted experiments of any kind. His *Epistola de magnete* (Letter on the magnet) was written while on a crusade under the direction of the king of Sicily, an endeavor in which he earned the title Peregrinus, meaning "pilgrim." Peregrinus's treatise provides the earliest known account of the north-south magnetic polarity.

POMPONIUS MELA (FLOURISHED IN THE FIRST CENTURY C.E.)

Mela was a Roman geographer whose system of five temperature zones remains in use today. He introduced these in *De situ orbis* (c. 43 C.E.), which divided Earth into northern frigid (cold), northern temperate (mild), torrid (very hot), southern temperate, and southern frigid zones.

Unlike many scientific works of antiquity, Mela's geography has remained influential well into modern times.

JOSEPH PRIESTLEY (1733–1804)

Priestley was an English chemist and naturalist who discovered oxygen, conducted fundamental studies of gases, and contributed to the understanding of photosynthesis in plants. In addition to oxygen, Priestley discovered eight other gases, including the element nitrogen, the nitrogen compounds ammonia and nitrous oxide, and the compounds hydrogen chloride and sulfur dioxide. He also invented soda water, making possible the creation of carbonated beverages, and his research into plant life led to the discovery that plants take in air and produce oxygen.

RHAZES (AR-RAZI; C. 865–C. 923)

Rhazes (see biography in Life Science chapter) was a Persian physician who also studied alchemy. Though his contributions lay primarily in the area of medicine, Rhazes is also credited as the first scientist to use hydrochloric acid. Hydrochloric acid, the first chlorine compound made by humans (salt is a natural chlorine compound), is produced by dissolving hydrogen chloride gas in water.

KARL WILHELM SCHEELE (1742–1786)

Scheele was a Swedish chemist whose record as a discoverer of new elements, compounds, and chemical reactions has long remained unequaled. In 1773 he proposed that air was composed of two gases, oxygen and nitrogen, and though he preceded Joseph Priestley (1733–1804) in his discovery of these elements, Scheele published his findings later, and is therefore usually not given credit. Scheele also discovered barium, molybdenum, tungsten, and manganese. He was the first to isolate chlorine and show that it could bleach cloth. However, he thought that it was a compound, and only later did English chemist Sir Humphry Davy (1778–1829) identify it as an element. Scheele also discovered or isolated a number of acids, including uric, tartaric, lactic, and hydrocyanic acid. He was the first to prepare the chemical compounds arsine and hydrogen sulfide, and his other discoveries included glycerine, copper arsenite, and the toxic gases hydrogen sulfide and hydrogen fluoride. Scheele also helped pave the way for photography by showing that sunlight removes salts from silver chloride, leaving only the metal behind.

SHIH SHEN (FLOURISHED C. 350 B.C.E.)

Shih Shen was a Chinese astronomer often credited with creating the first star catalogue. In about 350 B.C.E., he made a map showing some eight

Geber and the False Geber

The name Geber is used, sometimes confusingly, in reference to two men. The first of these was the Arab alchemist and physician Jabir ibn Hayyan (c. 721–c. 815), known to the West as Geber, and often credited as the father of Arab alchemy. Alchemy involves the belief that matter can be perfected (for instance, that ordinary metals can be turned into gold), and has little grounding in scientific fact. Yet alchemy also provided the basis for the genuine science of chemistry, and Geber is widely regarded as the father, or at least the ancestor, of scientific chemistry. He is also credited with the discovery of arsenic, sulfur, and mercury.

Even historians of science tend to confuse Geber with an individual known simply as the False Geber. Apparently a Spaniard who flourished during a period beginning in about 1310, the False Geber took on the name of the famous Arab alchemist as a way of adding to his reputation. He produced a number of important works on alchemy, including *The Sum of Perfection, Book of Furnaces, The Investigation of Perfection*, and *The Invention of Verity*, which explained and popularized alchemical principles. The False Geber, whose nickname hardly does him justice since he was apparently a great scientific mind in his own right, is also credited with discovering sulfuric acid.

hundred stars, and shortly thereafter the astronomers Gan De (Kan Te) and Wu Xien (Wu Hsien) developed their own star catalogues. More than six centuries later, Chen Zhuo (flourished c. 300 B.C.E.) would bring together these three catalogues in a single star map.

ABD AL-RAHMAN AL-SUFI (903–986)

Al-Sufi was an Arab astronomer who revised the catalogue of fixed stars established by **Ptolemy** (see biography in this chapter), and prepared an accurate map of the sky that became a standard work in the West for several centuries. He also wrote about a southern group of stars, today known as the Nebecula Major or the Greater Magellanic Cloud, based on reports from Arab sailors in the Malay Archipelago (modern Indonesia and the Philippines). A small mountainous ring on the Moon is named after al-Sufi, who had an enormous influence on the Arab astronomical studies of his time.

THALES OF MILETUS (c. 625–c. 547 B.C.E.)

Thales (THAY-leez) was a Greek philosopher and astronomer remembered as the father both of philosophy and the physical sciences. No doubt there had been other philosophers and scientists before his time, but Thales was the first historical figure to form a hypothesis about the nature of the world. By stating that "Everything is water," he was apparently suggesting that water is the primary substance of the world, which is in a fluid state like that of water. He is also credited with predicting a solar eclipse in 585 B.C.E., and with introducing geometry to Greece, but both stories are most likely myths.

EVANGELISTA TORRICELLI (1608–1647)

Torricelli was an Italian mathematician and physicist who in 1643 invented the mercury barometer, a device for measuring atmospheric pressure. A student of **Galileo Galilei** (see biography in this chapter), he expanded on some of his teacher's ideas regarding projectile motion, the form of motion when an object is shot or thrown through the air. In addition to his work in ballistics, the area of projectile-motion studies that involves shots fired from a gun or cannon, he developed an important theorem with regard to hydrodynamics, the study of the motion of fluids. His development of the barometer resulted from his interests in pumps and vacuums. Filling a long glass tube with mercury and placing his finger over the open end, Torricelli inverted the tube and inserted it in a large dish of mercury. As expected, the mercury began to drain out of the tube, all but three inches (76 millimeters). Torricelli realized that the weight of air pressing on the mercury in the dish balanced that of the mercury column.

NASIR AD-DIN AL-TUSI (1201–1274)

Al-Tusi was a Persian astronomer who established an observatory at Maragheh, now in Azerbaijan, under the patronage of the Mongol ruler Hülegü Khan (c. 1217–1265). He designed a number of instruments for the observatory, which became a center of scientific learning in Muslim central Asia. There al-Tusi prepared the *Ilkhanic Tables* (Hülegü was known as the Il-Khan), which contained twelve years' worth of astronomical observations and developed new hypotheses on the movement of planets. Many scholars consider his ideas the most important contributions to the understanding of cosmology, the branch of astronomy concerned with

Regiomontanus

Regiomontanus (re-je-oh-mahn-TAYN-us; 1436–1476), was a German astronomer and mathematician who played a key role in reforming astronomical studies in Europe at the beginning of the Renaissance, a period of intellectual and artistic rebirth that lasted from about 1350 to 1600 C.E. His real name was Johann Müller, but like many European scientists of the early modern era, he Latinized it.

With his teacher, the great Austrian astronomer and mathematician Georg von Peuerbach (1423–1461), Regiomontanus conducted the first significant European work in astronomy since the thirteenth century, when the Alfonsine Tables, a set of astronomical tables attributed to the Spanish king and scientist Alfonso X (1221–1284), were produced. However, as Peuerbach pointed out to Regiomontanus, the Alfonsine Tables were riddled with errors and badly in need of reform.

Among the many observations made by Regiomontanus was the comet of 1472, later to be known as Halley's comet after English astronomer Sir Edmond Halley (1656–1742). Peuerbach influenced Regiomontanus to begin a revision of Ptolemy's *Almagest,* but the result was something much greater: the *Epitome of Astronomy* (1496), which revealed errors in Ptolemy's work and greatly influenced a young **Nicolaus Copernicus** (1473–1543; see biography in this chapter).

the structure of the universe, between the time of **Ptolemy** and that of **Nicolaus Copernicus** (see biographies in this chapter).

ZOU YAN (FLOURISHED C. 270 B.C.E.)

Zou Yan was a Chinese philosopher who developed a system of five elements: earth, water, fire, metal, and wood. The system of elements, which was associated with the idea of the opposing *yin* and *yang* forces, became the basis of the Chinese Naturalist school, which advocated the idea of living in harmony with nature. These concepts later spread to Korea and other parts of East Asia.

RESEARCH AND ACTIVITY IDEAS

1. As discussed in the essay "Early Greek Theories of Matter: What *Is* Everything?" for nearly two thousand years, the four elements theory of the ancient Greeks held sway in the West. (The Chinese likewise adopted a five elements theory.) Divide the class into two groups, one of which will study and report on the ancient theory of the elements, perhaps by using some of the resources listed in the For More Information section, as well as the rival theory of atomism. The other group will study and report on the modern understanding of elements, including topics such as the periodic table. After considering the two viewpoints as a class, compare and contrast them through discussion. How would the composition of something such as a stone or a piece of wood be explained from each perspective? Why did people hold on to the unworkable four elements theory for so long, when in fact it is almost entirely inaccurate?

2. Much of this chapter concerns the model of the universe (that is, the solar system) established by Aristotle and Ptolemy in ancient times. Typically the word "model" has been used here figuratively, rather than referring to a literal model. However, just as classrooms today often contain literal physical models of the solar system, it is certainly possible to construct a physical model of Ptolemy's universe. (Refer to sources in the For More Information section; some of these provide actual drawings from the medieval period showing the universe as scientists envisioned it then.) Either construct a three-dimensional model as a class, or draw individual pictures. Then discuss the difference between the Ptolemaic system and the view accepted today, with regard to how those differences affect both science and daily life. For instance, how would it make you feel to believe you lived at the center of the universe, rather than (as is in fact the case) on a tiny planet at the edge of it?

3. Visit the *Muslim Scientists, Mathematicians and Astronomers* Web site (http://cyperistan.org/islamic/), choose a particular individual, and prepare a report on that person. Talk about that person's debt to Greek civilization and about the debt Western civilization in turn owes the individual, not just for preserving Greek learning, but also for adding to it. (An example would be Alhazen, who went far beyond the Greeks in his understanding of optics.) Physicists, alchemists, and astronomers are preferable as subjects, but even those thinkers noted for other achievements, for example, Averroës and Avicenna, both covered in the Life Science chapter, contributed to the physical sciences

and would make good subjects as well. Have these men received appropriate recognition from the West? Why or why not? Alternatively, you might research and report on Chinese, Indian, or other non-European scientists prior to 1800. It should be noted, however, that with the exception of Indian mathematics and Chinese achievements in technology and invention, the scientific activity in these regions had little direct effect on Europe and European-influenced civilizations.

4. A consistent theme in the history of the physical sciences, from ancient times even to the present, has been the relationship between religion and science. This is a broad subject, because it does not necessarily involve only Christianity. Nor does it always involve conflict: the Catholic Church, for instance, actually supported much scientific study during the late Middle Ages (c. 1100–c. 1500 C.E.). It also goes beyond the physical sciences, including topics such as the religious prohibition (both in pagan Greece and Christian western Europe) against dissecting bodies, as discussed in the Life Science chapter. As a class, try to come up with as many examples as possible of the relationship between science and religion, and discuss these. Among the topics especially relevant to the physical sciences are religion and the development of calendars; Christian acceptance of Aristotelian and Ptolemaic ideas, which led to controversy surrounding the ideas of Copernicus and Galileo; and debates over the findings of geologists as compared with the Bible. After this discussion, divide into four groups, each of which argues for a different position on the subject of religion and science: (1) religion is more important than science; (2) science is more important than religion; (3) religion and science can coexist in a friendly fashion; or (4) religion and science have nothing to do with one another.

5. Most of the progress in the physical sciences between 2000 B.C.E. and 1799 C.E. took place in the last two hundred fifty years of this period, thanks to the work of Copernicus, Galileo, Newton, and others. Much of this has to do with the scientific method introduced by Galileo and refined by scientists who followed him. Research the scientific method, and explain what it is. Give examples of the way that Galileo and others applied it, and talk about the ways that it influenced later progress in science. How is it still used today? One particularly fruitful area of discussion involves the application of the scientific method to areas beyond science. For instance, if a person applies the scientific method—drawing ideas from actual observations, and then testing those ideas—it would be very hard to maintain prejudices of any kind. How would the world benefit from

learning the scientific method, along with the related area of logic? (For more about logic, see The Greeks' New Approach to Mathematics in the Mathematics chapter.) What are the limitations, if any, of the scientific method? Does it stifle or enhance creative thinking?

FOR MORE INFORMATION

Books

Allan, Tony. *Isaac Newton.* Des Plaines, IL: Heinemann Library, 2001.

Ardley, Neil. *The Science Book of Gravity.* San Diego, CA: Harcourt Brace Jovanovich, 1992.

Aylesworth, Thomas G. *The Alchemists: Magic into Science.* Reading, MA: Addison-Wesley, 1973.

Beshore, George. *Science in Ancient China.* New York: F. Watts, 1998.

Christianson, Gale E. *Isaac Newton and the Scientific Revolution.* New York: Oxford University Press, 1998.

Cooper, Christopher. *Matter.* New York: DK Publishing, 1999.

Costello, Darby, and Lindsay Radermacher. *Astrology.* New York: DK Publishing, 1996.

Fullick, Ann. *Matter.* Des Plaines, IL: Heinemann Library, 1999.

Gay, Kathlyn. *Science in Ancient Greece.* New York: F. Watts, 1988.

January, Brendan. *Science in Colonial America.* New York: F. Watts, 1999.

Kallen, Stuart A. *Exploring the Origins of the Universe.* New York: Twenty-First Century Books, 1997.

Lampton, Christopher. *Astronomy: From Copernicus to the Space Telescope.* New York: F. Watts, 1987.

Lloyd, Gill, and David Jeffries. *The History of Optics.* New York: Thomson Learning, 1995.

MacLachlan, James H. *Galileo Galilei: First Physicist.* New York: Oxford University Press, 1999.

McTavish, Douglas. *Isaac Newton.* New York: Bookwright Press, 1990.

Nardo, Don. *Gravity: The Universal Force.* San Diego, CA: Lucent Books, 1990.

Nardo, Don. *Scientists of Ancient Greece.* San Diego, CA: Lucent Books, 1999.

Newcomb, Ellsworth, and Hugh Kenny. *Alchemy to Atoms.* New York: Putnam, 1961.

Reed, George. *Eyes on the Universe.* New York: Benchmark Books, 2001.

Sis, Peter. *Starry Messenger: A Book Depicting the Life of a Famous Scientist, Mathematician, Astronomer, Philosopher, Physicist—Galileo Galilei.* New York: Farrar Straus Giroux, 2000.

Stewart, Melissa. *Science in Ancient India.* New York: F. Watts, 1999.

Stringer, John. *The Science of Gravity.* Austin, TX: Raintree Steck-Vaughn, 2000.

Voelkel, James R. *Johannes Kepler and the New Astronomy.* New York: Oxford University Press, 1999.

White, Michael. *Isaac Newton: Discovering Laws That Govern the Universe.* Woodbridge, CT: Blackbirch Press, 1999.

White, Michael. *Galileo Galilei: Inventor, Astronomer, and Rebel.* Woodbridge, CT: Blackbirch Press, 1999.

Woods, Geraldine. *Science in Ancient Egypt.* New York: F. Watts, 1998.

Web sites

The Alchemy Web Site and Virtual Library. http://www.levity.com/alchemy/home.html (accessed on February 28, 2002).

"Biographies of Famous Chemists." *The WWW Virtual Library.* http://www.liv.ac.uk/Chemistry/Links/refbiog.html (accessed on February 28, 2002).

Chemistry: A History. http://www.nidlink.com/~jfromm/history2/chemist.htm (accessed on February 28, 2002).

The Galileo Project—Rice University. http://es.rice.edu/ES/humsoc/Galileo/ (accessed on February 28, 2002).

The Golden Elixir: A Website on Chinese Alchemy. [Online] http://helios.unive.it/~dsao//pregadio/ (accessed on February 28, 2002.)

"The Greek, Indian, and Chinese Elements." *The Proceedings of the Friesian School, Fourth Series.* http://www.friesian.com/elements.htm (accessed on February 28, 2002).

Hamilton, Calvin J. "Halley's Comet." *Views of the Solar System.* http://www.solarviews.com/eng/halley.htm (accessed on February 28, 2002).

"Indexes of Biographies." *School of Mathematics and Statistics, University of St. Andrews, Scotland.* http://www-groups.dcs.st-and.ac.uk/~history/BiogIndex.html (accessed on February 28, 2002).

Institute and Museum of the History of Science of Florence, Italy. http://galileo.imss.firenze.it/museo/b/index.html (accessed on February 28, 2002).

The Medieval Science Page. http://members.aol.com/McNelis/medsci_index.html#Aslb (accessed on February 28, 2002).

Muslim Scientists, Mathematicians and Astronomers. http://cyperistan.org/islamic/ (accessed on March 2, 2002).

Newton.org.uk. http://www.newton.org.uk/ (accessed on February 28, 2002).

The Physics Classroom. http://www.glenbrook.k12.il.us/gbssci/phys/Class/BBoard.html (accessed on March 2, 2002).

People in the History of Astronomy. http://www.geocities.com/CapeCanaveral/Launchpad/4515/HISTORY.html (accessed on February 28, 2002).

Presocratics. http://www.philosophos.net/phphers/PRESOCRATICS.htm (accessed on February 28, 2002).

"Ptolemy, the Man." http://www.seds.org/billa/psc/theman.html (accessed on March 2, 2002).

The Robert Boyle Project. http://www.bbk.ac.uk/boyle/ (accessed on February 28, 2002).

"Science Fiction Timeline." *The Ultimate Science Fiction Web Guide.* http://www.magicdragon.com/UltimateSF/timeline.html (accessed on February 14, 2002).

"Sir Isaac Newton: The Universal Law of Gravitation." *Astronomy 161: The Solar System.* http://csep10.phys.utk.edu/astr161/lect/history/newtongrav.html (accessed on February 28, 2002).

Starry Messenger. http://www.hps.cam.ac.uk/starry/starrymessenger.html (accessed on February 28, 2002).

"The Universe of Aristotle and Ptolemy." *Astronomy 161: The Solar System.* http://csep10.phys.utk.edu/astr161/lect/retrograde/aristotle.html (accessed February 28, 2002).

"The Periodic Table on the WWW." *Web Elements.* http://www.webelements.com/ (accessed on February 28, 2002).

Pence, Harry E. *Web Sites on the History of Chemistry.* http://webserver1.oneonta.edu/faculty/pencehe/chemhistory.html (accessed on February 28, 2002).

Index

Italic type indicates volume number; **boldface** indicates main entries and their page numbers; (ill.) indicates photos and illustrations.

A

C

D

E

F

G

H

I

M

N

O

Q

R

S

U

V

W